Better Homes and Gardens™ perennial gardening

WILEY

John Wiley & Sons, Inc.

Better Homes and Gardens® Perennial Gardening

Contributing Writer: Julie Martens
Contributing Project Editor: Michael MacCaskey
Contributing Designers: Sundie Ruppert, Lori Gould
Editor, Garden Books: Denny Schrock
Editorial Assistant: Heather Knowles
Contributing Copy Editor: Terri Fredrickson
Contributing Proofreaders: Susan Lang, Peg Smith
Contributing Indexer: Ellen Sherron
Contributing Photographers: Doug Hetherington,
    Dean Schoeppner, Denny Schrock
Contributing Photo Researcher: Susan Ferguson

Meredith® Books

Editorial Director: Gregory H. Kayko
Editor in Chief, Garden: Doug Jimerson
Editorial Manager: David Speer
Art Director: Tim Alexander
Managing Editor: Doug Kouma
Executive Director, Sales: Ken Zagor
Director, Operations: George A. Susral
Business Director: Janice Croat
Imaging Center Operator: Tony Jungweber

John Wiley & Sons, Inc.

Publisher: Natalie Chapman
Associate Publisher: Jessica Goodman
Executive Editor: Anne Ficklen
Assistant Editor: Charleen Barila
Production Director: Diana Cisek
Manufacturing Manager: Tom Hyland

This book is printed on acid-free paper.

Note to Reader: Due to differing conditions, tools, and individual skills, Meredith Corporation assumes no responsibility for any damages, injuries suffered, or losses incurred as a result of following the information published in this book. Before beginning any project, review the instructions carefully, and if any doubts or questions remain, consult local experts or authorities. Because codes and regulations vary greatly, you should always check with authorities to ensure that your project complies with all applicable local codes and regulations. Always read and observe all the safety precautions provided by manufacturers of any tools, equipment, or supplies, and follow all accepted safety procedures.

Better Homes and Gardens Magazine
Editor in Chief: Gayle Goodson Butler

Meredith Publishing Group
President: Tom Harty
Excutive Vice President: Doug Olson

Meredith Corporation
Chairman of the Board: William T. Kerr
President and Chief Executive Officer: Stephen M. Lacy

In Memoriam: E.T. Meredith III (1933–2003)

Photo Credits
Photographers credited may retain copyright © to the listed photographs.

Frank Peairs, Colorado State University, bugwood.org: 165BC
Jim Occi, BugPics, bugwood.org: 165TC
Clemson University, USDA Cooperative Extension Slide Set,
    bugwood.org: 165C

For general information on our other products and services or for technical support, please contact our Customer Care Department within the United States at (800) 762-2974, outside the United States at (317) 572-3993 or fax (317) 572-4002.

Wiley also publishes its books in a variety of electronic formats. Some content that appears in print may not be available in electronic books. For more information about Wiley products, visit our web site at www.wiley.com.

Library of Congress Cataloging-in-Publication Data

Better homes and gardens perennial gardening.
    p. cm.
Includes index.
ISBN 978-0-470-87844-6 (pbk.)
1. Perennials. 2. Flower gardening.
I. Better homes and gardens. II. Title: Perennial gardening.
SB434.B468 2010
635.9'32--dc22
                                         2010042156

Printed in the United States of America
10 9 8 7 6 5 4 3 2 1

grow your favorite flowers right outside your door. The inspiring images and easy-to-follow planting, growing, and care advice on the following pages will yield a bountiful display of beautiful blooms.

table of contents

understanding perennials

Perennials dress outdoor spaces with dynamic beauty. Textures, colors, and forms ebb and flow through the seasons in flower- and foliage-filled waves.

p.8
INTRODUCTION
Get to know perennials. These comeback beauties combine variety with versatility, handily filling many roles in the garden. Plants stage eye-catching drama that grows richer by the year.

p.10
PERENNIAL SECRETS
Although perennials present specific design obstacles and care needs that create a learning curve, they're a fantastic investment. Better still, there's a perennial to solve every landscaping problem.

p.16
PLANT NAMES
Explore perennial gardening, including plant names, basic garden design, planting, and seasonal care and maintenance. Discover how this book will help bring your garden dreams to life.

Introduction to Perennials

When it comes to garden favorites, it's tough to beat perennials.

In contrast to their annual cousins, these long-lived jewels grace a garden without fail for years. A perennial is a nonwoody plant that lives for more than two years and typically dies back as hard frosts embrace foliage. New growth emerges in spring, either from the ground or from remnants of woody stems. Some perennials, like heart-leaf bergenia or mondo grass, retain foliage year-round and in warmer regions stand as evergreen sentries amid seasonal change.

Multitalented performers

Perennials fill several of roles in the garden: star, supporting player, or chorus member. A clump of torch lilies with bold tint blooms commands attention, as does a full-size rodgersia leaf. Diminutive and feathery silvermound artemisia quietly complements other perennials, such as 'Autumn Joy' sedum, while also inviting closer inspection with its distinctive foliage.

As these versatile beauties grow through the season, plants alternate taking center stage. The swordlike foliage of crocosmia is striking in any season, yet it leaps to life when set ablaze by fiery flower spikes. The silver stems of Russian sage handily anchor a garden bed through the growing season, then when late summer blooms sparkle purple among the silvery haze, the effect stops traffic.

A celebration of variety

Diversity earns perennials a faithful following. Lacy, strappy, chunky, wispy—choose an adjective, and there's a perennial leaf to match. Some perennials tower to 6 feet or more; others hug the ground with neatly sprawling stems. Still others nestle in sumptuous billows in the garden, awaiting their turn in the seasonal spotlight.

Count on perennials to stage garden drama no matter the growing conditions. Plan a garden around deep shade, standing water, desert heat, a steep slope, or heavy clay soil, and you'll find the perfect perennial. In outdoor living settings, perennials dress views with seasonal charms that may include flowers, fragrance, or butterfly-attracting blooms.

For many gardeners, visions of rich, sweeping borders showcase these comeback bloomers in their best form, but perennials also draw a crowd when tucked into mixed borders, pots, or edible plantings. Perennials can stand alone or play a counterpoint to shrubs, bulbs, annuals, or even hardworking vegetables. They fit just as easily in tight quarters as they do in spacious environs.

Long-lasting beauty

Perennials keep time with the seasons. Anemone and bleeding heart awaken with the earliest rays of spring sunshine, greeting the arrival of migrating robins with their pastel shades. Other perennials, like monkshood and aster, bid the growing season farewell with brilliant tints. Some, like Lenten rose, never take a curtain call, lingering through winter with deep green leaves that stand out in snow.

The seasonal show is just one aspect of perennials' long-lived splendor. These plants grow stronger by the season, increasing in size and flower number as they age. Like well-seasoned performers, mature perennials enrich each scene they grace. While many live as long as 15 years in a typical garden setting, others, like peony, hosta, and false indigo, forge a legacy that can last up to 100 years.

Perennials promise—and deliver—versatile, dependable, and adaptable beauty.

Above left: **Peonies offer beauty that easily flourishes beyond a gardener's lifetime.**

Above center: **Summer perennials often unfurl flowers in bold shades, like red and yellow. White Oriental lilies balance the two strong colors.**

Above right: **Annuals such as ornamental cabbage (foreground) enhance perennial plantings.**

Opposite: **Perennials fill each growing season with eye-catching color, from soft pastels to fiery fall hues. Ignite autumn with blazing hues by pairing upright 'Autumn Joy' sedum with a dwarf fountain grass and hot pink asters.**

Perennial Secrets

Charming beauty and limitless potential top the list of reasons to grow perennials.

These reliable plants can be orchestrated to play symphonies of seasonal color that delight and inspire. Hidden in the midst of perennials' wonderful attributes, however, lie a few challenges.

Knowledge needed

To grow perennials successfully, you need to conquer a learning curve. Unlike annuals, which demand only one season's worth of attention, perennials' comeback personalities require a more sustained focus. Many gardeners mistakenly believe that perennials promise low maintenance and are a plant-it-and-forget-it package. While some plants feature easy-growing personalities, shrugging off disease or unfurling self-cleaning blooms, most perennials need attention. Ongoing care, such as staking, removing spent flowers, soil building, cutting down spent stalks, and dividing, makes perennial gardening a multitasking delight—and a great calorie-burning workout.

Above: **A common misconception about perennials is that they create a plant-it-and-forget-it garden. While some perennials are low maintenance, most require ongoing care throughout the growing season, including mulching, watering, and sometimes staking. Deadheading (removing spent blooms) is necessary to increase the number of flowers in plants such as yarrow.**

Many plants demand specific techniques you'll need to master to savor the fullest growth. Conversely, some care tactics apply to various perennials, allowing you to perfect newly acquired techniques throughout your garden. Because perennials require knowledge to grow, tending them easily becomes a lifelong pursuit filled with fresh learning opportunities.

Color isn't constant

Most perennials flower for a two- to four-week period. Beyond that color-filled time frame—and without careful planning—a perennial garden is mostly foliage. The trick is to compose a blend of perennials that flowers in sequence so your garden becomes an ever-building crescendo of seasonal beauty. This process isn't hard to perfect, and you can always count on annuals tucked among perennials to sound steady notes of color throughout the growing season.

Elbow room required

Because perennials live for more than one season, they're constantly growing and enlarging their borders. A 'Jack Frost' brunnera may start as a tidy clump of stems, but in ideal growing conditions can easily double in size from one year to the next. One false indigo stem can magically transform into a multistemed shrub over the course of several growing seasons. Some plants, like spotted bellflower, run rampant through a planting bed, trading a puddle of color for a river of bloom.

It's this changeability that gives a perennial garden its charm. From year to year, the dynamic nature of the plants maintains a lively scene—and keeps gardeners busy. When you design a perennial garden, avoid the temptation to overcrowd young plants and instead plan for growth.

You'll also need to increase the volume of plants you use if you want season-long color. Where three or four annuals will brighten a bed with nonstop blooms, you may need at least a dozen different perennials to ensure long-lasting color. That many plants need a larger planting bed than a few annuals, which also adds more garden chores.

In the long run, perennials are worth any extra effort you make to learn, plan, or tend. When you arrange a planting that combines individual perennials into a harmonious blend of color, texture, and bloom, you'll savor the beauty and discover the inspiration only perennials can give.

Specific perennials require differing levels of care, which you discover and learn over time. Tall foxglove spires frequently need staking. Attaching spikes to a single stake works best to support the bloom.

EASY GROWING
BEE BALM
BLACK-EYED SUSAN
CATMINT
DAYLILY (shown)
SIBERIAN IRIS
SPIDERWORT

CHALLENGING
BEAR'S BREECHES
CLEMATIS (shown)
RODGERSIA
SEA HOLLY
TORCH LILY

Perennials for beginner to experienced gardeners

Some perennials take off when planted in soil and multiply quickly without overtaking planting beds. Other perennials aren't necessarily difficult to grow; they just have specific demands or slow-growing natures that make success less certain. In the right region or where growing requirements are met, these plants would be called easy.

Perennials Solve Problems

Internationally diverse, perennials hail from every part of the globe.

You can grow agapanthus from South Africa, campanula from Russia, meadow rue from Spain, or peonies from China. If you prefer North American natives, look for bleeding heart, cardinal flower, coral bells, evening primrose, or hyssop.

Layered onto this geographical array of homelands, perennials also originate from a variety of growing conditions. Some, like Japanese water iris, rose turtlehead, and sweet flag, grow in standing water. Pinks and yellow corydalis thrive in fast-draining, slightly alkaline soil, while astilbe and primrose flourish in moist, well-drained soil and shade.

Perennials offer possibilities for every growing situation. As you contemplate digging into perennial gardening, approach it from the standpoint of solving landscape problems. There's a perennial that will thrive in every growing situation.

If you have a slope too steep for mowing, you can trade turf for a perennial groundcover. Near downspouts and low spots in your yard where water gathers after downpours, moisture-loving perennials can transform an eyesore into a beauty spot. Where lower rainfall dictates water restrictions, tap into the world of xeriscape plants, which grow and flower profusely with little moisture. Natural deposits of acid soil can support lovely perennials that will make you grateful for the locally low pH. Stop fighting to grow grass beneath shade trees—plant shade-loving perennials instead.

You can even find perennials that serve as lawn stand-ins—tidy, ground-hugging plants that withstand foot traffic and stay green year-round. In municipalities where surface runoff adds charges to your water bill, incorporating a rain garden filled with moisture-loving perennials will dissipate roof, driveway, or patio runoff into the soil and can reduce your water fees. Use the listing of perennials adapted to various growing conditions on the opposite page to draft solutions to your landscaping problems.

Above: **Whatever the landscape issue you confront, you can find a perennial adapted to those conditions. For soggy spots where water stands, count on a blend of (clockwise from bottom center) rodgersia, candelabra primula, and yellow flag for early season color.**

Perennial solutions
For every problem area in your landscape you'll find perennials that not only survive, but also thrive in the conditions available. Simply match the preferred growing conditions of each perennial to the site.

WET SOILS
CARDINAL FLOWER Brilliant red flowers in late summer to early fall.

GOATSBEARD Lacy, white flower plumes atop 3- to 5-foot-tall plants from early to midsummer.

JOE-PYE WEED Large mauve blooms; up to 6 feet tall when in late summer bloom (pictured above).

RODGERSIA Coarse texture, flower plumes in spring or summer.

SWEET FLAG Long-lasting swordlike foliage.

SHADE
ASTILBE Long-lasting flower stalks in summer (pictured above).

BARRENWORT Red, pink, white, purple, or bicolor blooms in early to midspring.

FOAM FLOWER White or light pink flowers in midspring.

HARDY BEGONIA Heart-shape foliage; pink flowers in late summer.

HOSTA Grown for foliage; many cultivars.

LENTEN ROSE Coarse-texture foliage; blooms in late winter to early spring.

LUNGWORT Early spring flowers and variegated foliage.

OLD-FASHIONED BLEEDING HEART Heart-shape pink flowers in spring.

WOODLAND PHLOX Fragrant blue, purple, pink, or white flowers in late spring.

ALKALINE SOIL
ANEMONE Late summer or fall flowers.

CORAL BELLS Many cultivars with colorful foliage (pictured above).

CREEPING BABY'S BREATH White flowers in summer.

GERANIUM Spring or summer flowers depending on species; foliage of many turns red in fall.

PINCUSHION FLOWER Blue flowers on wiry stems appear summer to fall.

PINKS White, pink, or red flowers in spring and summer; evergreen foliage.

DRY SOILS
BLUE FESCUE Ornamental grass with bluish green foliage.

CATMINT Fragrant foliage and lavender-blue flowers in early summer (pictured above).

FALSE INDIGO Pealike blue flowers in late spring followed by attractive seedpods.

LIRIOPE Dark green grasslike foliage.

PENSTEMON Desert species have bright flower colors, upright shape.

WHITE GAURA Airy white or pink flower stalks from midsummer to fall.

YUCCA Rounded clump of upright foliage.

FULL SUN
COREOPSIS Yellow flowers all summer (pictured above).

HOLLYHOCK Summer flowers on tall spikes early to midsummer.

MALTESE CROSS Silver foliage and scarlet flowers in early summer.

ORIENTAL POPPY Flowers with paperlike petals in late spring and early summer.

PEONY Large, fragrant flowers in late spring to early summer.

MOUNTAIN BLUET Blue-violet flowers in midspring to early summer.

TREE MALLOW Shrublike with white, pink, or purple-pink flowers all summer.

ACID SOIL
BEAR'S BREECHES Tall flower spikes in late spring to early summer and texture-rich foliage.

CINNAMON FERN Reddish brown fronds in center of plant.

FRINGED BLEEDING HEART Finely cut foliage; flowers all summer (pictured above).

GAYFEATHER Purple or white flower spikes in early to midsummer.

HEART-LEAF BERGENIA Shiny evergreen foliage.

JAPANESE IRIS Showy flowers in late spring or summer.

LENTEN ROSE Flowers in late winter.

Perennials
Solve Problems

Perennial solutions Perennial plantings transform an outdoor living area (at left) into a garden escape. Mingling flowering shrubs, such as hydrangea and shrub roses with long bloomers like black-eyed susan stages a season-long color show. Here are more site-specific perennials.

CLAY SOILS
DAYLILY Adaptable grower for tough conditions. Many colors available.

GERANIUM Many species with pink, purple, or white blooms for sun to part shade.

FALSE SUNFLOWER Also called heliopsis, this daisylike flower is a prairie native.

MONKSHOOD Late summer spikes of deep blue for shady sites.

OBEDIENT PLANT Rapid spreader with pink or white candles of bloom.

PEONY Fragrant pink, red, white, or yellow late spring blooms (pictured above).

YARROW Ferny foliage and drought-tolerant; golden yellow, white, pink, red, or salmon color blooms.

SANDY SOILS
ARTEMISIA Silvery foliage is the key feature of this perennial.

BLANKET FLOWER Long bloom season of orange-red daisies marked with yellow.

FALSE INDIGO Shrubby plant with spikes of blue blooms in spring (pictured above).

LAVENDER COTTON Herb with fine texture in silvery gray or green.

THYME Groundcover with pinkish purple blooms.

YARROW Adapted to full sun and dry soils with wide range of bloom colors.

YUCCA Succulent with spiky foliage and trusses of white bell-shape blooms.

SALT-TOLERANT
ARMERIA Also called sea thrift, this compact plant has grassy foliage and pink or white blooms (pictured above).

BLANKET FLOWER Bi-color daisylike blooms on mounded plants.

BUTTERFLY WEED Brilliant orange blooms highly attractive to butterflies.

CANDYTUFT White blooms in spring on mounded evergreen foliage.

DAYLILY Tough plant for almost any situation except deep shade.

HEN AND CHICKS Succulent with rosettes of green, pink or purple foliage.

PINKS Carnation relatives with grassy bluegreen foliage and fragrant pink, white, or red blooms.

DEER RESISTANT
ASTILBE Shade and moisture lovers with feathery plumes of bloom.

BARRENWORT Shade-tolerant groundcover with delicate looking blooms.

CARDINAL FLOWER Spikes of brilliant red blooms on plants that love moisture.

FOXGLOVE Clustered spikes of pink bells (pictured above).

LENTEN ROSE Late winter bloomer in shades of pink, white or purple.

ORNAMENTAL ALLIUM Perennial bulb with blooms of purple or white.

RUSSIAN SAGE Silvery gray foliage and purple blooms in summer.

COOL CLIMATES
DELPHINIUM Long spikes of blue, purple, pink or white.

GLOBEFLOWER Yellow springtime blooms with feathery centers (pictured above).

JAPANESE PRIMROSE Moisture-loving plant with globes of pink, purple, or white blooms in spring.

LADY'S MANTLE Chartreuse blooms over bluegreen foliage.

LUPINE Upright spikes of pealike blooms in many shades.

MONKSHOOD Fall bloomer for the shade.

ORIENTAL POPPY Crepelike blooms in spring in shades of orange, red, pink, or white.

HOT CLIMATES
BLACKBERRY LILY Orange blooms turn into black seed clusters.

BLANKET FLOWER Adaptable daisy for tough sites.

DAYLILY Trumpet-shape blooms in a wide range of colors.

HARDY BEGONIA Glossy green foliage with pink blooms.

MEXICAN SAGE Deep purple blooms on silvery plants (pictured above).

MUHLY GRASS Feathery foliage and white or pinkish blooms.

THREADLEAF COREOPSIS Finely dissected foliage with small yellow daisylike blooms.

Making Sense of Plant Names

When choosing garden phlox, knowing the correct botanical name ensures you're buying the plant you want—whether short, tall, pink, white, lavender, or mildew resistant.

Once you begin to discover perennials to grow in your garden, it's time to leap into the pool of plant taxonomy, the naming of plants. The reason you need to understand plant names is simple: Some plants, like coneflower, have several named varieties. If you want a coneflower with backward-curving orange petals, you need to understand the name in order to purchase the right one. Some perennial names, like *Campanula portenschlagiana*, are curiously long and complicated, or short and sweet, as in *Alcea rosea*. The purpose of plant names is to organize the world of plants. Most perennials have two types of names: a common and a botanical.

Common names

The common name of a plant is easy to pronounce and, at times, wonderfully descriptive. Names like blackberry lily, bleeding heart, goatsbeard, and fountain grass offer glimpses into a plant's personality or appearance. A common name can also reveal clues about a plant's origin, such as Ozark sundrops, or it can paint a picture of a flower, like rose turtlehead.

Common names are often confusing because the same plants may have different common names in different places. *Liatris spicata*, which we list as gayfeather, is also known as blazing star or button snakeroot. Bugbane (*Actaea racemosa*) is also sold as black cohosh, autumn snakeroot, or black snakeroot. The same common name can also refer to completely unrelated plants. Gayfeather and bugbane are from two unrelated plant groups, but share a same common name, "snakeroot."

Botanical names

A botanical name consists of two parts: a genus and a specific epithet. The genus is a closely related group of plants. It always begins with a capital letter and is written in italics. Think of a genus as a surname, for example, *Sedum*. The second part of a plant name, the specific epithet, is written after the genus and is also italicized. In the *Sedum* genus, there are specific members with identifying characteristics—such as *Sedum acre*, *Sedum spurium*, and *Sedum reflexum*.

Within a species, sometimes there are plants that are very similar but have one or more outstanding differences. These plants are called a variety of that species. *Sedum hispanicum* has a variety known as *Sedum hispanicum* var. *minus*, which grows only 4 inches tall.

A variety can be cultivated for a specific growth characteristic that occurs through natural mutation, plant selection by breeders, or hybridization. In these cases, the cultivated variety is called a cultivar. Cultivars for *Sedum spurium* include 'Dragon's Blood', with bronze-tinged leaves, and 'Red Carpet', with red tinted leaves that turn burgundy in the fall. Cultivar names are typically capitalized and set off with single quotes.

For easy reading, plants are listed by their common name throughout most of this book. But in the encyclopedia, the full botanical name for each plant is also used, so you can find the same plant at nurseries, catalogs, and in other books.

Name changes

As taxonomists study plants, they sometimes conclude that a plant is named incorrectly and belongs to a different genus or species. An example of that is bugbane. Now listed as part of the *Actaea* genus, it was previously—and still is, in some cases—known as *Cimicifuga*. If you see two names listed for a perennial in a catalog or on a website and you plan to find the plant at a local garden center, be sure to record both names. Sometimes grower nurseries have a stock of plant tags on hand, and they'll use what they have, which might use an older name.

TEST GARDEN TIP

Botanical latin

Plant names are often pronounced differently. Clematis might be KLEM-uh-tiss or kluh-MAT-iss. For *Phlox paniculata*, the species may sound like pa-nik-ew-LAH-ta or pa-nik-ew-LAY-ta. Don't worry about pronunciation rules. The bottom line on botanical names is that they are the key to getting the right plant.

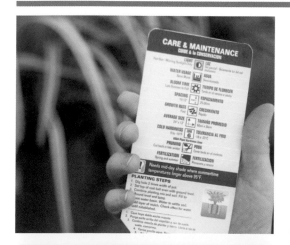

Plant names at a glance

Cultivar name

The cultivar name is assigned by the plant breeder. Popular cultivars are commonly referred to by their cultivar names in garden centers and mail order catalogs Example: 'Goldsturm'.

Genus name

The first word in a plant's botanical name is the genus. Think of this as a surname. There are several members of the *Rudbeckia* plant genus.

Species name

The second word in a botanical name is the specific epithet, commonly called the species. This identifies the plant specifically, separating it from all other plants in the genus. It is meaningless unless used in combination with the genus name. *Rudbeckia fulgida* is a specific species.

Common name

Common names fluctuate. One person might call this plant rudbeckia, while another calls it black-eyed susan.

selecting perennials

Narrow the field of perennials to grow by considering growing conditions and personal preferences.

p.20
GETTING STARTED

Determine what kind of garden best suits your home—and you. Browse garden magazines and take garden tours for ideas.

p.22
SUN VS. SHADE

Learn how to assess light patterns in your potential perennial garden area, and select plants that will thrive in your yard's conditions.

p.26
SOIL AND DRAINAGE

Some yards offer ideal soil for perennials; most don't. Learn how to transform poor soil into a perfect-for-perennials blend.

p.32
LIFESTYLE GARDENS

Plan a perennial garden that fits your everyday life, with beauties that bloom when you want them to and require little maintenance.

p.34
PERENNIAL SOURCES

Discover ways to save money, how to spot a healthy plant, and which perennials produce seeds that are easily saved and sown.

Getting Started

Gather information before designing a perennial garden.

A perennial garden yields ample opportunity to express your personal style. Whether you have a flair for drama, a penchant for exuberant color, or a quiet passion for understated beauty, you can showcase your preferences using perennial plantings.

If you've never gardened before, spend time looking through garden magazines, books, and catalogs. Photocopy or tear out pictures that catch your eye, and start an idea file. Visit public gardens and garden centers and photograph plants, combinations, or landscaping techniques that inspire you. Take local garden tours to glean yet more ideas.

Consider your own lifestyle interests too. If you're an avid recycler, you'll probably find the earth-friendly tenets of prairie, native plant, and xeriscape gardens appealing. If hosting family and other gatherings is a key

If your only available garden space is a container, fill it with perennials that unfurl different leaf colors and textures, and you'll stage an eye-pleasing scene.

part of your life, you may want gardens that enhance outdoor living areas and add beauty to indoor views.

Your home will also offer clues to your garden style. Picket fences and rambling front porches beg for cottage-style perennials, while clean, modern architectural features can be echoed with ornamental grasses and strong textural perennial compositions in the garden. If space is at a premium, perennials in containers are a logical—and beautiful—solution.

Your garden may sprout as a solution to a landscape problem, such as an area where grass won't grow because it's too shady or too wet. Consider indoor views of exterior areas, and plan perennial beds to spruce up scenery. You might develop a garden around a theme, such as a wildlife-attracting border, a cutting garden, or a garden for meditation. Your garden may feature unexpected, playful touches, or it may house a cherished collection of items with weather-resistant personalities.

Whatever the inspiration, you'll find perennials to carry out your vision with beauty and ease. Once you narrow your stylistic focus, you're ready to deal with the realities of your site.

Perennial gardens form a showcase for your personal style. Include artistic creations to share your flair for drama, whimsy, playfulness, or romance.

Plant collector's syndrome

Gardeners are drawn to plants in inexplicable ways. You're familiar with impulse purchases. In gardening circles, that's called a passion for plants. A plant catches your eye, and the next thing you know, you're trying to shoehorn it into your garden. In the best scenario, a garden born through improvisation looks fantastic. At worst, chaos reigns as the good, the bad, and the ugly grow side by side. Make collections work by following these simple steps.

Stick with a plan. Draft your perennial garden on paper—and use that as the final word on plant purchases.

Focus on a plant groups. Gather plants of one type, such as sedums, coneflowers, or grasses. Single-style plant groupings compose wonderful displays.

Choose a color. Monochromatic gardens are striking. Focus on plants that unfurl leaves, flowers, or stems in a specific hue, and you'll cultivate an artistic garden.

Set aside a bed. For all the plants you simply can't pass up, create a holding bed located away from your main garden. As you tend these plants, you'll discover their talents and demands, and whether there's truly a place for them in your garden.

Understanding Light:
Sun vs. Shade

One of the biggest influences for which perennials you'll grow is how much sunlight your garden site receives. The majority of perennials thrive in six hours of sun, but thanks to the many plants that unfurl fabulous foliage and beautiful blooms in lower amounts of light, you can plan a striking garden even in shady conditions.

Take inventory of sunlight

Gauge how much sunlight bathes your garden site. It's best to assess light patterns every hour or two in the course of a day, noting where shadows fall, linger, and pass. If you spy sunlight trails during spring, bare-branched trees give the illusion of sunny spots beneath. What you think is a sunny area may be swallowed by shade when leaves emerge. Buildings and walls also cast shadows; don't overlook those structures as you plot the sun's path.

Use marking flags and spray paint to indicate light and shadow in your yard, or create a light map on paper. Start with a few sheets of tracing paper, sketching a copy of your yard's outline on each page. About two hours after sunrise, observe where light and shade fall in your yard, and mark them on the tracing paper, noting the time. Repeat the process through the day, each time using a different sheet of paper. Stop recording about an hour before dusk. Use a pencil to mark shady sections of the yard on each page. Label sun and shade pockets to indicate whether they reflect morning or afternoon conditions. Layer the pages together, and you'll get an accurate picture of how much light your yard offers. Create a composite drawing to use as a one-page light map.

No hard-and-fast rules

Once you know your garden site's sun and shade characteristics, start choosing perennials. A plant's light needs are more fluid than static. For instance, if you plant a sun-loving plant in a shade-dappled spot, you won't necessarily kill it. You'll likely experience fewer flowers, shorter lifespan, less color, or gangly stems.

Regional influences

A plant's light requirements shift throughout the country. In the South, sun-loving perennials may need shade during the hottest part of the day, while in the Pacific Northwest, cloud cover can prevent sun lovers from flourishing. Where cool, wet summers prevail, perennials that nominally prefer partial shade can thrive in sunnier conditions.

Gardens planted beneath trees often boast a blend of sun and shade. Study sunlight patterns throughout the day and during seasons, then slip sun-loving perennials into sunny pockets.

The facts of light

As you read about specific perennials, you'll encounter growing requirements. Light needs are often expressed as full sun, part sun, part shade, or full shade. These terms refer to the sunlight a plant needs to yield top-notch performance. Unsure what these terms mean? You're not alone. Here's how to decipher the light code.

Full sun. Plants require at least six hours of sun per day.

Part sun. Plants should receive three to six hours of sun per day, preferably in morning or evening, not during the hottest parts of the day.

Part shade. Plants will thrive with three to six hours of sun per day, but definitely require shade during the afternoon, when sun is hottest. These conditions describe plants tucked beneath a tree where the sun slants in during the morning or on the east side of a building.

Full shade. Plants need fewer than three hours of direct sun per day. Filtered sunlight or light shade is necessary for the rest of the day. This could describe plants on the north side of a structure or under a spreading tree where sunlight briefly penetrates the canopy at some point during the day.

Dealing With Shade

Understanding sunlight is simple:

Either something receives sun or it does not. The intensity of sunlight varies based on time of day, with morning light offering a softer, gentler ray and afternoon sun burning with sizzle.

Shade presents a more complex scenario, full of nuances and degrees. There's the deep shade you find on the north side of a house, alongside a stone wall or privacy fence, or beneath a 70-year-old beech tree, where the sun only peeps from winter through early spring. Dappled shade dances beneath honeylocust trees, where small leaves filter sunlight to cast a filmy, shifting glow.

Deciduous trees offer seasonal shade. Spring sunlight under leafless boughs provides the perfect footing for ephemerals, plants like bleeding heart or wood anemone, which stage an early season flower show and then quietly disappear as leaves emerge and shade deepens. As the sun heads north for summer in the northern hemisphere, shade patterns shift and shorten, then silently lengthen as summer slips into fall. Observe seasonal light patterns as you plan your perennial garden and choose and situate plants.

Shade, shade, go away

You can make some shade do a disappearing act. If you have a tree with branches that cast dense shade, lighten the scenery below by removing lower limbs. This process, called limbing up, effectively lifts a canopy, permitting sunlight to

In a woodland setting, tall trees often cast light shade punctuated by shafts of sunlight. Count on reliable shade performers like astilbe to brighten shady gardens with colorful blossom spires. Plant a mix of astilbes that bloom at different points in the season to create a long-lasting flower show. Planting companions for astilbe include golden hakone grass, goatsbeard, and other ferns.

penetrate the leafy shade. During late summer and fall, sunlight can slant beneath limbed up trees to lighten deep shade. Selectively thinning can increase light to the ground below. Consider replacing solid fences with vine-covered lattice to increase light.

Dealing with dry shade

Dry shade under mature trees is one of the garden's toughest conditions, but perennials can splash color into these droughty, dark areas. For plants to thrive until they're established, they'll need frequent watering. Plants will deliver a modest flower show that slowly increases over time.

Sometimes shade comes from structures, such as buildings or fences. In these cases, you may deal with heavy shade that lingers for part of the day, until the sun shifts.

TEST GARDEN TIP

Plants for dry shade

Some perennials splash color into droughty, dark areas. Water plants until they're established.

Anemone

Barrenwort

Bear's breeches

Columbine

Coral bells

Lenten rose

Liriope

Mondo grass

Monkshood

Yellow foxglove

Flowers and foliage for shade
Different perennials perform in varying degrees of shade. Generally, plants that thrive in deep shade, such as these perennials, will also prosper in part shade. Try some of these flower and foliage favorites to pump up the beauty in shady corners of your yard.

BUGLEWEED
Mat-forming groundcover with blue flowers in spring; foliage in various hues—bronze, rose, white, green, purple. Zones 3–9.

FOAM FLOWER
Groundcover with white or pink blooms in midspring; evergreen in warm climates. Zones 3–8.

FOAMY BELLS
Groundcover with cut leaves in an array of hues and variegation patterns; white, cream, or pink blooms in spring. Zones 4–8.

HEART-LEAF BERGENIA
Shiny evergreen leaves and pink spring blooms; deer resistant. Zones 4–10.

HOSTA
Foliage plant in an array of hues and variegations. Zones 3–8.

JACOB'S LADDER
Blue, white, or pink blooms in spring; variegated leaf forms brighten shade. Zones 3–8.

LUNGWORT
Silver- or white-speckled, deep green leaves; some forms feature greater leaf variegation. Zones 4–8.

ROSE TURTLEHEAD
Upright, clumping plant with pink to white flower spikes in late summer and fall. Zones 4–8.

VARIEGATED SOLOMON'S SEAL
Arching stems hold cream-edged leaves that turn gold in fall. Zones 4–9.

YELLOW CORYDALIS
Yellow blooms dangle above lacy foliage spring through fall. Zones 5–8.

Soil

Some perennials, such as joe-pye weed (center), prefer rich, moist soil. Others, like 'Karl Foerster' feather reed grass (left and right), boast versatility, growing in moist or dry conditions.

Most perennials prefer soil that allows water to drain and offers nutrition to hungry

plant roots. There are exceptions to that rule—plants that flourish in lean, dry soil or in water-logged conditions, like those found in bogs or beside ponds or streams. Four components determine whether soil favors a water-loving great blue lobelia or a drought-tolerant sea holly: sand, silt, clay, and organic matter. Combined in the right proportions, these components form loam, the ideal soil for growing most perennials.

Soil components

The proportions of sand, silt, clay, and organic matter affects the ability of soil to hold or release water and nutrients. Soil with high clay content retains nutrients, but the tiny clay particles also trap water, creating a drainage issue. Prolonged rainfall causes waterlogged conditions as water displaces oxygen around plant roots. For plants like Japanese iris or sneezeweed, saturated soil and standing water are ideal. But if you try to grow perennials like yarrow or coreopsis, soggy soil is deadly. To tell whether your soil has high clay content, grab a handful of moist soil and squeeze it. Clay soil feels sticky and forms a tight clump.

Smaller than grains of sand but larger than clay, silt particles form soil that drains freely and holds nutrients. Cranesbill geranium, primrose, and black-eyed susan grow in soil with a high silt component. Silty soil feels powdery when dry, silky when wet.

Sandy soils drain very quickly and don't hold nutrients. Artemisia, catmint, and yucca all thrive in sandy soil. When you grab a handful of sandy soil, it feels gritty and, wet or dry, it won't hold together.

Organic matter transforms soil, giving it an ability to hold water and nutrients. When added to overly clay or sandy soil, organic matter transforms it into a soil that's loose and airy, able to drain and hold nutrients. When you pick up a handful of moist soil high in organic matter, the soil clumps together in your hand, but you can easily break the clump apart.

Working with soil

Once you know your soil components, you have two choices as you prepare to grow perennials.

You can choose perennials adapted to the soil conditions that you have, or you can change soil by amending it (see the chapter beginning on page 108) or improving drainage (see page 31).

If you opt to focus on selecting perennials to match your existing soil, you'll find some help below, along with the perennial lists on pages 12 to 29. As you study individual plants in the encyclopedia, you'll discover clues about pairing plants with appropriate soil. Each entry description includes "Site," which describes the conditions in which the perennial grows best. For sandy soil, look for plants that require excellent drainage. For loam to sandy loam, look for perennials that need well-drained soil. Infertile soil is the same as poor soil. If a site mentions soils of average fertility, that refers to any reasonably fertile soil.

see the chapter beginning on page 108 ... improving drainage (see page 31). ... the perennial lists on pages 12 to 29.

TEST GARDEN TIP

Sediment test

To determine soil type, conduct a sediment test. Place a handful of soil in a jar with 1 tablespoon of dishwashing soap. Fill the jar with water, shake, then allow it to sit. Soil components will settle in this order: sand, silt, organic matter, and clay. Larger particles (sand, silt, and organic matter) will settle in a few minutes or hours. Clay particles may take a week or more to settle. When the water is clear and you see distinct layers, measure the height of the total soil and each layer. Divide the height of each layer by the total height to discover which component dominates your soil.

Plants for lean soil Some perennials grow best when the soil dishes up a starvation diet to roots.

BLANKET FLOWER
Long-lasting red and yellow flowers in summer attract butterflies. Zones 4–11.

BUTTERFLY WEED
Striking orange blooms in summer and large seedpods in fall; attracts butterflies. Zones 3–10.

CENTRANTHUS
Reddish pink flowers open from early summer to fall; attracts butterflies. Zones 5–11.

LAVENDER
Fragrant purple flower spikes in summer. Zones 5–10.

PINCUSHION FLOWER
Light blue or pink flowers top wiry stems from summer into fall. Zones 5–10.

RUSSIAN SAGE
Tiny blue-purple blooms glow amid lacy, gray-green foliage from mid- to late summer. Zones 3–10.

STOKES' ASTER
Shaggy blue, pink, white, or rosy purple blooms from summer to fall. Zones 5–9.

WHITE GAURA
Starry pink or white flowers float on airy stems from midsummer to early fall. Zones 5–10.

Improving Drainage

The majority of perennials perform best in well-drained soil, where water moves easily, percolating downward through the plants' root zones. Soil that's well drained strikes a balance between allowing water to flow and holding it long enough so roots can absorb moisture. Soil that isn't well drained doesn't allow water to flow, and the surface may sport puddles for hours or days after a rainfall. Fast-draining soils permit water to rush through so quickly that plant roots can't grab a drop.

Poor drainage

How can you tell whether your soil drains well? A quick, easy gauge is to grab a handful of soil a few days after a soaking rain. Well-drained soil, even if it clumps somewhat, will crumble slightly as you pick it up. If soil clumps together and appears very wet, you could have an impervious layer underground—maybe clay or rock—that's not permitting water to drain freely downward through soil layers.

In some cases, you can improve poor soil drainage. In other instances, it's best to select perennials suited to your soil type and drainage. Swamp milkweed, a wetland native, is an ideal candidate for sites with moist to soggy soil.

Another common cause for poor drainage is soil compaction. In areas of high foot traffic or where vehicles frequently drive, soil can become compacted. In this condition, air pockets and channels that water typically flows through become compressed and disappear. When water encounters compacted soil, it can't flow downward and the soil quickly becomes waterlogged. Compaction often occurs in yards of newly built homes, where construction vehicles have removed top soil, replaced it with excavated clay subsoils, and then compressed it.

Steep slopes can also be poorly drained because water washes off and can't soak in. Slow the flow of water down a slope and prevent erosion by using basins around plants or channels to redirect the flow. If the soil inside a slope is especially well drained, surface runoff is less an issue. With a poor-draining slope, surface runoff can cause erosion.

Too much drainage

In coastal areas, the primary soil component typically is sand, which drains very quickly. When rainfall or irrigation water strikes sandy soil, it percolates through air channels so rapidly that plant roots don't have ample opportunity to absorb it. Adding organic matter to sandy soils can remedy the situation. More frequent irrigation is also likely necessary. Another option is to plan a perennial garden using plants that prefer sandy soils.

TEST GARDEN TIP

How to test soil percolation

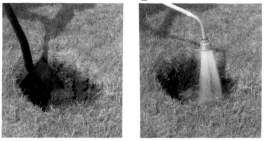

A percolation test reveals how quickly water drains from soil. Dig a hole that's 1 foot deep in the spot where you plan to have your garden. Fill the hole with water and allow it to drain. Fill the hole with water a second time. Ideally, the water should drain at a rate of 1 inch per hour. If it doesn't, you have a drainage problem.

Perennials for waterlogged soil

Dress a slow-draining, muddy spot in your yard with colorful, moisture-loving perennials. These plants are ideal candidates for creating a rain or bog garden. Typically, plants that endure wet conditions need more than four hours of sun daily.

CARDINAL FLOWER
Brilliant red blooms in late summer to fall lure hummingbirds. Full sun to part shade. Zones 3–9.

CINNAMON FERN
5-foot-tall green fronds encircle 36-inch, cinnamon-color spore stalks. Full sun to full shade. Zones 4–9.

HARDY HIBISCUS
Tropical-looking white, pink, or red flowers in mid- to late summer. Full sun. Zones 5–10.

JAPANESE GRASS SEDGE
A broad white stripe edged with green gives grassy leaves panache. Full to partial shade. Zones 5–9.

JAPANESE IRIS
Butterfly-like blue, purple, pink, or white blooms in late spring or summer. Full sun to part shade. Zones 5–9.

JAPANESE PRIMROSE
Pink, red, purple, or white flowers cluster atop short stems in late spring. Part shade to full shade. Zones 5–9.

JOE-PYE WEED
Flat clusters of mauve flowers top 6-foot-tall stems in late summer; attracts butterflies. Full sun to part shade. Zones 3–7.

QUEEN-OF-THE-MEADOW
Pink blossom spikes open above lobed leaves in early summer. Full sun to part shade. Zones 3–9.

SENSITIVE FERN
Green 2-foot fern fronds; attractive spore fronds resemble brown bead-covered spikes. Part shade to full shade. Zones 3–8.

SWAMP MILKWEED
Sweet scented pink blooms top 5-foot-tall stems in late summer; attracts butterflies. Full sun. Zones 4–9.

Improving
Drainage

Probably the most commonly encountered challenge

with new perennial gardens is poor drainage. If you discover that your soil doesn't drain quickly enough, don't be discouraged. There are several ways to transform a water-retaining nightmare into a beautiful dream.

Drainage trenches

A perforated pipe buried in a trench that slopes away from your planting area can shuttle water away from slow-draining soil. For a drainage pipe to work, you need a low spot in your yard where the water can drain. That spot should be at least 2 feet lower than the surface of your perennial bed or border.

To create good drainage, 6-inch-diameter perforated pipe works well. Space drainage pipes 10 feet apart. With a larger perennial border, place trenches parallel to one another as they run underneath the planting bed.

To get started, dig a trench at least 18 inches below the grade of the bed. Test the trench to make sure water flows from the bed to the drainage area by laying a garden hose at the upper end of the trench and turning on the water. If the water doesn't flow easily from one end of the trench to the other, adjust the depth of the trench accordingly. When the trench is set, lay the pipe in place, setting it on a bed of gravel or sand. Cover the pipe with gravel to keep soil from clogging perforations. You can skip the gravel layers if you use pipe wrapped with geotextile soil barrier. Backfill the trench with soil.

Mark the location of the pipe using stepping-stones, marking flags, or some other method to ensure that you don't dig there. You can plant perennials over the pipe if you select shallow rooted ones, such as astilbe, pinks, thyme, and others (see Test Garden Tip).

Raised beds

When no low spot eliminates the option of a drainage trench, consider raised beds. By lifting soil above the natural grade, you partner with gravity to improve drainage. Fill a raised bed with well-drained garden loam, and you're guaranteed good drainage.

Choose a material to edge beds and hold soil in place. Wooden options—landscape timbers, treated wood, or rot-resistant cedar—offer affordability but will need to be replaced in 8 to 10 years. Stone or interlocking pavers promise a permanent solution but require footings in areas where cold winters heave soil. If you use stone walls, incorporate planting pockets between some stones to accommodate trailing perennials. Dangling stems will soften the appearance of the wall and make it quickly look like an established part of the garden.

Soil at least 12 inches deep will grow the greatest variety of perennials. Avoid placing a raised bed against any structure. The bed will hold moisture against the building wall and could cause rot.

TEST GARDEN TIP

Shallow-rooted perennials

When soil depth is shy, try growing these perennials with shallow, fibrous root systems.

Astilbe
Blue fescue
Bugleweed
Coral bells
Lavender
Moss phlox
Pinks
Sedum
Thyme

Opposite: **Sometimes the solution to a drainage problem, particularly an issue related to runoff, is to create a dry creek bed, which catches and funnels water along a desired course.**

Raised bed how-to
Building a raised bed improves drainage and allows you to custom-blend soil for your perennials. Soil depth can vary from one end of a bed to the other. Aim for a minimum depth of 8 to 10 inches.

1 REMOVE
Take out any existing vegetation. Loosen the soil, using a rake, digging fork, or tiller. Remove roots, stones, or other debris.

2 EDGE
Establish an edge. Bricks or paver stones form a durable border; deep trench edging is a cheaper option (see pages 78–79).

3 ADD
Build up the existing soil level by adding amendments, such as organic matter, topsoil, or composted manure.

4 ENJOY
Apply mulch for a finished look. Add a 2-inch layer of compost once or twice a year to maintain soil level.

Match Your Garden to Your Lifestyle

Design a perennial garden to suit your daily routine. If your typical workday puts you in the garden around dusk, include lighting to enhance your enjoyment.

Your life patterns should play a major role in determining what kinds of perennials you grow.

Pay attention to lifestyle so you won't commit yourself to a garden you can't maintain, and one that will become an eyesore. Perennials offer such diversity that you can choose plants that cater to your family's schedule amd commitment to maintenance.

If you typically take a long vacation to escape the heat of summer, avoid planting perennials that display peak color in summer. Instead, stock your garden with spring-bloomers, such as bleeding heart, columbine, foamy bells, heart-leaf brunnera, jacob's ladder, and 'May Night' salvia. Include fall-flowering perennials to accent the post-vacation season.

Consider your daily and weekly routines as well. If your weekends are committed to away-from-home activities, fill your garden with low-maintenance perennials that can withstand neglect. A great place to spot performers that don't demand much upkeep is at public parks and commercial planting areas where minimal care is the rule. Durable perennials include hosta, Lenten rose, ornamental grasses, sedum, and yucca.

If daily commutes bring you home about dusk, stock the garden scene with white blooms and silver-tinted foliage to illuminate evening garden walks. The same style of garden also graces evening entertaining with glowing views. Silvery artemisia, lamb's-ear, and lavender reflect light at dusk, as does white-variegated foliage. White blooms of astilbe, garden phlox, hollyhock, iris, and peony infuse evening gardens with luminous life.

Take stock of time

Before you break ground on a perennial garden, inventory your time. How much can you realistically devote to gardening? The answer to this question should guide many aspects of your garden, from size to plant selection to soil preparation to irrigation. Careful soil preparation and an investment in automatic watering can forge a foundation for a beautiful perennial garden that doesn't require a lot of care.

TEST GARDEN TIP

The 15-minute gardener

Commit to spending 15 minutes a day in your garden, surveying the scene. As you take time to smell the roses, you'll also discover plants that need staking, invading pests, sprouting weeds, and dead flowers that need to be removed. Devote a few moments that same day or the next to deal with them. Many problems are nonissues when they're caught and conquered in the early stages.

To make the most of daily walks, tuck garden shears, twine, and a weeding/digging tool in a bucket you can carry or in a weatherproof tool station (an old mailbox works well) in the midst of the garden. When tools are handy, it's a breeze to tidy up as needed.

Plants for fall color
As the back-to-school blitz begins, strike up the color in your perennial garden with performers that come on strong from late summer through fall. These late-season stars sparkle in rich hues that suit the season. Many tower over other perennials. Stake or trim these plants early in the season to prevent an autumnal tumble of flower stems.

ANEMONE
Pink or white flowers with yellow centers dance atop long stems. Part shade to full sun. Zones 3–8.

ASTER
Daisylike blooms in pink, rose, white, purple, or lavender. Full sun. Zones 4–9.

CARYOPTERIS
Fluffy blue blooms among gray-green leaves attract butterflies. Full sun. Zones 5–9.

CHRYSANTHEMUM
Daisy flowers in classic fall hues: gold, orange, white, russet, bronze, purple. Full sun; part shade in the South. Zones 5–9.

FEATHER REED GRASS
Upright grass with golden, wheat sheaflike seedheads. Full sun to part shade. Zones 5–9.

GOLDENROD
Flowers unfurl in golden plumes atop nodding stems. Full sun to light shade. Zones 4–9.

HELENIUM
Yellow, orange, or red daisy blooms with brown to yellow button centers. Full sun. Zones 3–8.

MONKSHOOD
Tall flower spikes punctuated with deep purple blooms. Part sun to part shade. Zones 3–8.

MUHLY GRASS
Purple-pink to pink-red seedheads form clouds that glow in autumn light. Full sun to part shade. Zones 6–10.

RUSSIAN SAGE
Tiny lavender blooms glow amid lacy, gray-green foliage. Full sun. Zones 3–9.

Perennial Sources

You'll typically find a broad selection of perennials in a variety of pot sizes at locally owned and operated garden centers and nurseries.

You can find perennials in a variety of places—

and some don't come with a price tag. Take care when receiving divisions that you aren't also inheriting pest problems. Make sure the starts you receive aren't garden thugs that will quickly run through beds.

The cheapest way to get perennials is to start them from seed. Learn about that on page 39. Local plant sales, sponsored by garden clubs or charitable organizations, offer another option for inexpensive plants. You can purchase perennials at garden centers, discount stores, or home centers. You can also order plants online or from a mail order nursery.

Mail order nurseries are often the sole source of the newest perennials. Read online reviews of a company's service before committing to buy. Make sure you know what size plant you're getting. Some nurseries specialize in small plants, which is why their prices are much lower than their competitors.

Garden centers

Count on a local garden center to provide a broad, deep selection of perennials. Typically, garden centers organize perennials by name and growing conditions (full sun vs. shade). Plants are often well cared for, and you'll find healthy choices in displays. Garden centers are also a good place to find perennials in small pots, which can save money in the long run.

Be careful when you shop at garden centers not to select only perennials that are in bloom, which creates a seasonally lopsided garden based on your shopping window. If you shop in spring, for instance, and buy only what's in color, you'll have a lovely spring garden, but the show will likely fizzle as summer arrives.

Home centers

Hit the home center or big box retailer if you need a large number of uniform plants. The perennial selection at a home center is slimmer than at a garden center, and plants may not be as well tended. The best way to succeed with home center plants is to purchase them as soon as possible after they arrive. Most home centers receive plants on certain days of the week; phone ahead to learn the delivery schedule and shop shortly thereafter.

A home center is a great place to shop if you need large numbers of plants. Their prices will undercut garden centers or mail order nurseries. Compare prices and pot sizes at garden centers and home centers. Many home centers are switching to large pot sizes that command a high price. You may save money and be able to buy more plants if you shop at a garden center where 4-inch perennials are sold.

TEST GARDEN TIP

Plant sale shopping

A sale sponsored by a local garden club or charity is the bargain basement of the plant world. It's the place to scoop up treasures that aren't typically offered at local nurseries, to glean growing tips from other gardeners, and to save money. Take a wagon or cart to haul your selections.

How to choose a healthy plant

You can't judge a plant by its good looks. To pick the healthiest plant, take time to do a two-part visual inspection of the leaves and roots. It's easy to slip a plant out of a pot. Press gently on the sides of the pot, or squeeze it in your hands. Invert the pot while holding one hand over the top of the soil and cradling the stems. Don't pull the plant out by the stems.

HEALTHY ROOTS
Healthy roots are white, ivory, or tan and should reach to the edge of the pot. The soil should smell moist.

ROOTBOUND
Roots that are circling the bottom of the pot are a clue that the plant has been in the pot a long time. Before planting, tease out those circling roots and cut them off.

SICK LEAVES OR ROOTS
Damaged leaves might indicate disease—don't buy that plant. Roots that are slimy or mushy may be rotting. A foul, sewer-gas smell is a sign of root rot.

WEEDS
Weeds growing on the soil surface around the perennial are a clue that the plant may have been carried over from last year. The plant may be healthy—check the roots to be sure.

Smart Shopper Tips

After investing in soil preparation and addressing drainage issues, it's time to purchase plants. It's easy to stretch your dollar when you buy plants. As long as you understand what a healthy plant looks like and how plants are sold, you can assemble a custom-designed garden at a bargain price.

Bare-root perennials

When you purchase perennials, you'll find plants in several forms. Many mail order nurseries sell bare-root plants—without any soil—to save on shipping costs. Bare-root perennials are typically those that have fleshy roots, such as astilbe, balloon flower, or hosta, although fibrous-rooted perennials are often shipped nearly bare root, tucked into peat moss in plastic bags. Unpack and inspect plants upon arrival. Trim any broken roots prior to planting. A little mold on the surface of roots is okay, but if roots are mushy, contact the vendor and ask for a replacement.

Plant bare-root perennials as soon as possible. Bare-root perennials are sensitive to moisture and can easily rot during early spring when

When shopping for perennials, look for plants in one of two forms: bareroot and potted. Container sizes frequently vary from 4 inches to 1 gallon.

cool soil couples with frequent rainfall. If it's too early in the season to plant outdoors, slip bare-root plants into pots. Use pots large enough to accommodate the roots. Set the plant at soil level if you spot new growth emerging from the crown (the base of the aboveground portion of the plan); otherwise bury the crown 1 inch below soil level. Don't water until you see new growth emerging. Water plants when growth is already apparent. Keep the soil barely moist as new growth takes hold; avoid overwatering.

For dry plants, soak the roots for one hour in water before planting. If you must delay planting more than a few hours, store plants in their plastic bags in peat moss, in your refrigerator crisper (set to 35 to 38 degrees), or in a fruit cellar.

Potted perennials

At garden centers and home centers, you'll see perennials sold in a variety of container sizes: 4- to 6-inch pots holding small plants, and deep quarts and gallons housing large perennials. Sometimes you'll find groundcovers sold in shallow 12-inch-square flats. To plant these, slice the perennial into smaller sections with a knife and tuck individual clumps into the soil.

Dollar-wise shopping

In general, you can buy small plants, knowing they'll catch up with their larger, pricier counterparts in a year's time. When buying potted perennials, inspect all the pots in a display, and buy the one with the most stems or crowns per pot.

Another way to make the most of your purchasing dollar comes into play when you're purchasing more than one plant. With fibrous-rooted perennials that grow in clumps, sometimes it's more cost effective to buy one large plant and split it into three or four small plants than it is to buy three or four small plants.

TEST GARDEN TIP

Small plant savvy

Sometimes a tiny foliage tuft in a large pot means the grower has just moved the perennial up from a small container. In this case, the roots will be healthy, just barely visible as they begin to penetrate the soil. The plant may even fall out of the pot into your hand. If possible, buy the same type of perennial in a smaller pot—you'll save money and get the same plant.

A year in the garden One year from planting, perennials that started in a variety of pot sizes—4-inch, 1-quart, and 1-gallon—look pretty similar in size and create a lush, full garden. Use compost to help plants get a jump start. Add well-rotted compost to planting holes the first year and around crowns of plants in the spring of the second year. At the end of the second growing season, you'll see strong growth.

Grow-Your-Own Perennials

Stock a new perennial garden or fill out an existing one with plants you grow yourself. Choose one of two methods to grow perennials: divisions or seeds.

Start with plants

Many perennials are easy to divide and take hold from the smallest starts. You can glean divisions from various sources, such as friends or neighbors. As you walk in your neighborhood, if you spy a clump of perennials that could benefit from division, the owner may grant you a start for help in dividing the clump. Join a garden committee at your local house of worship, public garden, or community center. Many times, volunteers who maintain the gardens gain access to plant divisions.

Plants such as bee balm or coreopsis sprout from simple starts—you need only a trowel full of stems to start growing a sturdy clump. With fibrous-rooted plants like peony or blackberry lily, be sure to get a root that contains an eye or growing point. For trailing plants that root along the stems, such as goldmoss stonecrop or bugleweed, a few stems is all it takes to start a new plant.

Some perennials root easily from cuttings snipped from the end of a stem and stuck in soil. Good candidates for stem cuttings include butterfly weed, caryopteris, hardy hibiscus, and upright sedum. When taking stem cuttings, cut 4- to 6-inch sections near the growing tip. Harvest green, not woody, stem pieces. Strip lower leaves from the stem and slip it into a pot of soil. Poking a hole in the soil with a pencil, screwdriver, or other slender object makes sliding the stem in easier. You can dip the stem in rooting hormone to enhance the rooting process.

After placing the stems in soil, keep the soil moist. Check the stems in a few weeks to see if they're rooting. A simple tug—and ensuing resistance—usually reveals roots have formed.

Start with seeds

An alternative method to dividing perennials is to start from seeds. Some perennials start so easily from seed that they self-seed in the garden. Grow those from seeds yourself, or sprinkle seeds over prepared beds to sow new crops. Perennials take longer to germinate than annuals, but the results save money compared with purchased perennials.

Germination requirements vary by perennial. Some need sunlight to germinate; others require a period of cold. Some perennial seeds must be scarred prior to germinating, and others germinate only when they're sown at the peak of ripeness. Research the specific needs for seeds you want to sprout.

Consider saving your own seeds to reduce the cost of perennial plants. Seeds from hybrid plants yield plants that vary from the parents. The result could be pleasing or plain. Species perennials form seeds that produce fairly true to the parents. Some variation may occur, but that could mark the start of a new variety.

Opposite: **Create a lush perennial garden by dividing existing perennials in your own or a friend's garden. Self-sowing annuals also foster a feeling of fullness in a young perennial garden.**

Perennials with easy-to-save seeds
Allow a few flowers on these plants to set seeds. Harvest the seeds when capsules, seedpods, or flowerheads are dry. With many perennials, storing the seedpods in a bag or box allows them to dry. The drier the pods, the easier the seeds tumble free. Store seeds in a cool, dry, dark place.

BLACK-EYED SUSAN
Rub or shake over open paper bag or bowl. Zones 3–10.

BLANKET FLOWER
Store in cardboard box until dry; stir to separate seeds . Zones 3–11.

CATMINT
Roll between fingers over bowl; seeds and chaff will fall into bowl; softly blow away chaff. Zones 4–10.

COLUMBINE
Shake upside down over bowl. Zones 3–9.

DELPHINIUM
Shake upside down over bowl. Zones 3–10.

FOXGLOVE
Break open over bowl and let seeds fall out. Zones 4–8.

GLOBE THISTLE
Break open seedpods to allow seeds to fall away. Zones 4–9.

HOLLYHOCK
Store in cardboard box until dry; stir to separate seeds; if necessary, break seeds loose. Zones 3–8.

HYSSOP
Shake over piece of paper or bowl. Zones 5–10.

ORIENTAL POPPY
Shake dry seed capsules upside down over open paper bag or bowl. Zones 3–10.

designing with perennials

With experience, your design sense will evolve and showcase your personal style to enjoy and share with others.

p.42
DESIGN ELEMENTS

Combine line, form, texture, and color to create appealing perennial garden combinations. Learn how to bring your design ideas to life.

p.48
DESIGN PRINCIPLES

Repetition, contrast, balance, rhythm, and form are the design principles to keep in mind when developing your landscape. Add focal points to attract attention.

p.56
COLOR

Color is one way to inject individuality into your garden. Choose proven combinations, subtle monochromatic themes, or a riot of diverse hues.

p.64
COMBINING PLANTS

Learn how to exploit bloom time, height, form, and light and moisture needs to forge a cohesive, year-round design.

p.76
DESIGNING BEDS

A successful design starts with a theme and a plan. Analyze your site, and then create bed outlines. Add an edging treatment to give beds a finished look.

Elements of
Design

Gorgeous garden design begins with the basics:

line, form, texture, and color. When these design elements are combined with an inspired eye, the result can make you sigh with delight. Conversely, when these components are applied in a less-than-flawless way, the garden may still present beauty, but something will be missing that's hard to quantify.

Design components

Line refers to those aspects of a garden that lead and direct the eye, such as a plant, path, bed edge, sculpture, or structure. The lines of a garden give every guest's eye a guided tour. Some lines are strong and straight; others are pendulous and wavy. Form is similar to line, but it incorporates a three-dimensional component that reveals the shape of an object and how much space it occupies.

In typical applications, texture refers to how something feels and the look associated with that feel. In the garden, texture encompasses the overall visual appearance and interplay of the various parts—plants, structures, and surfaces. Color extends beyond the spectrum of literal hues and also embraces light, shade, harmony, and composition. Combining colors in a perennial garden is one aspect of the design process that, when woven with texture, form, and line, creates a magnificent garden scene.

Line

In a perennial garden, every plant, bed edge, path, and structure presents a line for the eye to follow. As you design your perennial garden, consciously consider how you can take the distinct lines of different objects and bring them together to compose and direct views. Think about where you want a viewer—even if it's you—to look. Do you want to draw the eye toward a long planting bed to the farthest point? Then place an object there, perhaps a tuteur (an oblisk-shape trellis), bench, or an upright ornamental grass, which will capture attention. Do you want to highlight a specific perennial combination that offers striking seasonal interest? Position that planting and surrounding objects to point the eye in that direction.

Lines can be curved and sweeping, or tidy and crisp. Bed edges can feature right angles and symmetrical organization, or they can be contoured and free-flowing. Pathways, too, strike a linear pose, serving a straight and direct line or a meandering approach. Trellises, arbors, sculptures, fountains, even plants can present vertical lines that draw attention upward. Balance vertical lines with horizontal ones that anchor the eye so it's not sent indefinitely skyward, but rather drawn gently back to earth.

An easy way to see how line expresses itself in your garden is to sketch the scene in winter. Every object—trees, arbors, benches, fences, or trellises—introduces lines. As you pencil in these lines on your drawing, observe how they relate to one another. Look for balance among lines and flowing transition between them. Consider the views from indoors and how line works from that angle. Make plans to fix linear issues that are disjointed, abrupt, or jarring.

Lines in the garden should deliver on their promise. A line leads the eye—somewhere. As you design your garden, make sure that a line leads to a prize of some sort: a focal point, a seating area, or a garden room. If a path bends out of sight around a corner, craft the view you have when you turn the corner, making it an "Aha!" moment in the garden.

Above left: **A weeping plant, such as golden hakone grass, creates a strong line that draws the eye downward. With a weeping line, place something of interest beneath the plant, such as a stone edging.**

Above center: **Curving lines give a garden an informal air. In a large garden space, a curving path adds a sense of mystery as it bends out of sight.**

Above right: **Large drifts of perennials arranged along a curving path form the perfect foundation for an informal, wildflower, or cottage garden.**

Opposite: **Formal garden design features bold, clear lines and sharp angles. A strong sense of symmetry prevails, and decorative touches, such as furnishings and fountains, also reflect the formal feel.**

As you lay out bed and path lines, test the line with your mower. Make sure you can easily swoop along curves. It's also wise to step back as far as you can—into a neighbor's yard, across the street, or upstairs—to view the proposed lines from a distance. Check that your eye travels smoothly along the line and doesn't dart around as it traverses the line.

Perspective and line

As you place planting beds and paths, use their lines to manipulate perspective and the consequent appearance of yard space. For instance, imagine you situate a planting bed in the midpoint of your yard. If you place a bench beyond that bed, toward the farthest point of the yard, that bench becomes the focal point, drawing the eye the length of the yard and effectively making the space seem bigger. If you place that bench between house and planting bed, the space seems smaller as the eye focuses first on the bench. With the simple use of line, you can create an ambience of cozy intimacy or gracious spaciousness.

Form

Form infuses lines with three-dimensional qualities, giving breadth and depth to garden components. A plant like catmint, which billows and spreads, has a mounded form, while gayfeather, with spiky blooms, has more of a cylindrical form. Some plants change form over the course of a growing season. For instance, a delphinium, when not adorned with towering flower stalks, sports a rounded mound of foliage. When flower buds emerge and blossoms unfurl, the plant shape is more conical to cylindrical.

Another way to understand form is to think about the density of a plant. An airy, open form describes a plant like white gaura. A solid form defines a plant like heart-leaf bergenia or hosta. Again, density of form can change during the growing season. An ornamental grass, for instance, may offer a fairly solid form early in the season with its mass of foliage, but when late summer arrives and seedheads shoot skyward, the form becomes more open.

In the perennial garden, combine forms to foster drama. Pair a lacy, airy astilbe with a broadleaf hosta. Plant a dense, rounded peony with dainty foamy bells. Juxtapose flower forms intentionally to stir interest. Fingerlike wands of goldenrod form a striking pose against lobelia spikes, as do the flat paddlelike blooms of joe-pye weed beside the rounded bells of hollyhock.

Rose companions Some
perennials pair naturally with roses, thanks to a low and mounding forms that create a petticoat to disguise a rose's "bare knees" (lower stems).

ROSE PLANTING PARTNERS
ARTEMISIA
BLUE FESCUE
CATMINT
CORAL BELLS
DAYLILY
LADY'S MANTLE
LAMB'S-EARS
LAVENDER
PINKS
SALVIA

Classic combinations
As you begin to plan perennial pairings, it's easy to focus on color. Another factor to consider is plant form. Juxtaposing forms gives a garden real eye appeal. Get started with these proven combinations.

ROUND FLOWER + WISPY FORM

A combination pairs a rounded flower with a wispy plant form, such as the wispy aspect of combining blue fescue and ornamental allium (and later-blooming lilies).

ORNAMENTAL ALLIUM + BLUE FESCUE ORNAMENTAL GRASS

'AUTUMN JOY' SEDUM + RUSSIAN SAGE

PEONY + 'POWIS CASTLE' ARTEMISIA

CONEFLOWER + PINCUSHION FLOWER

GOLDENROD + ALLIUM

SPIKE FLOWER + ROUNDED LEAF

Towering blossom spikes look lovely when planted alongside perennials that unfurl rounded leaves. The counterpoint of slender and curving forms creates eye-catching beauty and adds up to design success— every time.

LIGULARIA + HOSTA

DELPHINIUM + LADY'S MANTLE

CARDINAL FLOWER + CORAL BELLS

GAYFEATHER + SHOWY SEDUM

AIRY PLANT + SOLID PLANT

One way to mingle perennials is to place a plant with an airy, open form next to one with a more solid appearance. Many perennials qualify for this type of matchup. A perennial that seems open in form, like a meadow rue, can appear more solid when paired with a dense ornamental grass, like zebra grass.

ASTILBE + HOSTA

WHITE GAURA + SHOWY SEDUM

YARROW + FALSE INDIGO

FERN + HEART-LEAF BERGENIA

Texture

Intentionally mingling foliage texture gives a garden that magic factor t[...]kes you pause t[...]n the beauty. Glowing golden hakone grass plays a fine-leaf textural counterpoint to a broadleaf hosta.

In the garden, texture consists of several components.

Visual appearance as related to touch—what a plant feels like—is one aspect. The blossoms of bearded iris resemble richly hued velvet with fuzzy epaulets. With Oriental poppies, crepe paper blooms top pipe cleaner stems. Astilbe and meadowsweet unfurl flowers resembling feathery plumes, and foam flower and meadow rue open lacy blooms.

Leaves also introduce touchable content to the perennial palette. For instance, lamb's-ears appears soft and woolly, which it is. Yellow corydalis bears divided leaves perfect for tickling, many ferns resemble feathers, and some hostas unfurl seersucker foliage. Golden hakone grass resembles a soft waterfall, and the spiny foliage of globe thistle threatens danger. Each introduces texture to a perennial garden.

How a plant absorbs or reflects light is another aspect of texture. Light absorption enhances a leaf's textural appearance. The shiny leaves of bugleweed or Lenten rose stand out in a planting more than the matte foliage of campanula or hyssop.

Leaf or flower size also contributes to texture. Large leaves bear a bolder presence than small ones. For example, coral bells or hosta leaves present a stronger texture than fine ornamental grass foliage or a fern's divided leaves. A black-eyed susan flower has a stronger presence than airy foamy bells blooms.

Textural categories

Typically leaves and flowers are classified as coarse, medium, or fine textured. A coarse-textured plant has large leaves and flowers, large teeth along leaf edges, or rough surfaces. Fine-textured plants have small or narrow leaves and flowers or finely divided leaves. Medium-textured plants fall between coarse and fine and can take on either a coarse or fine appearance, depending on what it's growing near.

Texture isn't a characteristic cast in stone; it's truly relative. While coreopsis and muhly grass always appear fine textured, goldenrod can look fine textured next to a broadleaf hosta but coarse textured next to an airy ornamental grass.

Some plants don different textures at various points in the season. Lady's mantle flowers present a fine texture; its leaves, medium. Pincushion flower foliage is medium textured, but when flowers appear and dance atop wiry stems, the plant assumes a fine texture.

Design with texture

Use texture to your advantage when assembling a perennial bed. While combining flower colors is necessary, focus on foliage as well. Blossoms last a short time, but leaves linger. By carefully composing textural compositions, the garden border will strike interesting chords all season long. Use contrasting textures to introduce lively refrains and groupings of similar textures to play a soothing tune.

In shade gardens, texture saves the day when flowers fade and all that remains is green foliage. If you're facing a shady site, rise to the occasion by staging a textural drama punctuated with colorful foliage.

Play with texture to manipulate perspective in the garden. Fine-textured plants placed at the back of a garden give a sense of infinite expanse. Coarse-textured beauties planted at the rear of a large bed shrink a space, bringing the far end closer. Gardens viewed from afar benefit from a selection of coarse-textured perennials, which are easier to see.

TEST GARDEN TIP

Fabulous ferns

Count on ferns to inject textural interest in any planting combination.

Christmas fern
Cinnamon fern
Hay-scented fern
Japanese painted fern
Maidenhair fern
Ostrich fern
Sensitive fern

Tops in texture Perennials fall into three general categories of texture: fine, medium, and coarse. Mix plants from each category to create striking combinations. Medium-textured perennials can frequently function as fine or coarse textured, depending on their planting partners.

FINE-TEXTURED

ASTILBE Part shade to full shade (pictured)

BOLTONIA Full sun to part shade

LAVENDER Full sun

PRAIRIE DROPSEED GRASS Full sun

SILVERMOUND ARTEMISIA Full sun

MEDIUM-TEXTURED

BUTTERFLY WEED Full sun

FALSE INDIGO Full sun to part sun (pictured)

HYSSOP Full sun to part shade

LADYBELLS Full sun to part shade

SIBERIAN IRIS Full sun to part shade

COARSE-TEXTURED

BEAR'S BREECHES Full sun to part shade cool regions; full shade in hot areas

HEART-LEAF BRUNNERA Part shade (pictured)

HOLLYHOCK Full sun

HOSTA Part to full shade

RODGERSIA Part sun to full shade

Design Principles

Daylilies repeated throughout this garden bed represent the design principle of repetition. An edging of marigolds along each bed on either side of the path represents symmetry.

TEST GARDEN TIP

Asymmetrical design

Asymmetry occurs when dissimilar plants are planted on either side of the imaginary central axis in a bed. A large-leaf hosta tucked into one side of a bed and a trio of astilbe on the other side is asymmetrical, yet balanced. Another example of asymmetry is placing a New Zealand flax in a tall pot on one side of a garden and a clump of feather reed grass on the other side.

Simple design principles can help you create

a beautiful, unified perennial garden: balance, contrast, repetition, rhythm, focal point, and scale. You can approach design by mastering the elements (line, form, texture, color) or by manipulating the principles. Usually, if you execute the principles well, the elements simply fall into place. Whichever approach you take, trust that as you adapt these design basics into your garden design, the final result will be eye-catching, inspiring, and magical.

Balance

As you consider balance, think of perennials and objects in the garden as having visual weight. Some items are tall and square; others are billowing and round. When you have balance in a garden setting, you have equilibrium between all the parts when they're viewed from a particular angle. The balance may seem to disappear when you move to another position in the garden, but it remains. When there's balance, the garden exudes a feeling of harmony and stability.

Above left: **In a formal garden, symmetry typically prevails—in planting beds, pathway composition and design, and outdoor structures.**

Above right: **Containers placed throughout a garden introduce balance. Containers flanking the entrance to the lawn area don't have to be identical to add symmetry.**

In a perennial garden, imagine a central axis running through the center of the planting bed. Distribute the visual weight of the objects in the planting bed equally on opposite sides of that axis, and you achieve balance.

For instance, if on one side of the planting bed you have a false indigo that is 36 inches tall and wide, you'll want to balance that with something of a similar visual weight on the opposite side. You might use a tuteur with a vine, or even a pair of smaller plants that create similar bulk, such as aster and lady's mantle. The net effect is that when you step back and view the bed, there's an object on the left with a particular visual weight, and it's balanced by an object on the right.

To achieve balance, don't try too hard. If you concentrate on achieving balance, the look will be formal and possibly contrived. Aim to create a garden that's pleasing to your eye. Before you plant, consider the final look, either on paper or using potted perennials in the garden to see whether you have struck a point of balance. Most likely, you will, because our brains are wired to respond to balance.

Symmetry

Another way to think of balance is to consider symmetry. A symmetrical design presents balance—both sides of the planting bed are roughly equal in terms of visual weight of the objects. A pair of matching containers flanking a clematis-covered arbor embodies symmetry, as does a clump of coreopsis placed on either side of a delphinium. Symmetry is a key to executing formal garden design.

Contrast, Repetition, and Rhythm

The principles of contrast, repetition, and rhythm infuse a garden with interest and unity. Use these tactics to give your garden head-turning finesse.

Contrast

Sometimes called variety, contrast is probably the easiest concept for gardeners to grasp. After all, it's a cinch to gather a collection of plants that catch your eye. Achieving effective contrast involves mingling those plants in a border in a pleasing manner. For instance, if you plant daylily, ornamental grass, and sedge together, while you have a variety of plants, you don't have contrast because they all have a similar leaf and form. If you replace the sedge with an upright sedum and include a lady's mantle, you have a grouping that unfurls contrast through the growing season, adding drama to the garden.

Introduce contrast through plants, using texture, height, form, and color. You can also rely on hardscape elements to punctuate a perennial garden with texture. A steel-frame trellis, a stone bench, and a lively stepping-stone path each offers a different texture. Be careful not to overdo with contrast. When contrast rules in a garden, the result is chaos. Balance contrast with repetition.

Repetition

Repetition in the garden creates cohesiveness. It's the subtle sign, maybe only registered subconsciously, that separate parts of the garden or yard are part of a greater whole. You can repeat plants, using the same species or variety at several points in your planting bed, or you can repeat aspects of plants, such as color, texture, line, or form. Color is one of the strongest

A stepping-stone path creates rhythm in a garden, causing the eye to skip along in a game of mental hopscotch. This garden also features repetitive vertical elements: the picket fence posts and the sculptural black tuteurs.

motifs in effective repetition, striking balance and cuing the eye that separate parts of the garden are connected. You can also create repetition through objects or hardscape materials.

Rhythm

When you incorporate rhythm in a garden, you insert flow and movement. It's not the plants or the garden itself moving, but rather the eye of the person viewing it. When rhythm is at work, the eye is drawn neatly through a garden, following the repetition of plants, colors, or objects, or wending along a path or a series of terraces.

Arranging plants in a bed from tallest in back to shortest in front creates movement. Using plants that sway in the breeze, like ornamental grasses, sedges, or New Zealand flax, also generates rhythm. Interrupting a bed of low-growing perennials, such as pinks or groundcover sedum, with a tall clump of penstemon or Siberian iris or a stone sculpture, creates a sense of movement because the eye has to stop and travel around the interruption. Pathways, whether curving or straight, introduce rhythm. A curving path can physically cause a viewer to move in the garden to explore what lies around the bend.

TEST
GARDEN
TIP

Déjà vu in the garden

Repetition in the garden brings eye-pleasing unity to the scene. Introduce repetition using these tips.

Repeat a color, using plants, garden ornaments, mulch, or even a painted wall.

Tuck your favorite plant into many places throughout your yard.

Use the same material for all paths to create unity.

Build a fence to form a repetitive element across many areas of a yard.

Choose hardscape that echoes color tones. Brick pavers, outdoor furnishings, and oversize pots can reflect a color pattern that runs through your planting beds.

Spotlight on grasses
Ornamental grasses introduce elements of movement and rhythm to a perennial garden. With colorful foliage that lingers through winter, grasses also provide season-long interest.

BLUE OAT GRASS
Steel blue foliage; seedheads wheat color. 24 inches tall and wide. Seedheads to 40 to 64 inches tall. Zones 3–9.

'BOWLES' GOLDEN' SEDGE
Golden yellow leaves turn green as they mature. 24 to 36 inches tall and wide. Zones 6–9.

FEATHER REED GRASS
In winter, green leaves turn tan, purple-green seedheads turn gold. 3 to 4 feet tall; seedheads 5 to more than 6 feet tall; plant 2 to 3 feet wide. Zones 4–9.

GOLDEN HAKONE GRASS
Gold leaves striped dark green. 18 inches tall and wide. Zones 4–9.

MISCANTHUS GRASS 'MORNING LIGHT'
Green leaves striped with creamy white edges; pinkish seedheads fade to silver. 5 feet tall, 3 feet wide (seedheads to 6 feet). Zones 4–9.

MISCANTHUS GRASS 'POSITANO'
Green leaves have silver midrib; seedheads reddish. 5 to 6 feet tall (seedheads to 7 feet); 3 to 5 feet wide. Zones 5–9.

MISCANTHUS GRASS 'RIGOLETTO'
White-striped leaves; seedheads red fading to silver. 3 to 4 feet tall (seedheads to 5 feet tall. 30 to 36 inches wide. Zones 5–9.

MUHLY GRASS
Green leaves; purple-pink to pink-red seedheads fade to gold in fall. 12 inches tall (seedheads to 36 inches). 3 to 4 feet wide. Zones 6–10.

PORCUPINE GRASS
Horizontal yellow bands on green leaves; pinkish seedheads. 5 feet tall (seedheads to 7 feet); 3 to 4 feet wide. Zones 5–9.

SWITCH GRASS 'PRAIRIE FIRE'
Blue-green foliage turns red in summer; seedheads rosy red. 36 inches tall (seedheads to 4 feet); 24 inches wide. Zones 4–9.

Focal Point

As you envision your perennial garden, decide which part of the garden you want to emphasize. It could be a part of the garden that falls within a key viewing area as you stand inside the house looking out. It may be a section of your yard that stands opposite an area that is an eyesore; if so, use the focal point of a perennial garden to direct attention away from the problem area. Or it could just be the sunniest part of your yard or the area next to an outdoor living room.

If you're dealing with a large open area of your yard as the context for your perennial garden, consider using a kidney-shape bed. In that case, locate the focal point at the incurve—the part of the curve that dips in. With any curving bed, the naturally occurring spot for the focal point is the incurve. That's where the eye is drawn to rest.

Choose a focal point

You may already have the focal point in mind as you design and site your perennial garden. It could be a plant that you have come to love, an arbor or trellis, a sculpture, or a fountain. In a large yard, you could use a patio or seating area as a focal point.

If you select a plant as a focal point, be sure that it stages strong interest throughout the growing season. If it doesn't flower continuously, like black-eyed Susan or false sunflower, the plant must have striking foliage, such as bear's breeches, hosta, New Zealand flax, or ornamental grass—something that makes it stands out.

Design with the focal point

Once you decide where to place your focal point, design the rest of the garden in relationship to it.

Above: **Something as simple as a birdbath, sculpture, or gazing ball placed among perennials can serve as a focal point in a planting bed.**

Opposite, top: **You can count on a perennial that grows to a substantial size to hold its own as a focal point.**

Draw an imaginary line through the focal point in several directions to determine where to place other key plants or objects in your garden that will support and direct views toward the focal point. These become the axes of the garden. As you play with form and line around and along these axes, you will create a garden masterpiece.

Objects that highlight the primary focal point are called secondary focal points. They not only draw attention to the primary focal point but also introduce rhythm to the garden, as they draw or stop the eye en route to the primary focal point. In a kidney-shape bed, place a secondary focal point in one or both of the lobes of the kidney. If you choose to situate secondary focal points in both lobes, using the same perennial or plant grouping creates a stronger impact.

Perennials with presence A focal point plant commands presence in the garden with beautiful flowers or colorful foliage, or both. Whatever its size, it must stand out in the garden. Consider these focal point candidates.

FOR SHADY GARDENS

BUGBANE
Tall plant with slender wands of white to pink in midsummer to early fall. Zones 3–7.

CINNAMON FERN
Cinnamon-color spore fronds stand out in the center of green fronds. Zones 4–9.

GOATSBEARD
Plumes of creamy white flowers on top of tall stems in early summer. Zones 3–7.

HOSTA 'BLUE MAMMOTH'
Highly textured, seersucker, blue leaves up to 10 inches across. Zones 3–9.

RODGERSIA
Bold coarse-textured foliage; pink, red, or white flowers in spring or mid- or late summer. Zones 5–8.

FOR SUNNY GARDENS

ASTER
Blanketed with pink, purple, or white flowers in late summer and fall. Zones 5–9.

BUTTERFLY WEED
Brilliant orange flowers in summer are followed by seedpods. Zones 4–10.

FOUNTAIN GRASS
Flowing foliage all summer; fluffy plumes in late summer; stands all winter. Zones 5–9.

LAVENDER
Low-growing, bushy plant with vibrant purple flowers. Zones 5–10.

YUCCA
Strong, striking form all year. Zones 4–11.

Scale

Scale deals with the harmony of the garden, which hinges on size relationships—between you and your garden, and among various elements in the garden. When size relationships are in scale with one another, harmony reigns and the garden creates a peaceful, eye-pleasing scene. When scale is out of sync, one object engulfs another and looks out of place.

If you use a tall ornamental grass, such as switchgrass, which grows to 6 feet tall, next to a garden shed that's 7 feet tall, by the season's end the grass will dwarf the building. Plant a 3-foot-tall clump of ladybells next to the shed, and you'll have an eye-catching scene. The same principle applies when choosing which plants to position near one another in a grouping. For example, towering hollyhock skirted with liriope can look cartoonish.

An easy way to combine perennials with scale in mind is to arrange plants according to size—before planting. You can even do this in a wagon at a garden center as you contemplate perennial groupings. Place plants next to one another and see if the sizes complement each other.

Scale comes into play when you're selecting a sculpture, fountain, or arbor for your garden. Choose objects that are too small, and they'll be lost among the perennials. Too-large items will overshadow the garden and look out of place.

An easy approach for achieving scale is to arrange plants in a bed by height: short plants in front, tall in back.

A sliding rule

The guideline when selecting perennials for a planting bed is that the tallest plant height should equal no more than one-half the width of the bed. For a bed that's 6 feet deep, choose a perennial that's roughly 3 feet tall for the tallest plant. Step down other perennials from that size. A similar rule of proportion is true for decorative objects. Surround birdbaths, sculptures, or benches with plants that equal no more than two-thirds the height of the object in order to match the scale of the decorative object with the plants that surround it.

Once you master grouping perennials by size in pretty-as-picture combinations, you can plan to break the rules to orchestrate rhythm or emphasize a focal point. Use caution when planning abrupt changes in scale. If you incorporate too many changed into a garden, the net effect is restless and chaotic.

Choose structural elements that don't overwhelm plantings but rather complement them. A birdhouse introduces vertical interest among perennials; a vine climbing the post anchors the birdhouse to the bed.

Mix and match with scale

Using scale in the garden is all about creating smooth transitions between plants. For the smoothest shifts, pair small plants with medium-size ones or medium-size plants with large ones. If you want to stir up excitement, pair plants of vastly different sizes. Check out these examples; all the plants thrive in full sun and well-drained soil.

SMALL PLANTS—
12 INCHES TALL OR LESS

BELLFLOWER 'BLUE CLIPS' (shown) Blue flowers in summer. Zones 3–9.

BLANKET FLOWER 'BIJOU' Red and yellow flowers in early summer to fall; drought tolerant. Zones 3–8.

BLUE FESCUE 'ELIJAH BLUE' Grass with blue-green foliage. Zones 4–8.

DAYLILY 'EENIE WEENIE' Dwarf plant with yellow flowers. Zones 3–10.

GERANIUM Purple, pink, or white flowers in spring or summer; attractive foliage. Zone depends on species.

PINKS White, pink, or red flowers in late spring to early summer. Zones 3–10.

MEDIUM PLANTS—
12 TO 36 INCHES TALL

BEARDED IRIS (shown) Available in many flower colors; blooms in late spring to early summer. Zones 3–10.

COREOPSIS 'MOONBEAM' Pale yellow flowers all summer. Zones 4–9.

FOUNTAIN GRASS 'HAMELN' Almond seedheads in fall. Zones 5–9.

PURPLE CONEFLOWER Purple daisylike flowers in summer. Zones 2–10.

SALVIA 'MAY NIGHT' Purple flowers in summer. Zones 4–10.

SEDUM 'AUTUMN JOY' Deep rose flowers in fall; bronze seedheads in winter. Zones 3–10.

LARGE PLANTS—
3 FEET TALL OR MORE

BEE BALM (shown) Pink, red, or purple flowers in summer. Zones 3–9.

GARDEN PHLOX Many flower colors available; blooms in summer. Zones 4–8.

HOLLYHOCK Bold or pastel flowers on upright, sturdy stalks in summer. Zones 3–8.

JOE-PYE WEED 'GATEWAY' Large, airy pink flower clusters in late summer. Zones 3–7.

MISCANTHUS GRASS 'ADAGIO' Green-and-white striped leaves. Zones 5–9.

RUSSIAN SAGE Purple summer flowers and silver foliage. Zones 3–10.

Color in the Garden

Of all the design elements—line, form, texture and color—

color is the one that most people consider when they begin to design a perennial garden. Even if they aren't aware that they're actually designing a planting, most gardeners tend to choose perennials through flower or foliage color. By making careful selections, you can have perennials that bring color to the garden in nearly every season, through flowers, foliage, or seedpods.

Color has a physical and psychological effect on the human body and mind. Red and yellow cause blood pressure to rise; green produces relaxation. Emotionally, colors generate unique responses in different people. While red is exciting for some, it's irritating for others. For many, blue produces a soothing, cooling effect, but for some it's downright depressing

Use color effectively

Colors have a distinct impact on perception. Yellow, for instance, is a color that the eye sees first and faster than other colors, which is why school buses and warning signs feature that hue. Use yellow in the garden to highlight key features, such as a fountain or step. You can also choose an attention-grabbing yellow perennial to use as a primary or secondary focal point.

The cool colors—blue, green, and purple—tend to recede in the distance. In a small garden, incorporating these hues into the planting scheme will make the space seem larger. Cool tones have less light in them, which makes them disappear in low-light conditions, such as shade or evening gardens. If you plan to rely on something blue, green, or purple as a focal point, it will be most effective in a garden where sunlight or other reflected light floods the scene.

Red, yellow, and orange—the warmer shades—leap out, appearing closer than they actually are. This makes them excellent candidates for a large garden, where they can

Above: **Analogous colors, such as rose, purple, and lavender, are located near each other on the color wheel and look lovely together. Add in a complementary hue like yellow to give the combination pop.**

Opposite, top: **Creating a monochromatic color scheme, like this blue-tone tableau, produces a perennial planting that's guaranteed to be beautiful. Including containers that match the color palette enhances the effect.**

infuse a sense of intimacy. In a small setting, use these warm colors with care and intention, to avoid shrinking the space even more. A wonderful way to use red or orange in a tiny garden is as an accent color to highlight other hues. Be cautious with yellow, lest its prima donna personality create chaos by vying with other perennials for attention. Place yellow at the middle and back of borders to drum up rhythm and march the eye through the planting.

As you begin to contemplate color, grab some paint chips at a local hardware store or home center. Mix and match these until you find combinations that you like, then carry these with you to the garden center or use them as you peruse the color chart on pages 62–63, or the Perennial Encyclopedia (see page 174). Find perennials that match the shades you prefer. To ensure a season-long color show, use the bloom time chart on pages 70–75 to be sure you'll get a long sequence of bloom. Above all, as you plan your garden, choose colors that please you.

The color wheel The color wheel arranges the familiar colors of the rainbow in a circle. Use this wheel as a guide for planning perennial combinations.

By working with complementary, analogous, and triad colors, you're guaranteed to succeed with your color scheme. Use each of these groupings by season in your garden (complementary in spring, analogous in summer, and triad in fall) to create a planting that's dynamic, intriguing, and beautiful all year long.

COMPLEMENTARY COLORS are located across from each other on the wheel. Orange and blue, yellow and violet, and red and green are complementary colors.

ANALOGOUS COLORS—also called harmonious—are located beside each other on the color wheel. Blue and blue-violet, red and red-orange, and green and yellow-green are analogous colors.

TRIAD refers to colors that are separated by three colors on the wheel. Red, yellow, and blue are a triad, as are blue-violet, red-orange, and yellow-green.

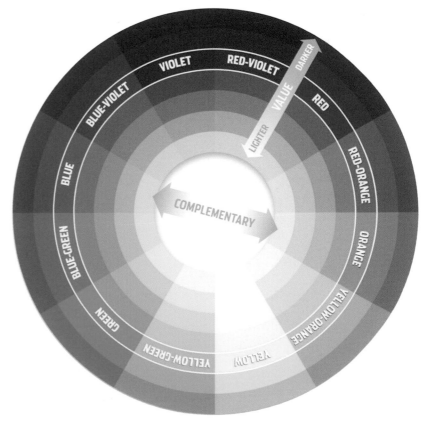

One-Color Gardens

For a simple but sophisticated approach to perennial garden design,

create a monochromatic planting. In this type of design, you use plants that unfurl leaves or flowers in a single color and in hues, shades, tints, and tones of that color. The result is a foolproof design featuring colors that don't clash or create too much contrast.

If your passion is red, a monochromatic garden celebrating that color could include expressions of red, such as burgundy, scarlet, orange-red, carmine, cerise, and pink. For a purple garden, you could work in plants showing lavender, blue-violet, violet, lilac, periwinkle, mauve, and eggplant. No matter what hue you choose to be the centerpiece of your garden design, you'll want to include a few touches of a complementary or analgous color throughout the planting to stir interest.

Single color strategy

A monochromatic scheme provides an opportunity to use color to open up a small or shade-shrouded garden. By planting perennials in pastel shades of pink, blue, or yellow, you can make a small space feel larger or turn up the light in a shady corner. Avoid using pastel hues in sunny spots if you'll view the area during the day, because the sun will wash out the colors, making them appear white. At dusk, however, these pale colors reflect light, forming a glowing welcome for after-dinner garden walks.

Count on gray to add neutral filler to the garden, forming a buffer zone that underscores subtle shifts between various expressions of the featured color. Group plants of a single color family just as you would different color plants. Create contrast by placing a dark shade next to a lighter tint and by blending foliage textures.

Remember to work colorful foliage into your design. You can find perennials and shrubs that bear leaves in a broad range of hues, including yellow, purple, burgundy, and blue. Use these foliage stars to accent and complete your monochromatic scheme.

Above: **In a monochromatic planting, include foliage plants and annual bloomers that suit the scheme. Here, burgundy-splashed 'Iron Cross' oxalis and annual impatiens add red tones to the garden all season long.**

Opposite, top: **In a blue garden, consider adding blue-tone pinks, like chives, to the mix. Use white as a foil that graciously interrupts the monochromatic scheme.**

Sculpture, furniture, or garden decor can also support your color choice—or introduce a contrasting accent. Look for hardscape that complements your color scheme, such as stepping-stones, tiles, or pavers. Mulch can play a supporting role in the design, blending in or interjecting a quietly subdued contrast. It's wise to surround a monochromatic garden with a swath of lawn or single-color path to provide a place for the eye to rest and serve as a foreground or backdrop to the monochromatic bed.

Shift your focus

Following a monochromatic approach transforms the design process into an exercise in considering aspects of plants beyond flower and foliage color. Form and texture—of both leaves and plants—play a stronger role in the perennial selection process when color is removed from the equation.

If you rely on flowers to carry the garden through the seasons, ensure that something is always blooming. An easy way to do that is to visit a full-service garden center every three weeks throughout the growing season to see what's in flower to give you ideas on perennials to include in your garden.

As with any perennial garden, a monochromatic planting is a work in progress. Make changes over time as you spot weaknesses in the color scheme or downtimes in the flower show. Interject daubs of complementary color if the overall effect shifts from monochromatic to monotonous at any point during the growing season.

Garden blues
Blue is one of the more elusive colors in the garden. While there are shades and tints of blue, varying from purple to pale lavender, true blues are hard to find. Satisfy your appetite for blue with a few of these blue-tone beauties.

BALLOON FLOWER
Blue-violet balloon buds burst open to reveal star-shape flowers from early summer to fall. Zones 3–8.

BLUE FESCUE
Compact grass with tufts of blue foliage. Zones 4–8.

CARYOPTERIS
Fluffy blue flower clusters fill stems from late summer to early fall. Zones 5–9.

CLUSTERED BELLFLOWER
Clustered violet bell-shape blooms top stems in early summer. Zones 3–8.

CORYDALIS 'BLUE PANDA'
Blue fishlike flowers dangle over fine foliage from midspring to early summer; repeat bloom in fall. Zones 5–8.

GLOBE THISTLE
Blue flower spheres stand on gray-green stems in midsummer and linger for weeks. Zones 4–9.

HOSTA 'HALCYON'
Steelblue leaves unfurl from spring through frost; reportedly shows some slug resistance. Zones 3–8.

MONKSHOOD
Blue blossoms cover spikes from late summer into fall. Zones 3–8.

NEW ENGLAND ASTER
Daisylike flowers cover mounding plants from late summer into fall. Zones 4–9.

SALVIA 'MAY NIGHT'
Deep blue flower spikes stand above foliage in late spring and linger for weeks. Zones 4–10.

Color from Foliage

Dark-leaf perennials, such as Hillside Black Beauty bugbane, introduce deep shades to the garden that form exquisite pairings with light-tone flowers or chartreuse foliage.

Set aside the color wheel, and you'll discover several other colors

that deserve a place in your garden. These hard-working hues earn top billing and solve problems in garden design. White, silver, gray, and black can infuse perennial combinations with that mystical wow factor.

White, silver, and gray

Because white reflects light, it's a showstopper in the garden, grabbing attention in a way that's second only to yellow. Pure white deserves particular consideration in conditions where light is lacking—a shady nook, a moonlight garden, or a woodland setting. Another excellent place to lean on white is in a planting bed backed with dark evergreens. Count on white to liven spring and fall settings, when sunlight is not as harsh as during high summer.

Pair white with green to cast an elegant ambience; mix it with pink, lavender, and other pastels for a demure, restful setting. Call on white to referee a clash between bold colors. Take care not to sprinkle white haphazardly throughout a planting. Too much can stir chaos,

pitting bold perennials against one another in a bid for attention.

Silver and gray put the finishing touches on a perennial bed, using their mellow personalities to coax other colors into harmony. Throughout the perennial garden, position silver and gray plants to soothe clashing colors, emphasize a deep-tone plant, or highlight a focal point plant. In low light situations, silver and gray reflect light, adopting a luminous quality. You can also rely on silver and gray plants to spark interest when nearby bloomers are not in flower.

Black

Most plants sold or labeled as black are actually a deep, deep shade of purple or burgundy. From a distance, these shades appear black. You can find "black" hollyhocks, irises, butterfly bushes, tulips, and roses—all featuring flowers in deepest shades. Dark foliage, such as 'Black Jack' sedum, black mondo grass, 'Black Adder' mountain flax, 'Hillside Black Beauty' bugbane, and 'Obsidian' coral bells also impresses.

Dark colors in a garden pair naturally with pastel hues. A pale pink catmint with a deep purple bearded iris forms a sizzling partnership that fills late spring and early summer with riveting beauty. Back a dark-flowered butterfly bush with Japanese silver grass for a sparkling summer scene. Dark foliage also delivers an eye-pleasing jolt when partnered with gold. Pair 'Black Beauty' or 'Obsidian' coral bells with 'Bowles' Golden' sedge, or 'Black Jack' sedum with porcupine grass, and you'll have season-long drama.

Site dark plants—whether the deep hue resides in flowers or foliage—in sunny areas of the garden. Tucked into shade, these bass-tone beauties tend to disappear.

Foliage

Leaves unfurl in many shades, tones, and tints of green. Take time to study the variations on a green theme at a garden center. Remember that the greenery in your garden will play background music through most of the garden season. When perennials aren't flowering—whether it's a momentary rest or a prolonged pause—greens take up the melody. Choose perennials with an eye toward a mix of green shades.

Foliage also offers other colors: gold, white, burgundy, blue, purple, rose, silver, and variegated. Incorporate striking leafy stars in your perennial design. Don't overdo variegated foliage; site it carefully for the biggest impact. Gold-leaf foliage plants tend to grow the strongest color in sunny sites, although a hot, dry footing can produce leaf scorch. White-leaf plants typically thrive in light shade.

A silver lining

Add a silver sheen to your perennial beds with plants that unfurl leaves in silver or gray shades. While most of these plants open blossoms at some point in the growing season, their foliage introduces a steady shot of color all season long. Rely on these perennials to stage a vibrant contrast with bold-color beauties or to infuse a garden with a soft glow at dusk.

SILVER-FOLIAGE STANDOUTS
ARTEMISIA
HEART-LEAF BRUNNERA 'JACK FROST'
CORAL BELLS 'PEWTER VEIL'
JAPANESE PAINTED FERN
LAMB'S-EARS
LAVENDER
LAVENDER COTTON
LUNGWORT 'SILVER SHIMMERS'
MULLEIN
ROSE CAMPION
RUSSIAN SAGE
SILVER SAGE
SILVER SPEEDWELL
YARROW 'MOONSHINE'

The spectrum of colors

Use this chart like a color wheel. From left to right the colors go from warm to cool. From top to bottom the colors decrease in intensity, with the top row being the strongest hue and the bottom row the palest tint. The colors across each row are of equal weight.

THE WARM RANGE

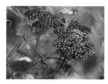
Yarrow 'Paprika'

Oriental poppy

Yellow and white bearded iris

Hosta 'Fire and Ice'

Red Asiatic lily

Lily 'Enchantment'

Yellow chrysanthemum

'Sea Foam' foam flower

Daylily 'Anzac'

Chrysanthemum 'Golden Grace'

Lily

Golden hakone grass

Pinks 'Ideal Crimson'

Orange Asiatic lily

'Sarah' chrysanthemum

Hosta 'American Sweetheart'

Autumn sage

Chrysanthemum 'Nicole'

Evening primrose

Hosta 'Golden Tiara'

Red-orange daylily

Black-eyed susan

Daylily

Green hosta

Daylily 'Fires of Fuji'

Yellow torch lily

Cushion spurge

Barrenwort

Crocosmia

Yellow corydalis

Lady's mantle

Hosta 'Don Stevens'

Butterfly weed

Coreopsis 'Baby Sun'

Lenten rose hybrid

Lady's mantle

THE COOL RANGE

 Artemisia 'Powis Castle'

Delphinium

 Cupid's dart

Clematis 'Ville de Lyon'

 Hosta 'Krossa Regal'

Globe thistle

Caryopteris

Bloody cranesbill

Lamb's-ears

Balloon flower

Geranium 'Johnson's Blue'

New England aster

Blue oat grass

Delphinium

Corydalis 'Blackberry Wine'

Spiderwort

Hosta 'Elvis Lives'

Blue anise sage 'Black and Blue'

Jackman clematis

Stokes' aster

Corydalis 'Blue Panda'

Columbine hybrid

Perennial salvia 'May Night'

Corydalis 'Berry Exciting'

Delphinium 'Butterfly Blue'

Japanese iris 'Iso-No-Nami'

Bearded iris hybrid

Centranthus

Creeping veronica 'Georgia Blue'

Siberian iris

Columbine hybrid

Clematis 'Niobe'

Heart-leaf brunnera

Clustered bellflower

Rose verbena

Lenten rose hybrid

Combining Elements

Creating striking perennial combinations begins with considering many aspects at once:

plant height, flower color, bloom time, light needs, texture, plant form, and more. Instead of trying to juggle these attributes and conceptualize your entire perennial border at once, focus on individual plant combinations. Plan a few key combinations that you want to include, and think about ways you can incorporate them into the same bed. You may want to lean on a foliage plant to bridge the gaps between combinations, or you could include some garden art or a container garden to keep the color going.

Consider flowering windows with the combinations you create. Make sure bloom times are seasonally spaced so you don't have a full-color summer sandwiched between a foliage-filled spring and a dull fall. Count on spring flowering bulbs for a guaranteed infusion of early season color.

Explore the world of hardy summer-blooming bulbs such as Asiatic lily, Oriental lily, and ornamental allium to punctuate a summer border with bulb-based color. Summer tropical bulbs can also work colorful touches into the summer garden that linger until frost. Tropical options include acidanthera, agapanthus, caladium, crinum, elephant's ear, or rain lily. These beauties grow quickly from bulbs and can be planted in beds or containers to accent perennial combinations.

Mimic seasonal color schemes

In the perennial garden, each season has a color palette that occurs naturally. Spring unfurls in pastel pinks and blues, with chartreuse or gold as an accent hue. Summer colors blaze strong, igniting bold shades, such as red, yellow, and orange. Fall overflows in a cornucopia of saturated jewel tones: purple, orange, gold, or burgundy. These color palettes suit the sunlight that occurs during these seasons—spring's soft

This fall border shines with artfully blended shades of pink and burgundy. The white seedheads of fountain grass add color and textural contrast to the combination.

light, summer's harsh rays, and fall's golden glow. As you craft perennial combinations, keep these natural palettes in mind and select plants that will complement the color show that nature is staging outside the garden.

Look to quiet times

Above all, don't overlook the quiet seasons of the garden when the flower show falls silent and foliage takes center stage. Consider the dormant season, too, when plants may sport stems or seedheads, or simply disappear. As you piece together combinations, factor in seasonal appearances and make sure that something—foliage, variegation, seedheads, strong form, or garden art—sparks interest when showy color slows down.

Practical pointers

As you begin to brainstorm plant combinations, remember the basics. Plants in a combination must have similar cultural needs. You can't successfully pair a sun-loving penstemon with a shade-requiring hosta, or a water-guzzling cardinal flower with a must-have-dry-feet Jerusalem sage.

Choose plants with overlapping flowering windows. In the excitement of creating combinations, make sure perennials actually share bloom times. As you look at Perennial Bloom Times on pages 70–75, make sure there's sufficient overlap in the flowering windows of plants you want to combine. Use caution when copying combinations shown in plant catalogs. Computer photo editing can easily place a fall-flowering aster beside a spring-blooming bleeding heart. Double-check bloom times against a secondary source.

Include shrubs, small trees, or evergreens in your perennial bed or near it, especially if you garden in regions where winter means snow. Branches with dark, curving lines add immense interest to winterscapes.

Off-season show
Your perennial garden can stage weeks of strong interest well into winter when you include these off-season showstoppers in the mix.

AMETHYST SEA HOLLY
Globe seedheads. Zones 2–10.

ANISE HYSSOP
Sturdy stems topped with erect seedheads that draw birds. Zones 5–10

BLACK-EYED SUSAN
Round seedheads draw birds for winter feeding. Zones 3–10.

BLUE FESCUE
Steel blue foliage and buff-color seedheads. Zones 4–10.

GOLDENROD
Strong stems add vertical interest; birds feed on seeds. Zones 4–9.

JAPANESE SWEET FLAG
Green and gold foliage. Zones 3–11.

LENTEN ROSE
Leathery evergreen leaves. Zones 4–10.

MISCANTHUS GRASS 'ADAGIO'
Buff foliage with tan seedheads. Zones 4–10.

Great Climbers

As you make your lists of must-have plants and can't-live-without-'em features for your perennial design, add vertical interest to the inventory. Vertical interest proves vital to garden design because it interrupts the chest- or knee-high flow with an attention grabbing pause. A stretch-for-the-sky object punctuates a perennial garden, an exclamation point that introduces pause, awe, or an inspired sigh. Upward mobility takes the design principle of line to a new level, breaking the horizontal plane that most perennials hug. The vertical line balances the horizontal plantings, lifting the garden to a new dimension.

You can answer the height question by incorporating perennials taller than 5 feet into plantings. This tactic works for many planting locations, but it can be a problem in areas plagued with high winds that wrestle towering perennials to the ground. Many skyscraping perennials also devour a large piece of garden real estate, as plants tend to form clumps as wide as they are tall. The other downside to tall perennials is that choices are limited, because the majority of perennials are shorter than 36 inches.

Vertical alternatives

A sculpture or tuteur can issue the needed interjection in a horizontal planting. As long as your tall selections display appropriate scale, these three-dimensional objects will simultaneously converse with surrounding plantings and perform a vertical soliloquy that captures the imagination and gives a garden that wow factor.

Above: **Count on perennial vines, like jackman clematis, to introduce color and vertical interest to planting beds. Train vines on a trellis or tuteur to punctuate a garden with a strong vertical element.**

A vine-covered trellis also adds height—and addresses other problems in the garden. Use vines to block an unattractive view, redirect vision, or splash a needed complementary color into a planting scheme without taking up precious garden frontage.

Most perennial vines remain in place over their support during dormancy; annual vines must be physically removed after frost. If you use a beautiful support beneath annual climbers, let the structure dress up the winter garden. Many vines require frequent trimming to keep them from swallowing sections of the garden, established trees, and structures; understand the vine's pruning requirements before planting.

Don't forget foliage

Rely on foliage to orchestrate interest in the garden when perennials aren't in bloom. As you select leafy beauties, piece together textural compositions that add artistry. Ornamental grasses introduce wonderful movement and texture to a perennial garden. In shade, rely on sedges, grass look-alikes, to fill this role.

Foliage can complete a color scheme. Many perennial and shrub varieties unfurl leaves in an array of colors—silver, burgundy, black, blue, gold, rose, and variegated. Research a color-leaf perennial to understand the ideal growing conditions for producing the boldest leaf color. Some require stronge light, some color best in filtered shade, and some demand a yearly pruning to generate new growth, which showcases the strongest hue.

TEST GARDEN TIP

Perennial vines

Some perennials are vines rather than ground-hugging plants. Here are some to consider in your yard.

Arctic Beauty kiwi vine
Carolina jessamine
Coral vine
Climbing hydrangea
Jackman clematis
Passionflower
Scarlet trumpet honeysuckle
Sweet autumn clematis
Trumpet creeper
Wisteria

Vines for vertical interest
Add dimension to your perennial garden with versatile vines. These classy climbers add drama to the landscape.

FRAGRANT
ARMAND CLEMATIS White flowers. Sun or light shade. Zones 7–9.

CONFEDERATE JASMINE White blossoms; evergreen foliage. Shade to part shade. Zones 8–10.

MADAGASCAR JASMINE Wnite blooms, evergreen foliage. Full sun to part shade. Zones 10–11.

PINK CHINESE JASMINE Pink blooms. Full sun. Zones 9–10.

SWEET AUTUMN CLEMATIS White flowers. Sun or shade. Zones 4–9. (pictured)

FINE-TEXTURE
ANEMONE CLEMATIS Pink or white flowers. Full sun. Zones 5–8.

CLIMBING BLEEDING HEART Yellow blooms. Part shade. Zones 7–9.

CLIMBING SNAPDRAGON Purple blooms. Full sun. Zones 9–10.

ITALIAN CLEMATIS American virgin's bower. White blooms. Sun or part shade. Zones 3–7.

SILVER LACE VINE White flowers. Full sun to light shade. Zones 4–8. (pictured)

BOLD-TEXTURE
CUP AND SAUCER VINE Purple flowers. Full sun. Zones 9–10.

DUTCHMAN'S PIPE Purplish brown blooms. Sun or shade. Zones 4–7.

GOLDEN HOPS Straw-color flowers. Sun or shade. Zones 5–8. (pictured)

MOONFLOWER White trumpet blooms. Full sun. Zones 8–10.

TRUMPET VINE Orange or golden yellow blooms. Sun or part shade. Zones 4–9.

Plan a Season-Long Show

When you're planning a perennial garden, it's natural to focus on flowers

for creating showy color every week of the year. Even in the coldest regions, it's possible to plan for blooms from March through November. In mild zones, it's not unusual for perennial displays to offer winter color, courtesy of plants like Lenten rose and primrose.

As you narrow the list of perennials for your garden, assemble your own blooming chart, like the ones on pages 70–75. Mark appropriate flowering months for the plants you'll be growing and note any quiet times in the seasonal bloom.

Use bulbs, annuals, and shrubs to embroider gaps with colorful interest. You can also lean on perennials with striking foliage (see pages 61 and 67) to touch up quiet bloom times with splashes of texture and color. Some perennials enhance the garden with lively color, form, or seedheads in winter (see page 65).

Make the most of your garden budget by including a few long-blooming perennials in your garden plan (see opposite page). Most perennials flower for an average of three weeks. Long-blooming perennials open blossoms for longer windows. Use these enduring bloomers to form a backbone of color in your garden, and then gradually as your budget permits add perennials that complement, contrast, and flower in shorter timeframes.

Buyer beware

Some perennials promise "strong" or "vigorous growth" or may be promoted as a "fast spreader." Use caution when adding these plants to your garden. Many perennials that carry these adjectives may be harmless performers that will grace your garden with sturdy growth and steady color. Others, however, may be garden bullies, perennials that quickly overtake beds and elbow other plants out of the way.

Opposite: **Ornamental grasses provide a long season of interest in a perennial garden, while beauties like white 'Casa Blanca' Oriental lily steal the spotlight for a few weeks.**

Clues you can spot on plant tags or in descriptions alert you to invasive potential. A plant that "readily self-seeds" will be tossing easily sprouting seeds into your garden. This trait can seem like a gift in an immature garden where you see more mulch than plants, but over time it can become a nightmare. But you don't have to avoid all self-seeders. One way to control spreading seed is to cut off seedheads before the seeds mature. This approach works well with self-seeders like goldenrod, joe-pye weed, and meadow rue.

If a description reports that a perennial "spreads by underground stems to form a well-rounded clump," you may be dealing with a plant that can surreptitiously overrun the garden, lawn, and your neighbor's yard too. It is possible to contain aggressive spreaders. Put them in beds confined by structures, driveways, or patios. Plant them in a bed by a lawn, and weekly mowing will keep spreading stems in check.

Try siting spreaders in less-than-ideal conditions. For instance, if a plant thrives in full sun, you can often curtail its wandering ways by tucking it in partial shade. Or you can use an old-fashioned approach and faithfully weed out new sprouts. With many spreading perennials, an annual spring weeding can bring the clump into order for the coming growing season. For a list of potential garden thugs, see page 141.

Long-blooming perennials

Take the guesswork out of organizing a season-long blossom procession by tucking a few flower powerhouses in the garden. These charmers exceed the average perennial three-week flowering window when growing conditions are favorable.

ASTER 'MONCH'
Daisylike lavender-blue flowers from midsummer through fall; treat as annual in Deep South. Pair them with yarrow and lady's mantle. Zones 5–10.

BLACK-EYED SUSAN 'GOLDSTURM'
Classic black-eyed daisy blooms from midsummer through fall. Pair them with 'May Night' salvia and Russian sage. Zones 3–10.

BLANKET FLOWER
Orange, yellow, and multicolor daisies from early summer to fall. Pair them with white gaura and blackberry lily. Zones 3–11.

DAYLILY 'HAPPY RETURNS'
Yellow daylily flowers from early summer to frost. Pair them with clustered bellflower and Husker Red penstemon. Zones 2–11.

GARDEN PHLOX
Look for mildew resistance on tag or description; flowers from mid- to late summer. Pair them with centranthus and catmint. Zones 4–8.

GAYFEATHER
Flower spikes open in early to midsummer; deadhead for repeat bloom. Pair them with black-eyed susan and showy sedum. Zones 3–10.

GERANIUM 'ROZANNE'
Violet-blue blooms unfurl from early summer to fall; leaves turn mahogany in fall. Pair them with bearded iris and anise hyssop. Zones 5–8.

SEDUM 'AUTUMN FIRE'
Flower buds form in midsummer, open pink in late summer, linger into winter. Pair them with false indigo and false sunflower. Zones 3–10.

SPIDERWORT
Violet-blue blooms open spring to fall if soil is kept consistently moist. Pair them with cardinal flower and joe-pye weed. Zones 3–11.

YELLOW CORYDALIS
Nonstop flowers midspring to fall. In full shade, pair with hosta and lungwort. In partial shade, pair with woodland phlox and ladybells. Zones 5–10.

Perennial bloom times

Arranged alphabetically by common name, this chart shows the bloom period of many popular perennials (E=early, M=mid-season, L=late). It also displays peak times for other decorative features, such as exceptional foliage, winter structure, or ornamental seedheads. Pink bars show typical bloom times; purple bars represent visual interest. Consult this chart to make beds and borders that look good from spring to fall.

| | BLOOM TIME |
| OTHER INTEREST |

PLANT NAME	SPRING (E M L)	SUMMER (E M L)	FALL (E M L)	WINTER (E M L)	PLANT NAME	SPRING (E M L)	SUMMER (E M L)	FALL (E M L)	WINTER (E M L)
Allegheny foam flower					Bear's foot hellebore				
Anise hyssop					Bee balm				
Artemisia					Bethlehem sage				
Asiatic hybrid lily					Big blue lobelia				
Aster					Bigleaf ligularia				
Astilbe					Bigroot geranium				
'Autumn Joy' sedum					Black-eyed susan				
Baby's breath					Blanket flower				
Balloon flower					Blue oat grass				
Barrenwort					Bluebeard				
Bearded iris					Boltonia				
Bear's breeches					Bush clematis				

PLANT NAME	SPRING			SUMMER			FALL			WINTER		
	E	M	L	E	M	L	E	M	L	E	M	L
Butterfly weed				▓	▓							
Cardinal flower					▓	▓						
Carpathian bellflower				▓								
Catmint			▓	▓	▓	▓	▓					
Cheddar pinks				▓								
Chinese astilbe					▓							
Christmas rose	▓							▓				▓
Chrysanthemum							▓	▓				
Clustered bellflower				▓								
Columbine			▓									
Columbine meadow rue			▓									
Common beardtongue				▓								
Common sage			▓	▓	▓		▓					

PLANT NAME	SPRING			SUMMER			FALL			WINTER		
	E	M	L	E	M	L	E	M	L	E	M	L
Compact pincushion flower				▓	▓							
Coneflower					▓	▓	▓	▓				
Coral bells				▓	▓	▓	▓					
Cowslip		▓										
Creeping baby's breath				▓								
Creeping phlox		▓										
Creeping veronica		▓										▓
Crested iris		▓										
Crimson pincushion flower					▓							
Crocosmia					▓							
Daylily					▓	▓						
Delphinium				▓								
English primrose		▓										

DESIGNING WITH PERENNIALS • BETTER HOMES AND GARDENS   71

Plant Name	Spring E	Spring M	Spring L	Summer E	Summer M	Summer L	Fall E	Fall M	Fall L	Winter E	Winter M	Winter L
Evening primrose, sundrops				■	■							
False indigo			■	■								
False solomon's seal	■	■										
Feather reed grass				■	■	■						
						■	■	■				
Fern-leaf yarrow				■	■							
		■	■	■	■	■						
Fleabane			■	■								
Foamy bells			■	■								
		■	■	■	■	■	■	■				
Fragrant bugbane					■							
Frikart's aster					■	■						
Garden phlox					■							
Gayfeather			■			■						
Germander, wall germander					■							
Giant coneflower					■	■	■					

Plant Name	Spring E	Spring M	Spring L	Summer E	Summer M	Summer L	Fall E	Fall M	Fall L	Winter E	Winter M	Winter L
Globe thistle				■	■							
Gloriosa daisy							■	■	■			
Goatsbeard				■								
Goldenrod							■	■	■			
Ground clematis				■	■							
Hardy begonia							■					
Hardy hibiscus					■							
Heart-leaf bergenia			■									
			■	■	■	■	■	■	■	■	■	■
Heart-leaf brunnera			■									
			■	■	■	■	■					
Helenium							■					
Hollyhock				■								
Horned violet			■	■								
Hosta					■	■	■					

PLANT NAME	SPRING			SUMMER			FALL			WINTER			PLANT NAME	SPRING			SUMMER			FALL			WINTER		
	E	M	L	E	M	L	E	M	L	E	M	L		E	M	L	E	M	L	E	M	L	E	M	L
Hybrid agastache (hyssop)													Lamb's-ears												
Hybrid anemone													Lavender 'Blue Cushion'												
Hybrid astilbe													Lavender cotton												
Hybrid foam flower													'Lavender Mist' meadow rue												
Hybrid lobelia													Lenten rose												
Hybrid mullein 'Summer Sorbet'													Liriope												
Hybrid speedwell													Louisiana iris												
Hybrid violet													Lungwort												
Hybrid yarrow													Maiden grass												
Jacob's ladder													Maiden pinks												
Japanese iris													Maltese cross												
Joe-pye weed													Meadow rue												
Lady's mantle													Meadowsweet												

Bloom-time chart. Each plant's bloom period is shown as a shaded bar across the season/stage columns (E = Early, M = Mid, L = Late).

PLANT NAME	SPRING E	M	L	SUMMER E	M	L	FALL E	M	L	WINTER E	M	L
Moss phlox	▓	▓	▓	▓	▓	▓	▓					
Nettle-leaved mullein				▓	▓							
Obedient plant					▓							
Old-fashioned bleeding heart		▓										
Olympic mullein				▓								
Oriental hybrid lily					▓							
Oriental poppy		▓										
Ornamental onion				▓	▓	▓						
Ornamental oregano					▓							
Ozark sundrops				▓	▓	▓						
Pacific bleeding heart	▓	▓		▓	▓							
Peach-leaf bellflower				▓								
Peony		▓	▓									

PLANT NAME	SPRING E	M	L	SUMMER E	M	L	FALL E	M	L	WINTER E	M	L
Perennial fountain grass			▓	▓	▓	▓	▓	▓				
Perennial salvia					▓	▓						
Pincushion flower					▓	▓						
Pink coreopsis					▓	▓						
Purple coneflower					▓	▓	▓	▓				
Queen-of-the-prairie					▓							
Reblooming bearded iris			▓		▓							
Reblooming daylily					▓	▓						
Rodgersia					▓	▓	▓					
Rose campion					▓							
Russian sage					▓	▓	▓					
Sea holly					▓							
Shasta daisy					▓							

Plant Name	Spring E	Spring M	Spring L	Summer E	Summer M	Summer L	Fall E	Fall M	Fall L	Winter E	Winter M	Winter L
Showy evening primrose		■	■	■	■	■						
Siberian iris				■								
Siebold primrose		■	■									
Smooth white penstemon				■	■	■	■	■				
Snowdrop anemone		■	■									
Solitary clematis			■	■	■	■	■	■	■			
Spike speedwell				■	■	■						
Spotted bellflower				■	■	■						
Star astilbe				■	■							
Stokes' aster			■	■	■	■	■					
Switch grass				■	■	■	■	■	■			
Threadleaf coreopsis			■	■	■	■						
Thrift	■	■	■									
Torch lily				■	■	■						
Tree mallow				■	■	■						
Turk's-cap lily						■	■					
Variegated solomon's seal		■	■	■	■	■	■					
Wherry's foam flower		■	■	■	■	■	■	■	■			
White gaura						■	■	■	■			
Woodland phlox		■	■	■	■							
Woolly thyme			■	■	■	■	■	■	■			
Woolly yarrow		■	■	■	■	■	■					
Yarrow		■	■	■	■	■	■					
Yellow corydalis		■	■	■	■	■						
Yellow foxglove				■	■							
Yucca	■	■	■	■	■	■	■	■	■	■	■	■

Discover Inspiration

Before you actually push a shovel into soil to break ground on your perennial paradise, formalize your thoughts about why you want a garden. The best inspiration for a beautiful garden is a clear focus, a purpose that helps drive and motivate decisions, actions, and choices. When your focus is firmly resolved, the rest of the garden falls naturally into place.

Begin with "why"

The easiest way to unravel your inspiration is to ask yourself why. Why do you want to grow perennials? The reasons may revolve around wanting to improve a view—from a kitchen, home office, or outdoor living area. You may have a passion for fresh flowers and want to trade store-bought bouquets for homegrown. Some gardeners desire to attract birds and butterflies for backyard nature watching.

Your rationale may involve problem solving, such as hiding an eyesore, transforming an area where grass won't grow, or dressing a damp spot with beautiful plants. Your locale may have increasing water restrictions that make you want to swap a water-guzzling lawn for drought-tolerant perennials. Or you may have

an awkward area that's challenging to mow. Plant it with perennials, and your mowing headache is gone.

Perhaps you have a side yard that's overlooked and neglected. A perennial garden with a bench or swing can make that spot a destination where your family enjoys spending time. Or maybe now your children are grown and you no longer need the play area they enjoyed. Convert it to perennials, and you'll savor an echo of the laughter of your children among the flowers.

Sometimes location dictates purpose. If your front yard is the only area where you can grow perennials, you'll need to develop a garden that extends a warm greeting. You might need to sandwich a perennial border between a patio and a swimming pool or play area. You'll want to arrange this garden to take advantage of tighter quarters and provide pleasant views from multiple sides, while stocking it with some child-friendly perennials.

Consider multiple priorities for your garden—a primary focus, and then secondary reasons you want perennials. Use these prioritized desires to guide your decisions as you build and plant the garden.

Celebrate style

Discover and express your personal flair in the perennial garden. Formal or casual, old-fashioned or modern, alpine or over-the-top cottage—there may be nearly as many perennial garden styles as there are perennial gardeners. You might want to plant a mixed border, incorporating perennials as one aspect of the scene, but also including trees and shrubs.

Choose a style that complements your home—or not. If you're converting an entire yard into perennial gardens complete with structures, you can veer away from following a style that suits the location, especially if the garden is hidden from the house with a hedge or fence.

With front yard perennials, it's important to marry garden design to architecture. Select cottage or prairie garden style for Craftsman bungalows or ranch homes. Xeriscape gardens complement Southwest stucco and adobe homes; formal plantings with strong lines pair nicely with traditional colonial architecture.

Opposite: **A front yard perennial garden trades turf—and maintenance chores that go with it— for year-round beauty. This garden includes torch lily and garden phlox, plants that beckon butterflies.**

TEST GARDEN TIP

Front Yard Garden Tips

Make a lasting first impression with a front yard perennial garden. Follow these tips to welcome guests and greet passersby with perennial charm.

Establish order. Foster order by limiting the number of species (5 to 10), planting them in groups, and repeating them throughout the garden.

Think big. Plan for planting beds large enough to accommodate the mix of plants necessary to convey order.

Make it flow. Repeat plant forms and textures to unify plantings.

Frame the door. Make the front door your focal point and steer design lines in that direction.

Coordinate color. Select perennial foliage and flowers to complement your home's exterior or front porch furnishings.

Make a site inventory
Before breaking ground, take an inventory of what your site offers so your garden can capitalize on and blend into existing features.

1 MAKE A SKETCH
Pencil a rough drawing of the area you plan to put the garden. Be as accurate as possible, but don't worry about crafting a to-scale sketch. Mark permanent features, such as fences, paths, existing plants, or play areas.

2 SNAP PHOTOS
Take pictures from surrounding spots that will provide viewing points for the garden—including interior rooms. Include photos of areas bordering the garden site and anything that's especially attractive or problematic. Refer to these photos as you design the garden.

3 CREATE A MUST-HAVE LIST
This list should include the things you must have in the garden: certain plants (especially trees or shrubs), large rocks, oversize containers, or fountains. Use this list to incorporate items that are on hand or in your budget.

4 MAKE A WISH LIST
This list should include items you hope to introduce into your garden one day.

5 COMPLETE A SITE ANALYSIS
Record light exposure and other environmental conditions for your proposed site. These answers will help guide you as you choose perennials.

Put Pencil to Paper

Once you have defined the "why" behind the garden and have an idea

about the style you want to pursue, it's time to begin sketching. Use a piece of plain or graph paper to draw an outline of your garden area. You don't need a plan that's drawn to scale, although a certain amount of accuracy makes planning easier. A scale that adapts well to perennials is 1 inch on the paper equal to 2 feet in the garden.

Inside and around the outline of your garden, sketch any trees, fences, or structures that interact with or affect the garden. Pencil in the line of the house, so you know where that is in relationship to the garden. If the garden is being designed with reference to a deck, patio, or particular interior room, include that area on your drawing.

As you sketch the garden bed, dividing it into thirds makes plant placement easy. With beds viewed from one side, stairstep perennials, filling the front third of the bed with low-growing plants, the middle third with mid-range plants, and the back third with taller types. If you design an island bed that will be viewed from all sides, place the tallest plants in the center of the garden and step down height as you work toward the edges.

Note any particular aspects of the site on the drawing—wet spots, windy corners, proximity to trees, or sun exposure. Keep the worksheet handy as you begin to choose plants. You might even draft a short list of plant requirements, such as drainage, light needs, or long bloom, to facilitate plant selection.

Opposite: **A striking monochromatic blend, such as these delphiniums and solitary clematis, often begins with one plant that catches the gardener's eye. Other perennials are added based on bloom time, color, and other attributes. The entire combination may bloom on paper long before it's tucked into the soil.**

Tackle the plants

Make a master list of plants. Start with those you have on hand or can obtain from friends or neighbors, and include plants you intend to purchase. Avoid the mistake of trying to incorporate too many plant species. Repetition and larger clumps stage an eye-pleasing scene. To make assembling combinations easy, arrange plants in order of height. Use this list to create a bloom chart similar to the one on pages 70–75 for your own garden. As you fill in flowering windows and times of foliage interest, you'll notice gaps. Flip through the Perennial Encyclopedia (see page 174) or peruse the perennial lists throughout the book to supplement your plant list. Look for perennials that flower and introduce foliage interest to the garden. Remember not to plan heavy flowering windows during seasons when you're typically out of town.

When you're ready, begin adding plants to your garden plan. Start with perennials that offer the same color, either through flowers or foliage. Once you pencil in those plants, place companion perennials you want next to them, slowly building combinations until the garden plan is complete.

TEST GARDEN TIP

How Many Plants?

To determine how many plants you need for your garden, you must understand plant spacing. When you place perennials in the garden bed, space them according to their mature size. If a plant spreads 24 inches, you should place it 24 inches from the plant beside it. If that same plant nestles against a fence or object (like a birdbath), place it 12 inches away.

When you arrange young plants in a new garden, you'll see plenty of soil (or mulch) between plants. Don't react to that by planting perennials too tightly. You'll only wind up dividing and moving plants as they reach their mature size. Instead, fill in the gaps with annuals until perennials spread.

Penny-pinching design
Grow a perennial garden on a shoestring budget without skimping on results. Try a few—or all—of these tips to trim the investment in your first-year garden.

Find free plants. Get perennial divisions from friends or neighbors. Even strangers are usually willing to share plants with new gardeners. Just ask.

Shop plant sales. Look for locally sponsored plant sales by civic groups, garden clubs, or church fellowships. Avoid sales with professionally grown plants; those perennials cost more.

Start small. Use a combination of seeds and small plants to jump-start the garden. Sow seeds of one type of perennial in a swath; tuck a few small plants of the same variety into that swath. The small plants will give first-year flowers; seed-grown plants will catch up in size and flower power next year.

Plan for bloom. Pint-size or bare-root perennials flower the first year. Plan on a few of these in your garden. Include a couple larger plants of the same type for a showy splash right away.

Designing Beds

A successful design starts with a theme of your choosing and a plan drawn on paper. Analyze your site, and then create bed outlines. Add an edging treatment to give beds a finished look.

How to define bed shape

Use a supple garden hose or rope to outline a bed edge. This option gives you versatility—it's easy to pick up the edge and move it. Choose this method for the first run in creating the shapes of your bed.

Or sprinkle flour along a proposed bed edge for an easy-to-see outline. Flour isn't rainproof, so downpours may dissipate lines. Use flour when you're fairly sure of the shape and about to begin breaking ground.

Break out the spray paint for a final marking that's not easily changed or removed. Paint provides a good choice when greater time will pass between determining bed shape and starting work on the garden.

A sweeping perennial border and a confined perennial cottage bed have this in common:

Both require decisions regarding bed shape and size. Sometimes, as with the confined cottage bed, you may not have much choice in the matter. Surrounding objects, such as structures, driveways, patios, or fences may dictate dimensions.

In an open space, freedom to design a large border or island bed can overwhelm you as you wrestle with balancing garden dreams with budget or time constraints. To narrow your options, consider various possibilities for the bed. For instance, do you favor a formal or informal look? With a formal garden, you'll incorporate more straight lines than curves; with an informal style, you'll have more curves than straight edges.

Consider possible shapes. A simple shape, like an oval, kidney bean, or half-circle, lets plantings shine.

Nearby objects may influence bed shape. A fence enclosing your yard is a natural backdrop for a perennial border that curves in and out along the straight edge. Or you may want to create your perennial bed against a structure, such as a garden shed or garage. A solid backdrop for a perennial border reduces airflow, which can increase chances of powdery mildew, a problem that plagues pincushion flower, garden phlox, and bee balm. In that planting situation, choose mildew-resistant varieties.

Form can follow function. For a perennial bed serving as a patio backdrop, you definitely want the bed to wrap around the patio. If you want a cutting garden, provide space for large clumps or even rows of perennials, leaving access to all points of the bed for easy flower gathering. A garden intended to host wildlife should offer ample elbow room for layers of plants to provide adequate shelter and food to critters—and nearby seating areas to offer handy vantage points for wildlife watching.

Check interior views of proposed exterior beds. If you sit near a particular window in your home, arrange a perennial garden to enhance that view. By allowing inside and outside spaces to interact, the perennial garden becomes an integral part of your home's living experience.

Practical pointers

In most settings, property dimensions and structures will guide bed length. Bed width can vary, even within the same border. In beds less than 24 inches wide, planting layers are one or two plants deep. This limits plant combination potential. A bed width that permits consistently beautiful perennial layering is 36 inches deep.

Above left: **Consider the view of your garden from indoors. A well-placed focal point in the foreground can lead your eye to the beds beyond.**

Above right: **A pathway that curves out of sight is an intriguing way to lead the visitor through the garden, encouraging exploration.**

Edge Your Beds

Garden edging dresses beds with the outdoor equivalent of a string of pearls.

A neat bed edge gives a garden a polished, professional finish—but it's much more than good looks. Edging also serves a purpose, establishing an effective border control over the potential turf war between perennials and surrounding grass.

Look at edging as another aspect of structure in your garden, a material that can provide year-round interest. Select from a variety of manufactured edgings or create your own using natural or recycled materials. Stones, shells, or large-diameter broken branches provide effective, organic edging. Natural materials decompose over time, which makes them an excellent choice when your garden is a work in progress and you haven't yet discovered that perfect edging.

A twist on the classic Southern bottle tree is bottle edging, which features upside-down glass bottles inserted into the soil around beds. Colored glass evokes the most charm. Push bottles into the soil to varying depths to create an undulating effect. Recycle past-its-prime garden gear into an edging, such as terra-cotta pots placed upside down along beds or tool heads with broken handles shoved into the soil.

Evaluate your options

Approach edging from a budget-minded stance by starting with deep trench edging. To create this edge, use a sharp square-point shovel or spade to dig into sod 4 inches away from the planting bed. Dig 4 to 6 inches deep, and

Edging can be purely functional, or it can combine beauty with function. Mortared stone dresses a bed with pleasing curves.

lift out turf, roots and all. Clear the trench of soil, roots, and rocks. Fill it with mulch for a classy look. Refresh a trench edge at least once a season to keep grass out of beds.

Over time, as funds permit, exchange the trench for a dressier touch with masonry, metal, wood, or plastic edging. Of the four materials, plastic is the cheapest and may last the shortest time. Masonry offers a pricier, more durable, and permanent edge. Without mortar in joints, bricks and pavers do permit grass, perennials, and weeds to grow between them. Choose a masonry type that complements your home's exterior for a coordinated, formal look.

For whimsical shapes and peek-a-boo charm, look for intricately patterned aluminum, wrought-iron, or steel border fences that promise strength and enduring quality. Wrought iron and steel benefit from an antirust treatment for greatest durability. Metal is a wonderful choice for a formal or traditional-style garden.

Wood edging may be crafted from bamboo, willow, or other woods and can be counted on to enhance a garden's cottage or Asian ambience. Wood in contact with soil will decompose at some point; plan to replace edging over time.

Edge the edging

No matter what edging you use, create a mowing strip so you can easily maneuver the mower alongside the edging. Clear a shallow trench to accommodate mower wheels or lay down a strip of mulch or recycled rubber mulch. Without a mowing strip, you'll have to string-trim every bed.

A deep trench edge treatment gives planting beds a neat appearance that's easy to maintain. A quick pass with a string trimmer along bed edges keeps the look very sharp and clean.

TEST GARDEN TIP

Edging option

To halt grass spread into beds, many gardeners apply a targeted spray of glyphosate along bed edges. The chemical has a short life in soil but will harm frogs and aquatic wildlife; don't use it near water features. A chemical approach is handy if you have multiple large beds or, conversely, one or two short edges that are the sole reason you might need a trimmer.

planting plans

Take the guesswork out of designing a perennial garden with plant-by-number plans. Copy a plan as is, or create a custom design by replacing plants with perennials of similar size and flower color.

p.**86**
GARDEN SOLUTIONS
Perennials excel at solving landscape problems. Get creative with a garden plan for seaside conditions, a shady border in a woodland setting, or plantings tucked beside a flight of steps.

p.**92**
SHRUG OFF DROUGHT
Perennial gardens don't have to guzzle water to be beautiful. Eye-catching low-water-use gardens can also attract wildlife, create a cottage-style look, or showcase native and prairie plants.

p.**102**
COTTAGE APPEAL
Cottage gardens feature over-the-top color and floral abundance. These adapt to sun or shade, sloping sites, or a sunny spot where you want to stage a strong autumn show.

Made for the Shade

One aspect of creating a perennial garden

for a shady space is learning to look carefully at foliage texture. In a sunny garden, bold, plentiful blooms easily steal the show throughout the growing season. In the shade, blossoms often unfurl subtle hues and leaves can unfold fabulous variegations. Low light truly celebrates the intricate variations of leaves in many tones of green, showcasing textural differences.

The garden pictured above capitalizes on shade, filling a part to full shade location with an exquisite blend of foliage textures. Flowers— bleeding heart in spring, yellow foxglove in summer, and hybrid anemones in fall—enhance the scene through the seasons. Other bloomers,

including ligularia, fringed bleeding heart, and Virginia knotweed also help complete the seasonal show. The fragrance of a sweetly scented hosta casts a perfumed spell over the garden in summer.

Plants in this garden thrive in moist, loamy soil. If your garden offers less desirable footing, mix moisture- and nutrient-retaining compost into the soil at planting time.

Duplicate this garden in your yard by following the planting diagrams opposite. Plans are presented both in plan view (top) to indicate proper plant spacing, and in elevation view (bottom) to show what the garden will look like at maturity.

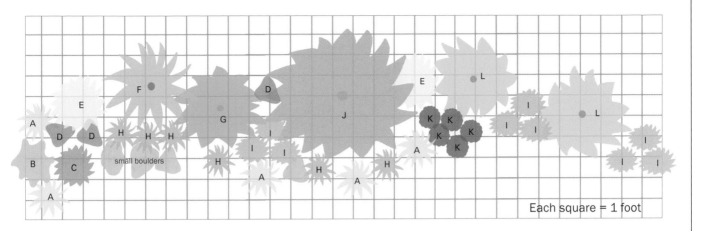

Each square = 1 foot

small boulders

PLANT LIST

A. **5 Yellow-green hybrid hosta** such as 'Piedmont Gold': Zones 3–9

B. **1 Blue-green hosta** such as 'Hadspen Blue': Zones 3–9

C. **1 Green with gold edge hosta** such as 'Golden Tiara': Zones 3–9

D. **3 Caladium** (*Caladium bicolor*): Zones 8–11, annual elsewhere

E. **2 Yellow-green hosta** with blue-green edge such as 'Captain Kirk': Zones 3–9

F. **1 Siebold hosta** (*Hosta sieboldiana*): Zones 3–9

G. **1 Blue-green with gold edge hosta** such as 'Tokudama Flavocircinalis': Zones 3–9

H. **6 Lungwort** (*Pulmonaria saccharata*) such as 'Mrs. Moon': Zones 4–8

I. **9 Woodland phlox** (*Phlox divaricata*): Zones 4–9

J. **1 Cutleaf Japanese maple** (*Acer palmatum* 'Dissectum Rubrifolium'): Zones 6–10

K. **5 Impatiens** (*Impatiens walleriana*): Annual

L. **2 Large yellow-green hosta** such as 'Sum and Substance': Zones 3–9

TEST
GARDEN
TIP

Striking shade combos

Many shade-loving perennials present spotlight-worthy performances, either with beautiful blossoms or luxurious leaf texture. Try these three techniques to add sparkle to your shade garden.

Foliage color. Leaves that unfurl blades in shades of gold, white, pink, or variegated patterns will infuse a low-light garden with eye-catching color no matter the season. Gold foliage in particular turns on the light in a shady corner, adding a luminous glow.

Bold bloom. Count on colorful flowers to pack a punch in a shade planting. Whether blossoms are short- or long-lived, their window of color livens a shady scent.

Textural tapestry. Mix and match plants that have contrasting foliage textures to weave interest in the garden that's independent of bloom time. Beautiful texture combinations can carry a garden—in sunlight or shade—with artful ease through the growing season.

Seaside Solution

Don't let sweeping winds, sandy soils, and salt spray get your garden down. Work with nature rather than battling it to turn a barren site into a spectacular garden.

Everything that makes an oceanside setting

so desirable for vacationing also makes it unique for growing perennials. Yet you can transform a seaside paradise into a perennial haven by choosing plants adapted to the growing conditions. Some perennials naturally thrive in sandy soil and tolerate salt spray—like the ones in this perennial garden plan. These comeback beauties also flourish in cool conditions, surviving even harsh New England winters.

The three biggest challenges of seaside plantings are salt spray, wind, and sandy soil. Winds carry salt spray inland dozens of miles, coating plant leaves encountered along the way. Salt can damage perennials, burning leaves and stunting growth. Wind topples tall plants and also wicks moisture from the soil and leaves, creating an intensely dry environment. Sandy soil doesn't naturally retain water, adding to the drought conditions of an oceanfront garden. Sandy soil also lacks the ability to hold nutrients, so you must amend the soil by adding organic matter and fertilizing plants.

Even with these less-than-ideal environs, you can find perennials that withstand the ocean's triple threat of salt, wind, and sand. Plants like yucca possess sturdy foliage that isn't fazed by salt spray. The foliage of lamb's-ears takes shelter in the hairy surface, which keeps salt from harming the plant. Sedum leaves boast a naturally waxy surface that is virtually impervious to salt spray.

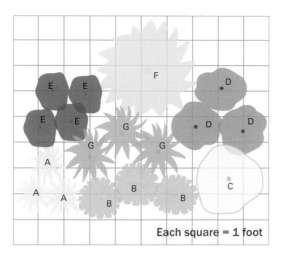

Each square = 1 foot

PLANT LIST

A. **3 Miniature daylily** *(Hemerocallis hybrid)* such as 'Stella de Oro': Zones 3–10

B. **3 Lamb's-ears** *(Stachys byzantina)*: Zones 3–10

C. **1 Gooseneck loosestrife** *(Lysimachia clethroides)*: Zones 4–10

D. **3 Rose campion** *(Lychnis coronaria)*: Zones 4–10

E. **4 Maltese cross** *(Lychnis chalcedonica)*: Zones 3–10

F. **1 False sunflower** *(Heliopsis helianthoides)*: Zones 3–9

G. **3 Large daylily** *(Hemerocallis hybrid)* such as 'Lady Lucille': Zones 3–10

TEST GARDEN TIP

Seaside planting secrets

Planting perennials that survive seaside conditions is one aspect of gardening at the shore. Here are three other ways to alleviate the harsh environment for plant survival.

Windbreak. Choose natural windbreaks, using plants, or build a fence or retaining wall to interrupt the wind. For plant windbreaks, select a fast-growing evergreen, such as juniper or pine, or a double layer of a structurally substantial grass, like pampas grass. Windbreaks protect perennials from salt spray as well as insulate them from drying winter winds.

Compost. Give sandy soil an ability to hold water and nutrients by adding compost in liberal amounts. Annually add 1 to 3 inches of compost to the top of sandy soil around plants, placing it as mulch. As the compost breaks down, it increases the amount of organic matter in the soil.

Plants. Without an established windbreak, larger perennials may not establish well in a seaside garden. Start with small plants and water infrequently but deeply to help them sink deep roots. Consider setting up a short-term windbreak using a temporary fence while new plants are taking hold.

Design for Slope

When you tame a sunny slope with steps, take advantage of the microclimate you create to grow plants that thrive in the conditions found around stone and pavement. This palette of low-growing perennials originates on stony mountainsides in their native settings. Some plants self-seed into cracks and exposed soil. Others, like low-growing sedum, slowly spread, filling in open spots.

Many of these plants can also be tucked between stepping-stones to transform a path into a living, textural masterpiece. Select plants that handle foot traffic between small stepping-stones. Between large stepping-stones, beside paths, or in areas you don't typically walk, use groundcover perennials that don't tolerate footsteps.

Established stair or stepping-stone plantings soften hard surfaces, prevent soil erosion, and elbow weeds out of the way. They also eliminate the need for string trimming.

Consider adding stones and boulders to a stairway garden to help hold soil in place and moderate the microclimate. The garden shown above features sedum growing in cracks between steps; if your steps or walk has no gaps, eliminate these spreading plants.

Slabs of stone used as stairs provide the perfect place to tuck in rock garden perennials that appreciate good drainage and a sunny site.

TEST GARDEN TIP

Tips for slope gardens

Simple strategies to address slope problems:

Deep roots. To help hold soil in place, choose perennials that form dense, far-reaching root systems, such as daylily, false indigo, and California fuchsia.

Water wisdom. Use drip irrigation or a soaker hose to slowly apply water directly to soil, which increases water absorption and reduces runoff.

Prevent erosion. Pin landscape fabric to the slope prior to planting. Cut slits to plant through the fabric.

PLANT LIST

A. **3 White stonecrop**
(*Sedum album*) such as
'Chubby Fingers': Zones 4–10

B. **5 Goldmoss stonecrop**
(*Sedum acre*): Zones 3–10

C. **1 Purple leaf violet**
(*Viola riviniana* Purpurea Group):
Zones 4–9

D. **6 Sea thrift**
(*Armeria maritima*): Zones 3–10

E. **4 Creeping thyme**
(*Thymus coccineus*): Zones 4–10

F. **1 New Zealand flax**
(*Phormium tenax*): Zones 8–11

G. **4 Purple-leaf sedum**
(*Sedum* spp.) such as 'Purple
Emperor': Zones 3–10

H. **1 Sea lavender**
(*Limonium latifolium*): Zones 5–11

I. **2 Oregon stonecrop**
(*Sedum oreganum*): Zones 2–10

J. **1 Two-row stonecrop**
(*Sedum spurium* 'Voodoo'):
Zones 4–10

Each square = 1 foot

Water-Wise Beauty

Trade a water-guzzling landscape for an easy-grows-it escape

that's a symphony of color from spring to frost. Filled with drought-tolerant beauties, this garden begs for attention—but not in terms of care. The perennials don't demand more than an occasional pruning to keep them looking their best.

Silvery foliage weaves a ribbon of unifying color through the garden, complementing the purple wands of English lavender and the lipstick pink electricity of tall garden phlox. Catmint, lavender cotton, Russian sage, and yarrow carry the silver melody. Purple coneflower and Firecracker penstemon play a striking counterpoint. The cobalt blue birdbath blends with the cooling silver foliage yet also stands out as a vivid focal point.

Typical of plants that thrive in dry environs, these perennials require excellent drainage to flourish. Improve heavy soil by adding compost. For mulch, choose gravel of some sort, using whatever appeals to your design sense. Gravel is the mulch of choice for plants that prefer good drainage because it moves moisture quickly away from plant crowns, which helps prevent fungal diseases.

This drought-tolerant garden is filled with easy-to-grow perennials that need minimal care, yet it provides cooling bursts of color throughout the year.

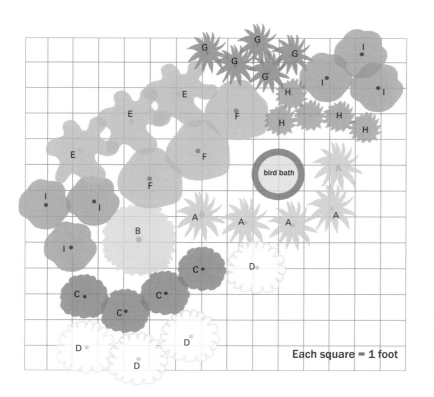

Each square = 1 foot

TEST
GARDEN
TIP

Drought tolerant by design

Reducing the amount of water you need to maintain your landscape begins with design. With a few simple techniques, you can limit the water you use to keep your yard looking good.

Group plants by thirst. In a xeriscape planting, plants are grouped according to how much water they need. The thirstiest perennials occupy a space near the water source for ease in watering. Plants that need only occasional watering fill spaces farther from the water source. The most drought-tolerant plants stage color along the perimeter, the farthest point from the water source.

Downsize lawn. Reduce the amount of turf by planting low-water-use perennials, such as groundcovers, ornamental grasses, or prairie plants. Site the lawn in an oasis zone, a high-use irrigation zone in your garden near other water-loving perennials.

Stage shade. Cast a pool of cooling shade over perennials that tend to wilt during the intense heat of the day. Count on a tree with a high canopy, or add a pergola, arbor, or lattice house to filter the sun.

PLANT LIST

A. **5 Catmint**
(*Nepeta × faassenii*):
Zones 3–10

B. **1 Yarrow**
(*Achillea* 'Moonshine'):
Zones 3–10

C. **4 English lavender**
(*Lavandula angustifolia*),
such as 'Hidcote' or 'Munstead':
Zones 5–10

D. **4 Santolina**
(*Santolina chamaecyparissus*):
Zones 6–10

E. **3 Russian sage**
(*Perovskia atriplicifolia*):
Zones 3–10

F. **3 Purple coneflower**
(*Echinacea purpurea*):
Zones 3–9

G. **5 Firecracker penstemon**
(*Penstemon eatonii*):
Zones 4–10

H. **5 Pineleaf penstemon**
(*Penstemon pinifolius*):
Zones 4–10

I. **6 Garden phlox**
(*Phlox paniculata*):
Zones 4–8

Welcome Wildlife

Turn your yard into a bed-and-breakfast for flowers. This garden design features native plants with tough personalities that stand up to heat, drought, and even roadside salt without missing a blooming beat.

Turn your yard into a bed-and-breakfast for wildlife by planting a garden that provides for their needs. You'll love this critter-catering garden because while it's dishing up nectar and shelter, it's also delivering armfuls of flowers. This garden design features native plants with tough personalities that stand up to heat, drought, and even roadside salt without missing a blooming beat.

Sited in a boulevard between street and sidewalk, this wildlife garden showcases perennials that flourish with minimal water once established. These street-smart beauties are fuss-free growers, demanding little in the way of staking, pruning, or fertilizing. In the western third of the country, substitute drought-tolerant hyssop, penstemon, salvia, sedum, or yarrow for plants like bee balm and turtlehead.

The garden's simple rectangular design makes it easy to adapt to multiple settings in a yard. You can even transform the blocky form into a curve by repeating some of the central plants to fill in the expanded shape.

Some gardeners call it the hell strip—that bit of ground between the sidewalk and street that provides an inhospitable environment for growing plants. The solution is to grow tough native plants adapted to minimal maintenance. This planting is just a year old.

TEST
GARDEN
TIP

Walk on the wild side

Try these perennials to attract critters of all sorts to your garden.

Aster	Lupine
Bee balm	Perennial sunflower
Butterfly weed	Prairie dropseed
Coneflower	Sedge
Goldenrod	Yarrow
Joe-pye weed	Yucca

PLANT LIST

A. **4 Blue false indigo** (*Baptisia australis*): Zones 3–10

B. **5 Coneflower** (*Echinacea purpurea*): Zones 3–10

C. **3 Smooth aster** (*Aster laevis*) such as 'Bluebird': Zones 3–8

D. **4 Goldenrod** (*Solidago rugosa* 'Fireworks'): Zones 3–9

E. **4 Bee balm** (*Monarda didyma*) such as 'Jacob Kline': Zones 3–9

F. **3 Rose turtlehead** (*Chelone lyonii*): Zones 4–10

G. **4 Tall gayfeather** (*Liatris scariosa*): Zones 4–10

H. **6 Garden phlox** (*Phlox paniculata*) such as 'Shortwood': Zones 4–9

I. **2 False sunflower** (*Heliopsis helianthoides*): Zones 3–9

J. **5 Switchgrass** (*Panicum virgatum*): Zones 3–9

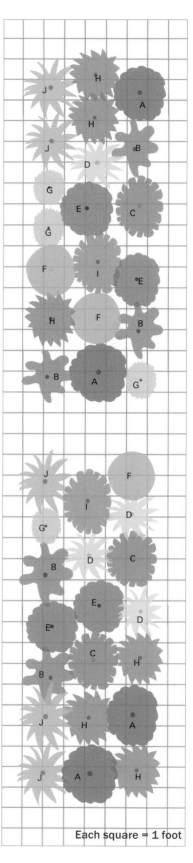

Each square = 1 foot

Spotlight on Grasses

Graceful foliage that dances on the breeze

earns ornamental grasses a place in any garden. Tall grasses offer a strong vertical element for garden design, and shorter types introduce wonderful texture and color to border edgings. Grasses play a textural counterpoint to broad-leaf perennials, such as sedum and hollyhock, and quietly complement the round shape of black-eyed susan and coreopsis blooms.

This border plan features strong seasonal interest from early summer through late fall. Annual zinnias team with perennial bloomers to unfurl flowers that beckon butterflies all summer long. Ornamental grasses produce arresting leaves with variegations and hues, fanning the flames of summer color. Seedheads form on the grasses in late summer, adorning the garden's dress with a new accessory.

As the seedheads mature in fall, birds flock to the garden to feast on seeds, continuing to forage through the seedy buffet well into winter. Include some grasses native to your region in your garden to ensure that seeds ripen when local bird species need nutrition. In spring, birds will also tease out strands of dried grasses from the garden or the compost pile to construct their nests.

TEST
GARDEN
TIP

Grass know-how

Grasses add a dynamic element to the perennial garden. Follow these steps to make the most of them.

Choose wisely. Ornamental grasses are either clumping or spreading. Clumping types form neat clumps that slowly grow wider in the garden. Spreading types run rampant through open soil and do best when planted in spaces confined by sidewalks, driveways, or other substantial barriers.

Go vertical. Count on grasses to add height to plantings. Ornamental grasses are an option for places where you need the form of a shrub but without the permanent branch structure.

Brighten winter. Allow seedheads and leaves to remain in place as the snow flies to interject interest in winter garden scenes.

Prune annually. In spring, before new growth emerges, clip remaining stalks. Use hedge shears or electric hedge clippers for a quick and easy job.

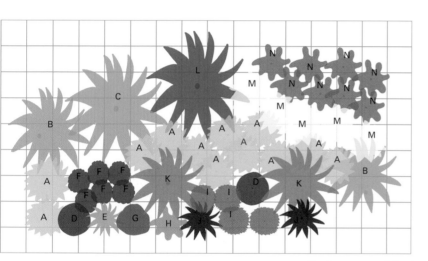

Each square = 1 foot

PLANT LIST

A. 12 Black-eyed susan (*Rudbeckia* spp.): Zones 3–9

B. 2 Maiden grass (*Miscanthus sinensis* 'Gracillimus'): Zones 4–9

C. 1 Variegated eulalia grass (*Miscanthus sinensis* 'Variegatus'): Zones 4–9

D. 2 'Autumn Joy' sedum: Zones 3–10

E. 1 Silver variegated Japanese sedge (*Carex morrowii* 'Variegata'): Zones 5–9

F. 6 Tall zinnia (*Zinnia elegans*): Annual

G. 1 Low-growing sedum such as *Sedum sieboldii*: Zones 6–9

H. 1 Prickly pear (*Opuntia compressa*): Zones 6–9

I. 4 Pink coreopsis (*Coreopsis rosea*): Zones 7–9

J. 2 Japanese blood grass (*Imperata cylindrica* 'Red Baron'): Zones 4–9

K. 2 Fountain grass (*Pennisetum alopecuroides*): Zones 6–10

L. 1 Zebra grass (*Miscanthus sinensis* 'Zebrinus'): Zones 4–9

M. 5 Daylily (*Hemerocallis* spp.): Zones 3–10

N. 8 Hollyhock (*Alcea rosea*): Zones 3–10

Native Knock Outs

Late summer arrives in a blaze of floral glory when you design a garden filled with native perennials. When spring bloomers fade and fizzle as rainfall dwindles and the sun drives temperatures skyward, these tough beauties come into their own. Native plants shrug off pests and diseases, just as they dismiss drought.

Late summer has a way of making a garden look spent and tired, scraggly and mean. Native plants transform summer's stern conditions into a beauty pageant where blooms and butterflies compete for attention. Count on native plants to lure nectar-sipping creatures—bees, butterflies, hummingbirds, and other insects—to your garden. Natives also beckon numerous bird species that come to feed on some of the insects. When you build a perennial garden around native plants, you build an ecosystem. Include multiple birdbaths—pedestal models and ground-level types—to increase the animal species that frequent your garden.

With its blocky form this garden design adapts easily to any sunny setting. Use it for a front yard facelift, a side yard showcase, or a backyard barbecue backdrop.

Native prairie plants, such as coneflower and gayfeather, form the backbone of this vibrant summer garden that scoffs at the heat and dry conditions of the season.

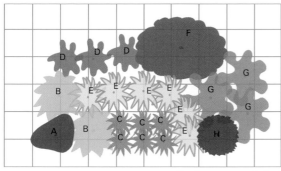

Each square = 1 foot

PLANT LIST

A. **1 Dwarf New England aster** *(Aster novae-angliae)* such as 'Purple Dome': Zones 4–10

B. **2 Thread-leaf coreopsis** *(Coreopsis verticillata)* such as 'Zagreb': Zones 4–10

C. **6 Coneflower** *(Echinacea purpurea)* such as 'Magnus': Zones 3–10

D. **3 Hollyhock** *(Alcea rosea)*: Zones 3–10

E. **6 White blazing star** *(Liatris spicata)* such as 'Floristan White': Zones 4–10

F. **1 Butterfly bush** *(Buddleia davidii)* such as 'Black Knight': Zones 5–10

G. **3 Russian sage** *(Perovskia atriplicifolia)*: Zones 3–10

H. **1 'Autumn Joy' sedum**: Zones 3–10

TEST GARDEN TIP

Praise for prairie plants

Stock your garden with prairie natives and you'll discover qualities beyond beauty that make these plants outstanding.

Water misers. Prairie plants practice water conservation—once established they're drought tolerant and don't require supplemental irrigation.

Erosion preventers. Long-lived, far-reaching roots search out moisture and prevent soil erosion.

Movers. Native ornamental grasses introduce movement to the garden in any season.

Chemical free. Prairie natives don't require fertilizer or insecticides to thrive.

Heat lovers. Searing heat doesn't faze prairie plants, which look fresh when summer sizzles—without watering.

Welcome in winter. Plant texture, color, and seedpods keep the good looks going in the off-season.

Top Drought-Tolerant Perennials

CONEFLOWER

RUSSIAN SAGE

SEA HOLLY

SHASTA DAISY

Low-water-use plants stock a garden with

colorful flowers that thrive in summer heat and dry soil. These water misers shrug when seasonal drought rolls in, tossing open blooms without so much as a sip of irrigation.

Drought-tolerant perennials do require care during their first season of growth. Provide plants weekly deep watering to encourage deep roots. Avoid overwatering; check the soil to see if it's dry before you irrigate. Once plants are root established, actively growing new roots, you're on your way to a drought-tolerant paradise.

If you choose to surround plants with gravel mulch, realize that stone retains heat, absorbing sunlight during the day, radiating heat at night. When you have a gravel covering exposed to sunlight (not covered by foliage), it can moderate the growing environment near the soil to the point that plants emerge sooner in spring and die back later in fall. In cold-winter climes, apply mulch to perennial crowns after the soil freezes for an extra layer of insulation and to ensure plants don't emerge during winter thaws.

This list offers a selection of water-saving, eco-savvy perennials for every growing region. Not all of these plants appear in the Perennial Encyclopedia (page 174). Some are too regionally specific to merit inclusion. Look them up online or at a local library to learn about their attributes.

NORTHEAST
ARTEMISIA
BLACK-EYED SUSAN
BLANKET FLOWER
BUTTERFLY MILKWEED
CATMINT
CONEFLOWER
COREOPSIS
CRANESBILL
DAYLILY
GAYFEATHER
GLOBE THISTLE
GOLDENROD
HOUSELEEK
LAMBS' EARS
LAVENDER
MULLEIN
SEA HOLLY
SPOTTED DEADNETTLE
SPURGE
WAND FLOWER
YARROW

SOUTHEAST
BARRENWORT
BLUE ANISE SAGE
COREOPSIS 'Zagreb'
FALSE INDIGO
PINKS
RUSSIAN SAGE
SEDUM 'Autumn Joy'
SHASTA DAISY
SHRUB VERBENA
SPEEDWELL 'Georgia Blue'

BASKET-OF-GOLD

ROCK CRESS

LAMB'S-EARS

CALIFORNIA FUCHSIA

COREOPSIS

PENSTEMON

TORCH LILY

KANGAROO PAW

MIDWEST
ALPINE ALYSSUM
BASKET-OF-GOLD
COREOPSIS
GOLDEN FLAX
JOE-PYE WEED
LAVENDER COTTON
LILY TURF
MEXICAN HAT
OX-EYE DAISY
OZARK SUNDROPS
SNEEZEWEED
SNOW-IN-SUMMER
ST. JOHNSWORT
WILD THYME

ROCKY MOUNTAINS
BROWN SEDGE
CANDYTUFT
GAZANIA HYBRIDS
ICE PLANT
KASHMIR SAGE
LUPINE
OREGANO, cascading
   ornamental varieties
PENSTEMON CULTIVARS
PUSSYTOES
ROCK CRESS
SANDWORT
SHOWY GERANIUM
SULFUR FLOWER
TWINSPUR
WHITE FIREWEED
WILD HYSSOP
WOOLLY SUNFLOWER

NORTHWEST
ANEMONE
CAMPION
CAPE FUCHSIA
CENTRANTHUS
CINQUEFOIL
CRIMSON SCABIOUS
DALMATION BELLFLOWER
FLEABANE
GEUM CULTIVARS
GIANT FEATHERGRASS
GIANT SEA KALE
HEART-LEAF BERGENIA,
   Bressingham Hybrids
LAMB'S-EARS
MYRTLE SPURGE
PEARLY EVERLASTING
PURPLE TOADFLAX
TORCH LILY
WALLFLOWER 'Bowles' Mauve'
WHITE GAURA

WEST
BEAR'S BREECHES
CALIFORNIA FUCHSIA
CALIFORNIA TREE POPPY
CURRY PLANT
FEVERFEW 'Aureum'
FLOWERING TOBACCO
FOOTHILL PENSTEMON
HONEYWORT 'Purpurascens'
JERUSALEM SAGE
KANGAROO PAW
MEXICAN BUSH MARIGOLD
MEXICAN TULIP POPPY
SALVIA, MAY NIGHT
SOUTH AFRICAN GERANIUM
STICKY MONKEY FLOWER
TALL VERBENA
TANSY 'White Bouquet'
TORCH LILY

Front Yard Cutting Garden

Your home will make a colorful first impression when you fill the front yard with flowering perennials. Whether you situate the bed front and center or closer to the house, the spread of blooms will enchant with its seasonal show. If your front yard features a slope that makes for tricky mowing, trading turf for colorful perennials can make weekly mowing headaches disappear.

Raising perennials along the edge of your property scores points with passersby who savor the scene, but your enjoyment is linked solely to coming, going, and maintenance. Enhance your ability to partake of the perennial pleasures by stocking the garden with plants you can cut for bouquets. Campion and daisies create fresh, simple arrangements; toss in a few sprigs of boxwood for greenery. Combine various daisies for an elegant vase display; peachleaf bellflowers form a long-lasting bouquet. You can easily increase the flower power in a garden like this by tucking in a few classic cutting annuals, such as cosmos, tall verbena, or zinnia.

When dealing with a deep border, whether it's a 7-footer like this one or as small as 3 feet, it's a good idea to include stones in the planting to provide a place to stand while gathering or tending to plants. In a hillside setting, choose large stones that can also act as a retaining station, helping to hold the soil in place.

With front yard flowers, formalize the entry with a gate or arbor. A pair of boxwood bookends the gate in this setting, accenting the entrance.

An exuberant mix of long-stemmed perennials is perfect for a cottage garden look. At the same time, this group of plants provides plenty of blooms for bouquets.

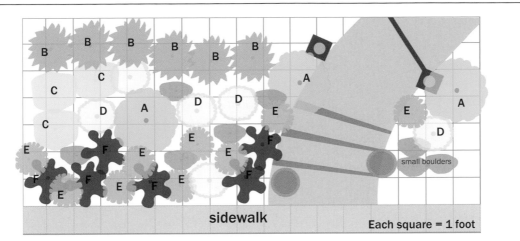

B B B B B B B
C C
C D A D D
A E
C E
E E E F
E F E E F
F E F F F
F E E F F E
small boulders

sidewalk

Each square = 1 foot

PLANT LIST

A. **3 Boxwood** (*Buxus* spp.), Zones 5–9
B. **6 Delphinium** (*Delphinium* Pacific Giant Series); Zones 4–10
C. **3 Peach-leaved bellflower** (*Campanula persicifolia*): Zones 3–10
D. **6 Shasta daisy** (*Leucanthemum* ×*superbum* 'Becky'): Zones 4–9
E. **9 Goldmoss stonecrop** (*Sedum acre*): Zones 3–10
F. **6 Rose campion** (*Lychnis coronaria*): Zones 4–10

TEST GARDEN TIP

Perennials for bouquets

FLOWERS

Balloon flower: Fat balloon-shape buds burst to reveal starry blooms.

Hyssop: Spiky flowers add vertical element to arrangements. Flowers in blue, lavender, pink, rose.

Lavender: Lavender-blue flower spikes weave fragrance into bouquets.

New England aster: Daisylike blooms in shades of purple, lavender, or vibrant pink.

Ox-eye or false sunflower: Cut a single bloom for tiny bouquets or entire branches for larger displays.

Yarrow: Flattened gold, red, pastel flowerheads form chunky focal points in bouquets. Use fresh or dried.

FOLIAGE

Artemisia: Silvery leaves that are linear, fernlike, or feathery. Pair with burgundy blooms or foliage for a striking bouquet.

'Brunette' blackberry bugbane': Grow for lustrous dark, fernlike foliage.

Coral bells: Leaves in shades of bronze, chartreuse, burgundy, deep maroon, green, orange, or silver.

Hosta: Select foliage in shades of blue, green, variegated, or chartreuse.

SEEDHEADS

Switchgrass: Use seedheads to introduce an airy element.

Corner Cottage Garden

Romance blooms in this corner cottage garden filled with delphiniums and roses.

Cottage garden style typically fills a small space with jostling perennials that crowd the cramped quarters with nonstop color. In this plan, a perennial border adapts cottage concepts to a protected pocket garden, blending fragrance and color. A stone wall and a shrubby hedge provide a neutral backdrop for the delphiniums and roses, which predominate in the mixed bed.

Cottage gardens typically feature sun-loving perennials, and this border is no exception, showcasing plants that thrive in full sun. A blend of foliage types, flowering periods, and artful touches ensures a season-long progression of color, interest, and beauty. Many of these perennials bear flowers suitable for cutting. Gather bouquets during peak bloom times and you won't miss the blossoms in the border.

Include a few shrubs and vines in a sweeping cottage border to provide interest during winter when perennials subside. Gardeners in cold-weather regions may want to substitute Shasta daisies for the marguerite daisies, pink yarrow for the cistus, Asiatic lilies for the Peruvian lilies, perennial salvia for the Mexican bush sage, English lavender for the Spanish lavender, and chives for the society garlic specified in this plan.

Each square = 1 foot

Delphinium know-how

Fill your garden with delphinium drama. These stately, spired beauties grow best in evenly cool conditions. Delphiniums are short-lived perennials, with plants surviving five years in the Pacific Northwest and three years elsewhere. Follow these tips to succeed with delphiniums.

Plant in rich, well-drained soil in a sunny location.

Add compost three times each growing season: in early spring, after flowering, and in late fall.

Insert stakes early in the season to protect the flowering stem where gusting winds are typical.

Encourage a second flowering by cutting off spent spikes when blossoms fade.

Replace plants regularly to ensure that you'll always have a delphinium presence.

PLANT LIST

A. **3 Rose-type geranium** (*Pelargonium hortorum*) such as a 'Graveolens': Annual

B. **1 Medium-size rose** such as 'Fragrant Memory': Zones 5–10

C. **1 Marguerite daisy** (*Argyranthemum frutescens*): Zones 10–11, annual elsewhere

D. **5 Moss phlox** (*Phlox subulata*): Zones 2–9

E. **1 Medium-size rose** such as 'Double Delight': Zones 5–10

F. **2 Medium-size rose** such as 'Chicago Peace': Zones 5–10

G. **20 Tall delphinium** (*Delphinium* hybrids): Zones 3–10

H. **3 Rock rose** (*Cistus creticus*): Zones 7–10

I. **7 Peruvian lily** (*Alstroemeria* cultivars): Zones 8–10

J. **10 Society garlic** (*Tulbaghia violacea*): Zones 7–10

K. **3 Mexican bush sage** (*Salvia leucantha*): Zones 9–11

L. **3 Spanish lavender** (*Lavandula stoechas*): Zones 8–10

Fall Color

Breathe life into a perennial garden with a late-season border that explodes with floral fireworks in fall's jewel tones. Deep purple and sizzling pink asters, brilliant yellow goldenrod, dusky blue fescue, and vibrant scarlet chrysanthemums sparkle in a border that can stand alone or fit neatly into an existing perennial planting.

This grouping of autumn favorites features dwarf versions of popular plants, creating a garden that's easily tended by eliminating flopping, need-to-be-staked tall varieties. The suggested goldenrods form tidy mounds compared to the taller, more open shape of their cousins. In this garden, goldenrod fills a groundcover role instead of headlining as a towering showstopper plant.

The flowers of these perennials linger nicely in fall's lower temperatures, bearing up even when temperatures tumble below 40°F. Use this garden plan to grace a driveway without blocking views, surround a patio, or greet trick-or-treaters in a front yard.

Group autumn's most brilliant bloomers—asters, mums, and goldenrod—for a high-impact display. Supplement the show with texture from ornamental grasses.

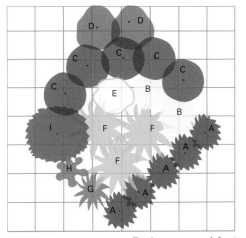

Each square = 1 foot

PLANT LIST

A. **5 Spike speedwell** (*Veronica spicata*) such as 'Goodness Grows': Zones 3–9

B. **2 Yarrow** (*Achillea* spp.) such as 'Moonbeam': Zones 4–10

C. **5 Chrysanthemum** such as 'Foxy Nana': Zones 5–10

D. **2 'Purple Dome' aster** (*Aster noveae-angliae* 'Purple Dome'): Zones 4–10

E. **1 Dwarf white aster** (*Aster* hybrids), such as 'Snow Flurry': Zones 4–8

F. **3 Dwarf goldenrod** (*Solidago* hybrids) such as 'Golden Baby' or 'Golden Fleece': Zones 4–9

G. **1 Blue fescue** (*Festuca glauca*) such as 'Elijah Blue': Zones 4–10

H. **1 Lamb's-ears** (*Stachys byzantina*): Zones 4–10

I. **1 Pink New England aster** (*Aster novi-belgii*) such as 'Alma Potschke': Zones 4–10

TEST GARDEN TIP

Pinch for flowers

What's the secret to a gorgeous fall display? Early summer pruning, especially for autumn performers like aster, boltonia, and chrysanthemum.

Asters and boltonia that grow over 36 inches tall tend to flop right about the time they're entering a full flush of bloom. By cutting plants back by one-third to one-half in early summer, when stems are about 12 inches tall, you'll encourage bushy, branched plants. The pruned perennials will lose their floppy tendencies and produce more flower buds. Other fall bloomers that benefit from an early summer trim are Russian sage and 'Autumn Joy' sedum.

With chrysanthemums, pinch off forming flowerheads until the Fourth of July. The result of this persistent pinching is a bushy, full plant with large flowers that last longer because they open during cool fall days.

planting the garden

Because perennials remain in the same place for years, it's vital to give them an ideal footing. Before breaking ground to bring your garden dreams to life, build a good foundation. Great gardens begin with great soil.

p.**110**
SOIL TESTING

Crafting ideal soil for perennials starts with taking a soil test. Act upon the results by adding materials to adjust soil pH, improve drainage, or enhance fertility.

p.**114**
BED PREPARATION

Once you define the bed shape and mark the edges, it's time to clear existing vegetation. Learn the best time to dig and how to work amendments into the soil.

p.**120**
PLANTING

The act of planting requires little time or effort, even in a large border. Explore the process, including storing perennials prior to planting, selecting digging tools, and mulching.

p.**128**
PERENNIALS IN POTS

When planting space is at a premium, grow perennials in containers. Discover which perennials thrive in containers, tricks to tend them, and what to do with them in winter.

Soil Testing

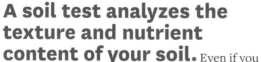

A soil test analyzes the texture and nutrient content of your soil.

Even if you have gardened in your yard for years, if you've never tested it before, it's worth the effort. Test results will reveal the texture by percentage, detailing how much sand, silt, and clay is in your soil. Texture dictates soil type, determining whether you have sandy soil, a mostly clay blend, or fertile garden loam.

The test also reveals soil pH, which influences nutrient availability. Soils that are extremely acidic (low pH) or alkaline (high pH) tie up nutrients so that plant roots can't absorb them.

While pH needs vary by perennial, most require a pH between 5.5 and 6.5 to flourish. You can adjust pH using lime or sulfur.

Most lab reports also state how much nitrogen, phosphorus, and potassium is in the soil, along with a measure of organic matter.

Test methods

Typically, a basic soil test is inexpensive and home test kits are available at garden centers or in garden catalogs. These tests provide generalized results with limited accuracy. For a more precise test that includes recommendations for addressing soil structure, organic matter, or nutrient issues, find a local soil-testing lab.

Contact your county extension offices for local lab suggestions. If that lead doesn't prove fruitful, contact a local land grant university or state department of agriculture. Once you find a local lab, it's worth calling to learn specific testing procedures you should follow or certain days the lab handles soil tests. To learn the basics of how to take a soil test, see below.

Test results

The soil test results provide the numeric breakdown of your soil content and include suggestions for soil improvement. Typically, the lab asks what kinds of plants you'll be growing. It lumps all perennials into one category, so the recommendations you receive will be rather general.

A soil lab usually suggests how much of each type of fertilizer, lime, or acidifying

Opposite: **A home soil test kit involves dipping a test strip into a soil solution and interpreting the outcome with a color key.**

agent you should add to improve soil. These recommendations are normally given in rates of pounds per 1,000 square feet. You'll need to do some math to adapt the measurements to your planting bed. Add amendments to the soil just before you till your planting bed. Work the materials into the top 6 to 8 inches of soil, mixing them in evenly.

Most tests address organic matter generically, suggesting you add it regularly, but without specifying a rate. In general, it's wise to apply a 2-inch layer of compost (organic matter) to perennial gardens annually. It's easier to apply in spring, before plants leaf out and while the soil is accessible. In warm regions, you may want to make two 1-inch applications—one in spring, one in fall. You can gently work this material into the soil using a hand cultivator or set it in place as mulch. Over time this annual application of compost will increase the amount of organic matter in your soil.

Step-by-Step Soil Sample

Gathering a soil sample to send to a testing lab takes less than 10 minutes. Test accuracy hinges on sending the lab a composite sample from your garden area. Follow these steps to collect the sample.

1 DIG
Dig a trowelful of soil from each of 10 testing sites in your garden plot. Before digging, remove any mulch or compost covering soil. Take the soil from the top 6 inches of the bed and add it to a bucket.

2 MIX
When all 10 soil samples are in the bucket, mix them together thoroughly. Break up clods, and remove any sticks, stones, or other debris.

3 SEND
Label a gallon zipper storage bag according to lab instructions. Add the recommended amount of soil to the bag (usually 1 to 2 cups). Seal the bag and send it to the lab.

Soil Amendments

The soil test may carry recommendations for adjusting soil pH, organic matter content, or nutrients.

A variety of amendments exist, from general types that can be applied to most soils to items that target specific problems. Some amendments come from the ground; others are by-products of food or plant processing.

Organic matter

Interview a dozen perennial gardeners, and you'll discover a dozen different types of organic matter. One reason for the variety of amendments is regionality. Various materials are readily available in different geographical areas. For instance, many South Florida gardeners favor sugar cane waste; Maine gardeners enjoy seaweed and composted fish soil additives. If you garden near the High Plains of Texas, you might be using cotton burr compost; in the Pacific Northwest, mushroom compost.

Organic matter increases pore spaces in a soil, which in turn improves the soil's ability to retain water and nutrients. Some types of organic matter, such as composted cow manure (readily available in dairy farming

Healthy soil contains roughly 25 earthworms per square foot. As worms tunnel, their castings stimulate soil microbe populations and enhance nutrient availability to plant roots.

regions), offer high levels of nutrition that's released as the material breaks down. Manures in particular can contain high salt levels; make sure you're adding well-composted manure (aged several months) to your garden to avoid burning plants.

Amendments derived from woody plant parts, such as chopped leaves, rotted sawdust, or wood chips, offer fewer nutrients and linger longer in soil until they've broken down. If you use a shredded bark mulch to double as a compost treatment, you may not need to refresh that layer for two years; on the other hand, if you use rotted manure-based compost, you'll need to replace it annually.

You can find organic matter through several sources. Many garden centers or landscape businesses sell organic matter in bags or bulk form. Bagged organic matter (dehydrated manure, compost, and leaf mold) provides a source that's free of weed seeds. If your city gathers leaves and yard waste in a citywide composting program, you may be able to obtain the composted product. You can also brew your own compost.

Some soil additives—the meal products—are used more as fertilizer than organic matter. Cottonseed meal and blood meal provide an excellent source of nitrogen to plant roots. Bonemeal releases phosphorus and calcium into the soil.

TEST GARDEN TIP

Timing is everything

Ideally, plan your garden through summer and use fall to prepare the soil. Then let it sit over winter. In this situation you can layer on readily available organic matter, such as chopped fallen leaves, and let the weather and worms improve your soil as the seasons change. This method works well when you're expanding an existing garden.

Living soil additives

Healthy soil teems with life, from easy-to-see worms and insects to invisible microbes, such as fungi, nematodes, and bacteria. Soil microbes engage in a host of beneficial activities, including increasing nitrogen, defeating pests, and building stronger roots.

Organic gardeners promote products designed to increase microbial activity in soil. *Biostimulants* and soil activators increase the number of microbes already living in soil. *Bioinoculants* contain living microbes you add to soil. When applying living microbes, focus on the word "living"—and follow instructions carefully to avoid killing the invisible creatures. Follow these tips for the best success with microbes.

Microbes have a definite shelf life. Use them before the date indicated on the package.

Avoid storing microbes in sun or heat. If storage instructions aren't on the package label, open the package carefully to discover correct storage conditions.

Most microbes must be applied to moist soil and within a specific temperature range. Apply them after rain or irrigation.

Microbes thrive in soils high in organic matter. Make annual applications of composted organic matter to keep microorganisms well fed.

Preparing for Planting

Clear existing vegetation from garden sites using one of several methods.

Which process you choose depends on how much time you have, how much effort you want to invest, and what kind of vegetation you're removing.

If you're dealing with turf or a groundcover, physical removal will work effectively. For a planting bed laced with pernicious weeds, such as quackgrass, dandelions, mugwort, or wiregrass, you'll need an aggressive stance to eradicate plants.

Whichever method you use, define the bed edge before beginning. Use a sharp spade to slice into vegetation. With the blade inserted into the soil, rock the spade back and forth to form an accessible trench. If you use an herbicide to remove vegetation, create a physical barrier or shield using cardboard, plastic, or lumber to prevent any spray from drifting onto surrounding plants.

Physically removing vegetation

Removing plants by hand involves intense labor but offers a low-cost approach to clearing a bed. When digging vegetation by hand, budget roughly an hour to hand clear 100 square feet, although that estimate varies based on the type of vegetation you remove. Sod comes up easily, as do some groundcovers. If you face deep-rooted perennial weeds, you'll dig deeper, which will slow your overall progress.

When clearing vegetation by hand remove as little soil as possible. The top few inches of soil is the most fertile. As you start removing the first chunks of existing vegetation, examine the soil beneath. You shouldn't see any grass rhizomes, plant roots, or rooted stems. If you do, dig a little deeper and remove more soil.

When working with a groundcover that roots along stems, search around in the proposed garden site and locate crowns of the plant. Focus on digging those out; the remaining stems should pull up easily.

Using an herbicide

An herbicide deals with weeds and turf in short order, killing the aboveground portion of plants, roots, or both. It's an excellent choice when time is short. Read the package label; typically you can plant in an herbicide-treated area within 10 to 14 days.

One of the most commonly used herbicides for killing grass and weeds is glyphosate. If you aspire to an organic garden, you may not want to use herbicides. Many professionals in the prairie restoration movement, which generally embraces organic principles, use an herbicide like glyphosate, which becomes inactive in soil after a few days, to prepare planting areas and wipe out existing non-native plants.

An excellent use for herbicides is planting a slope garden. Spray plant tops with herbicide, and roots will remain to hold soil in place. When greenery dies down, you can dig through the remaining roots to plant perennials. Within two years you won't see any sign of the previous vegetation.

If you need to wipe out weedy roots, spray plants in late fall, when carbohydrates are moving from leaves into roots. At this time, herbicide move more readily into roots, and you should be free of problem weeds come spring.

Opposite: **Use a supple garden hose to define a bed outline. View the bed from interior rooms and outdoor living areas. When you're satisfied with the shape, outline the edge with flour and start digging.**

TEST GARDEN TIP

Sod stories

When you remove turf, you're left with a pile of sod. Recycle those pieces using a few of these ideas.

Patch and repair bare spots in your lawn.

Add pieces to the compost pile. Toss turf onto the pile upside down, so the grass will decompose and not root into your compost pile.

Create a berm. Stack sod pieces upside down on top of one another to form a berm or raised planting area. Cover the stack with equal parts compost and top soil, and add a 2-inch layer of mulch. Allow the stack to settle for two to four weeks, then plant. If you want to cover the berm with turf, place a few of the sod pieces right side up on the soil-compost mixture.

Share with others. If you can't use your sod, ask neighbors or gardening friends if they would like it.

Turf's up Learn the basics about how to remove existing turf in a potential planting site.

TO REMOVE TURF WITH A SPADE, start with a sharpened blade. Starting along your defined edge push the spade under the grass. Use short pushes to slice about 1 inch under turf. You may start the process standing up, but you'll need to kneel before you finish. This task is easier when you have a helper who can pull sod back as you cut it free.

A MANUAL SOD CUTTER requires muscles and elbow grease to operate. Its main benefit over removing turf with a spade is that it keeps you off your hands and knees. Otherwise, it's not any easier in terms of physical labor. Use this method for a small garden area.

RENT A MECHANICAL SOD CUTTER if you're clearing a large garden space. This method lifts sod easily and in strips that form ready-to-use patches for bare spots in your lawn. A mechanical sod cutter can shave hours of labor from clearing a garden site.

CHOOSE AN HERBICIDE for weed-infested turf or when you're short on time. Use a sprayer that delivers large droplets. Don't spray on a windy day or you risk damaging nearby plantings. The herbicide must coat foliage to kill the plant, so don't mow or trim leaves before spraying. Use a spreader sticker with the herbicide to help it stick to plant leaves.

Preparing for Planting

If you're not in a hurry to get your garden in the ground, you can eliminate much of the labor from the preparation process by using slower methods to clear existing vegetation. These labor-saving techniques prepare beds that can be ready for planting in three weeks to six months.

Smothering

The smothering process composts existing vegetation in place and enhances your new garden with a layer of organic matter. It's an effective way to deal with troublesome, persistent weeds.

Smothering works by depriving plants of sunlight. You spread layers of material over existing plants, starting with a layer that allows no sunlight to penetrate. Choices include cardboard, 10 layered sheets of newspaper, or dark plastic. Select a material that decays, and you won't have to remove it when the plants die. Use mulch, such as compost, grass clippings, straw, or chopped leaves, for the second layer. Typically, a smothered bed is ready for planting in 6 to 12 months. Many gardeners start a layered bed in fall, when autumn leaves are available and lawns are poised to go dormant. In this case, the bed will be ready for spring planting.

"Lasagna gardening" takes smothering to new heights, adding layer upon layer of compostable material. Start with a light, impervious layer and build upon that. This technique works well in situations in which you know you'll be constructing a new bed in a certain place. Throughout the year, add layers as they're available. For instance, gather chopped spring tree and shrub prunings and layer them on the bed. Add grass clippings all season, and layer compost or straw when it's available. Finish the layers with chopped fall leaves. At any point during the process, if the layers are

Use solarization to clear soil of weed seeds, disease spores, nematodes, and insect eggs. Cover the soil with plastic to trap the sun's energy, which can heat soil to over 140°F.

deep enough or the soil beneath is diggable, you can bury kitchen waste in the same area to attract and feed beneficial soil organisms. By spring, you'll have worm-rich soil high in organic matter.

Solarization

With solarization, you harness the sun's energy to bake the soil above 140°F, the temperature that kills weed seeds, insect eggs, disease spores, and nematodes. While potential garden problems fry, beneficial fungi and bacteria survive. Solarization is an excellent choice for a heavily weed-infested site.

To solarize the soil, cut down weeds and till up roots with a heavy-duty tiller. Rake weeds and stems, and rake a second time to even out the soil. Water the area thoroughly to soak the top 4 to 6 inches of soil. Cover the soil with a sheet of clear construction grade plastic (1 to 6 mil), stretching it tightly. Seal any seams with clear tape to trap heat generated beneath the plastic. Use heavy blocks or bricks to hold down the edges until you can bury them to anchor the plastic and retain heat. In four to six weeks, the soil will be sufficiently heated and you can plant.

In the Northern hemisphere, the best time to solarize soil is when the sun is at its highest point in the sky: during June and July. This method works best in a garden site that receives at least six hours of direct sun daily.

TEST
GARDEN
TIP

Tough weeds

When you deal with tough weeds, such as tap rooted dandelion or spreading quackgrass, don't give up. Try one of these methods to bid weeds good-bye.

Spray and till. Use an herbicide to kill pernicious weeds. When the weeds are dead, rake them out by tilling the soil. Tilling brings weed seeds to the surface, so wait a few weeks for those seeds to sprout, then spray again. A third till-and-wait period will ensure a weed-free garden.

Solarize. Solarization kills even the most persistent weed seeds and roots, and the soil is ready to plant in four to six weeks.

Smother. If time is not an issue, smothering persistent weeds over winter will kill them.

How to smother vegetation

An easy approach to killing turf is to smother the soil. This technique composts the grass in place, which enhances soil organic matter. A smothered bed is generally ready to plant in 6 to 12 months.

1 MOW
Use a mower or string trimmer to cut existing turf and weeds as close to the soil as possible. Allow clippings to remain in place. They'll help smother existing vegetation. Make sure you know where the bed edges are; mark them, if necessary.

2 LAY DOWN NEWSPAPER
Place newspapers over the designated planting area, creating a layer at least 10 sheets thick. Newspaper inks aren't toxic to plants or soil.

3 WET NEWSPAPER
Wet the newspapers to hold them in place. If you're covering a large area, you may need to combine Steps 3 and 4, working to cover a small portion of the bed at a time, to prevent newspapers from drying and blowing away.

4 PLACE MULCH
Cover the newspapers with a 4- to 5-inch-thick layer of organic matter, such as grass clippings, straw, shredded leaves, or composted manure. Mix materials, if necessary, to create a 4- to 5-inch depth.

5 WATER MULCH
The organic layer needs to stay in place for several months. If you notice it's breaking down, add more organic material (you can use a different material) to maintain the 4- to 5-inch layer. Avoid letting the organic matter dry out. If rainfall is scarce, water the mulch on occasion. The edges tend to dry faster than the center.

Preparing for Planting

Use a digging fork to work amendments into the soil. Avoid standing or walking on the soil. Instead, lay down a board and stand on that to reach the middle of the bed.

When you have removed existing vegetation, it's time to work amendments into the soil.

This task is the most labor-intensive aspect of planting a perennial garden. The goal in working the soil is to improve drainage on lower levels, if needed, and to work organic matter into the upper 6 to 8 inches of soil.

Adding amendments

As you blend in amendments, try to create gradual changes in the soil from top to bottom. Work in amendments from the top down, aiming to increase organic matter in the topmost layer, where the majority of soil organisms and plant feeder roots are. Lower soil layers may need only to be broken up to enhance drainage. Before digging, make sure soil isn't overly wet or dry (see Just-Right Soil, below).

Mix in amendments by hand, using a digging fork or round-point spade. Digging by hand is more labor intensive, but the results prove just as effective as using a rototiller. Hand-digging makes sense in a small garden or to save money. Going over the ground two or three times with a spade will effectively blend amendments into the soil.

For a large garden, rent or borrow a rototiller. A tiller isn't effective in rocky soil or a bed filled with tree roots but works fabulously fast in sandy or loamy soil. In clay soils, don't churn the same area of soil too much to avoid compacting lower layers where digging tines strike.

In soil with many tree roots, a digging fork (also called a spading fork) maneuvers well without damaging roots. A digging fork also makes quick work of soil preparation in sandy soil.

To mix in amendments, add a 1- to 2-inch layer of organic matter on top of the soil and work it into the top 6 to 8 inches. If digging by hand, use a digging fork to turn forkfuls of soil on its side, mixing in the amendments as you turn the soil. Repeat the process, adding another 1 inch of organic matter plus any other amendments. Dig these amendments in 3 to 4 inches deep. This amending method yields a gradual decrease in organic matter from the soil surface to deeper layers.

The best digs

Choose a round-point spade for efficient digging. Also called an irrigation spade, round-point shovel, or digging shovel, this tool has a straight shaft, which allows you to dig efficiently. A round-point spade makes quick work of creating or redefining a bed edge. Shovels with a bent shaft are better suited to scooping than digging. Use one to define a bed edge, and you'll wind up with an inclined edge.

Just-right soil

Avoid working soil that's overly wet or dry or you may make the soil structure worse, not better. This is most important for soil with clay particles; sandy or high silt soils aren't an issue. Before digging, grab a handful of soil and squeeze it.

JUST-RIGHT SOIL CLUMPS IN HAND When soil is right for digging, it forms a ball that breaks apart easily when touched. No water drips from it as you squeeze.

TOO-DRY SOIL DUST CLOUD Soil that's too dry to work won't clump together. Too-dry soil creates a dust cloud if you dig in it, and topsoil blows away. If you work too-dry soil, a hard crust forms on the surface when water touches it.

TOO-WET CLUMPING SOIL When you squeeze a clump of soil that's too wet, you end up with a wet, muddy hand. Too-wet soil sticks to digging tools and, if you dig in it, forms hard clods that clump together.

Plant Placement

The hardest part of planning your perennial garden is definitely the preparation work.

Planting even a large border takes a small fraction of time compared with clearing vegetation and blending amendments into soil.

Before planting, transfer your garden design from paper to the planting bed. For each perennial, you need to know the mature size. If your perennials are in pots with plant tags, look for that information on the tag. For bare-root perennials or starts obtained from neighbors or friends, research mature size in the Perennial Encyclopedia (page 174).

Arrange your perennials in the garden, starting at one point and working outward. Place the plants slowly and carefully, situating them at the correct spacing for their mature size. To learn more about plant spacing, see the tip box, How Many Plants? (page 79). You may want to let the potted perennials sit on the bed for a few days to view the design from several angles (inside and out) and confirm that you're satisfied with it.

Best time to plant

Aim to plant perennials at a time of year when they'll be able to sink roots with the least amount of stress. In cold climates, planting in late spring or early summer provides perennials an entire season to grow before winter cold arrives. Fall is an ideal planting time in mild regions, where winter brings moist soil and cool air without freezing temperatures. For climates with clearly defined wet and dry seasons, plant perennials at the start of the rainy season and allow rainfall to irrigate the plants.

Before planting, arrange perennials on the soil according to your garden design. Stand back and inspect the placement, then begin tucking plants into soil.

Mulch

New perennial beds need a layer of mulch to maintain soil moisture and suppress weeds. You can add mulch after planting, which works well when you're dealing with large perennials (quart or gallon size). For small and bare-root perennials, it's often easier to mulch the bed before planting. To plant, simply pull back mulch and dig a planting hole.

Mulch quality and type vary immensely. You don't have to pay top dollar to get the best mulch product; you can find inexpensive sources of quality mulch. Many communities gather and compost yard waste and offer it to gardeners at little or no cost. Before taking advantage of what appears to be the best mulch bargain in town, discover how the compost is processed. If it's not turned but just sits and decomposes, you may take home compost laced with weed seeds and disease spores. In that case, the bargain is a problem in the making. Often you can find well-composted manure free for the taking at stables or farms. In coastal areas where there's a fish-based industry, many companies offer free fish waste compost.

Mulch sold in bulk is cheaper than bagged products. Look for discounted bagged mulch during end-of-season sales at seasonal garden centers, the kind sold at grocery or warehouse stores during the growing season.

When you use organic mulch, such as bark, pine straw, shredded leaves, or compost, you can usually identify potential problems by scent. If you detect an odor of ammonia, vinegar, sulfur, or alcohol, that mulch could actually burn plants. In general, if you can't stand the mulch smell for about 10 seconds, you don't want that mulch. Mulch that's safe to place around plants has a damp earthy odor.

TEST GARDEN TIP

Planting depth

Most perennials flourish when their crowns are planted at the same depth as in the growing container. Test planting depth by laying a tool handle across the planting hole with the perennial placed at the proposed planting depth in the hole. Adjust the soil in the planting hole accordingly. When the crown is even with the tool handle, the plant is at the proper depth. Exceptions to the ground-level planting rule include:

Above grade. Perennials prone to rot grow better when their crowns are slightly above soil level. These include daylily, lady's mantle, lamb's-ear, and bearded iris.

Shallow depth. Perennials that crave moisture thrive when their crowns are 1 or 2 inches below grade. Examples (as well as how deep to plant) are bee balm (1 inch), bugbane (2 inches), hosta (1 inch), and peony (1 inch deep in warm climates, 2 to 3 inches deep in cold zones).

Deep planting. Perennials with tuberous or bulbous roots need deeper planting—about 4 inches below the soil surface. Examples include crocosmia, ornamental allium, and variegated solomon's seal.

Mulch how-to Learn proper mulching techniques with these simple steps.

MULCH TO PROPER DEPTH Apply a 2- to 4-inch layer. Thicker layers can lead to rodent or pest problems. If mulch breaks down quickly in your region, it's better to apply two thin layers over the course of a year than to apply one thick layer.

MULCH AWAY FROM CROWN Pull mulch about 2 to 4 inches away from perennial crowns. Mounding mulch over crowns can lead to rot and provide a safe haven for voles and other plant-munching critters.

WATER AFTER APPLYING Water dry mulch after applying it to help hold a dry, light material in place, rather than let the wind blow it away.

The Lowdown on Mulch

When choosing mulch, you want a natural-looking material that doesn't rob nutrients from soil. Some mulches, such as wood chips, saw dust, and straw, draw nitrogen out of the soil as they decay, which can cause nutrient issues for plants. If possible, use wood-based mulches that are well rotted or take longer to decompose, such as high-

STRAW

Risk of weed seeds: Yes

Nitrogen impact: Slight

Availability: Widespread

Cost: Inexpensive

Durability: 1 year

Comments: Keep bales wet for several weeks to germinate all seeds before applying

CHOPPED LEAVES

Risk of weed seeds: No

Nitrogen impact: Slight

Availability: Widespread

Cost: Free or inexpensive

Durability: 1 year or less

Comments: Best if partially decomposed

FRESH WOOD CHIPS

Risk of weed seeds: No

Nitrogen impact: Severe

Availability: Widespread

Cost: Free or inexpensive

Durability: 1–4 years

Comments: Use after composting

SAWDUST

Risk of weed seeds: No

Nitrogen impact: Severe

Availability: Local to regional

Cost: Free or inexpensive

Durability: 1–3 years

Comments: Use only after several years of decomposition: do not use sawdust from treated wood

MUNICIPAL COMPOST

Risk of weed seeds: Yes

Nitrogen impact: None

Availability: Local, most often urban and suburban areas

Cost: Free or inexpensive

Durability: 1 year or less

Comments: Quality varies significantly, depending on municipality.

PACKAGED COMPOST

Risk of weed seeds: No

Nitrogen impact: None

Availability: Widespread

Cost: Expensive

Durability: Several months

Comments: Better used as a soil additive than a mulch

PINE STRAW

Risk of weed seeds: No

Nitrogen impact: Slight

Availability: Local to regional

Cost: Inexpensive to moderate

Durability: 1–2 years

Comments: May be blown away in windy areas

SPOILED HAY

Risk of weed seeds: Yes

Nitrogen impact: Slight

Availability: Local

Cost: Free to inexpensive

Durability: Several months to a year

Comments: Wear dust mask while applying spoiled hay since it may contain mold spores

quality shredded hardwood bark. When you must use a wood-based mulch that's not decomposed, add a slow-release fertilizer to the soil surface before applying the mulch.

Some mulches offer greater longevity than others. Grass clippings and spoiled hay last a few weeks to a few months; cocoa hulls, pine straw, and fresh wood chips last one to three years. If you tap into a locally available compost source, such as seaweed, spent mushroom soil, or chopped leaves, you'll spend little to nothing on mulch.

One last concern with mulch is floatability. Some mulches pack down when wet; others, such as pine bark, tend to float. Avoid using lightweight, easily blown or floated mulch near inground swimming pools or ponds, or on hillsides.

SPENT MUSHROOM SOIL
Risk of weed seeds: No

Nitrogen impact: None

Availability: Very local

Cost: Free to inexpensive

Durability: Several months to a year

Comments: Adds organic matter but not significant amounts of nutrients

COTTONSEED HULLS
Risk of weed seeds: No

Nitrogen impact: None

Availability: Very local

Cost: Free to inexpensive

Durability: Several months to a year

Comments: May be blown away in windy areas

SEAWEED
Risk of weed seeds: No

Nitrogen impact: None

Availability: Local to regional

Cost: Free to inexpensive

Durability: Several months

Comments: Adds valuable micronutrients to the soil

COCOA HULS
Risk of weed seeds: No

Nitrogen impact: None

Availability: Widespread

Cost: Expensive

Durability: 1–3 years

Comments: Deliciously fragrant

SHREDDED HARDWOOD
Risk of weed seeds: No

Nitrogen impact: Limited

Availability: Widespread

Cost: Moderate

Durability: 1–3 years

Comments: In recent years quality has declined and may vary widely

SHREDDED PINE BARK
Risk of weed seeds: No

Nitrogen impact: Limited

Availability: Widespread

Cost: Moderate

Durability: 1–3 years

Comments: Use instead of pine nuggets, which can tie up nitrogen

SALT MARSH HAY
Risk of weed seeds: No

Nitrogen impact: Limited

Availability: Local to regional

Cost: Moderate

Durability: 1 year

Comments: Some concern about environmental impact of harvesting

SHREDDED CYPRESS
Risk of weed seeds: No

Nitrogen impact: Limited

Availability: Widespread

Cost: Moderate

Durability: More than 5 years

Comments: More durable than most mulches but less beneficial to soil

Planting Perennials

After setting a perennial into soil, begin to backfill the planting hole, tamping soil into the empty spaces. When the soil is even with the surrounding bed, add mulch.

Tucking plants into beds requires some attention to detail,

but mostly it's an easy, approachable task. Dig a hole that's no deeper than the height of the root ball and a few inches wider than the container. Remove any rocks you unearth while digging. With a bareroot perennial, form a mound in the base of the planting hole to hold the crown and allow roots to spread out and down.

The right tool

Tackle perennial planting with a variety of digging tools. Specialized tools suited to specific tasks make quick work of planting, but you can manage your garden with a few key implements. A digging spade or round-point spade creates a sharp, straight bed edging. It's also useful for digging holes for large perennials. A short-handle shovel, sometimes sold as a contractor's shovel, works well for digging small holes. The short handle is easy to manage while on your knees, which makes it handy for planting.

A transplanting spade has a long, narrow blade that fits neatly between established perennials. It's the digging tool of choice when you're working in an existing planting bed, maneuvering and digging around plants. For small perennials in 2- or 4-inch pots, a hand trowel or hoe speeds up planting, especially when soil is loose and easy to dig.

Pots, roots, and crowns

When dealing with container perennials, water plants thoroughly before planting. To remove plants from pots, invert the container with one hand splayed over the soil and cradling the stems. If the plant doesn't slide out easily, lay the container on the ground and roll it, pressing down with your hands using some force. You can also step on the pot, but use light pressure to avoid damaging the plant.

After removing the plant from the pot, if roots blanket the outside of the soil, tease some free or slice about one-half inch into the root ball at several points. The idea is to loosen and free roots to branch into surrounding soil after planting. If you don't deal with roots, they'll tend to circle inside the planting hole, which will stunt top growth.

Before planting, brush soil away from around the base of the stems so you can see the crown. This will help you place the plant at the correct planting depth (see page 121).

Remove a biodegradable pot before planting as long as roots aren't poking through the pot and the pot isn't decaying. A dry, intact biodegradable pot can actually restrain roots after planting, preventing them from invading surrounding soil.

Post-planting care

After planting, place mulch around perennials, covering any exposed soil. If you mulched before planting, replace mulch around plants. Water thoroughly, soaking the top 8 inches of soil. Dig into soil away from plants to determine saturation depth. Watering settles soil and removes air pockets. If water starts to run off before soil is adequately soaked, stop for 30 to 45 minutes before resuming irrigation.

New perennials need evenly moist soil to root and establish. Typically 1 inch of water per week, delivered through rainfall or watering, is sufficient. Pull back mulch and check soil moisture 3 to 4 inches deep to determine if you need to water. Established perennial gardens need about ½ inch of water per week. Moisture-craving plants need more; drought-tolerant plants need less.

How to plant container-grown perennials

1 DIG
Dig a generous hole. For 4-inch or smaller pots, dig with a trowel. For larger pots, use a spade. In old beds where the soil hasn't been worked in a while, make the planting hole one to two times wider than the nursery pot, but no deeper. Dig so the sides of the hole slope toward the center of the bottom. In well-prepared beds, dig the hole as wide and deep as the pot.

2 CHECK THE DEPTH
Check the depth of the hole by setting the pot in it. Make the plant crown level with the surrounding soil. Planting too deep invites stem and crown rot; planting too high may retard plant growth. Check the level by laying the handle of your spade, a ruler, or other straight object over the hole. The top of the container soil should be even with the bottom of the handle.

3 REMOVE THE PLANT
Take the plant out of the pot by flipping it over, keeping one hand stretched over the soil around the plant. Tap the pot with your other hand until the plant is free of the container. If a plant won't come out, roll the pot back and forth on the ground while firmly pressing on it with your hands or your foot.

4 TEASE APART
Tease apart any potbound roots encircling the root ball. Or make shallow slices around the root ball with a sharp knife, cutting from the bottom to halfway up the root ball.

5 SET THE PLANT
Set the plant in the hole, evenly spreading the loosened roots. Recheck the planting depth and adjust the depth of the hole so the plant's crown is at the right level.

6 BACKFILL
Backfill the hole halfway, firming the soil with your hands. Then fill the hole with water to settle the soil. When the water has been absorbed, finish backfilling the hole; firm the soil and water again. Use a gentle spray, such as from a water breaker or fan-spray sprinkler, to avoid splashing soil out of the hole.

How to plant bare-root perennials

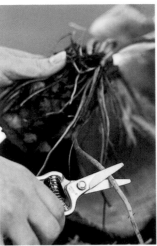

1 CHECK THE ROOTS
Bare-root plants have no soil around their roots. Nurseries often wrap the roots in moist sphagnum peat moss before shipping to prevent drying while the plants are en route. Remove it before planting.

2 TRIM
Trim any dead or broken roots. Try to keep as many roots intact as you can. The bigger and healthier the root system at planting, the faster a plant will take off when growth begins in the spring.

3 SOAK ROOTS
Fill a bucket with water and soak the roots to rehydrate them. Leave them in the bucket for at least one hour and no more than two hours. Adding a root starter to the water is beneficial.

4 DIG
Dig a hole as wide as the spread-out roots and as deep as the roots reach. You can do this while the plant soaks or just before planting.

5 FORM MOUND
At the center of the hole, form a mound of soil to hold the plant at the right depth and help anchor it while you fill the hole. Scrape the dirt at the bottom of the hole into a high enough pile that the crown or eyes (buds on the roots) sit at the soil surface.

6 LET ROOTS SOAK
Leave the plant to soak in the bucket until you are ready to plant it.

7 SET
Set the plant on the mound and evenly spread its roots over the soil. Backfill the soil halfway, and then fill the hole with water.

8 FINISH
After the water has been absorbed, finish backfilling the hole. Firm the soil and water again. Move the mulch back around the plant or add a layer. Thoroughly water again and keep the soil moist until the plant becomes established.

Planting Perennials in Containers

Just because your real estate won't accommodate an inground planting bed doesn't mean you can't tend a perennial garden. Perennials can grow anywhere, even in containers. On a deck, balcony, rooftop, patio, or porch, containers bring the beauty of perennials within reach of every gardener.

Count on potted perennials to interject an element of surprise in beds and borders, forming arresting focal points that present seasonal and vertical interest. Confining perennials to containers also permits you to grow plants that wouldn't normally survive in your garden's conditions.

Tips for pots

Select containers that give perennial roots room. Choose a minimum pot diameter of 12 inches; larger is better. Wooden half barrels, and stone, faux stone, or concrete containers stand up to weather and are frostproof. Extend the life of wooden containers by tacking pieces of treated lumber beneath the pots to raise them above a constantly moist footing. Terra-cotta tends to crumble in regions with freeze-thaw cycles. Elevating the container above the ground can help slow water-related damage.

With large, heavy containers, situate the pot before filling it with soil and planting it. Place the container on bricks or pot feet to enhance drainage. Every container needs drainage holes on or near the bottom. If your container boasts lightweight construction, use a heavy item in the bottom to help prevent toppling in strong winds.

Perennial pointers

The design principle of balance comes into play when selecting perennials for a pot. A general guideline is that mature plant height shouldn't exceed more than one and a half times the height of the container. If your container is 18 inches tall, the perennials in it should grow no more than 27 inches tall. Typically, potted perennials don't attain the same height that they would if they were planted in a bed.

All perennials in a container should have the same light needs; nutritional needs can vary slightly. In a pot, nutrition comes from soil and supplemental fertilizer you provide. Frequent watering washes nutrients from soil, potentially depleting an already limited supply. By combining one or two perennials with greater nutritional needs, such as garden phlox and daylily, with plants like coneflower and coral bells that prefer leaner soil, your pot will have sufficient fertility to satisfy each plant's appetite.

Hedge against winter damage by choosing perennials that are at least one zone hardier than your hardiness zone. For instance, if you garden in Zone 5, fill your pot with perennials hardy to Zone 4. Soil volume in the container isn't enough to protect plant roots from winter temperature extremes. Learn more about winter care for containers on pages 156–157.

Consider gathering several different pots together to stage container drama. Balance one large container planted with a substantial perennial, such as New Zealand flax or golden hakone grass, with a medium pot and a cluster of smaller pots. You could also use containers as a cleverly disguised holding bed to grow small perennials to size or to hold plants until new garden areas are ready.

Opposite: **Low-maintenance succulents and sedums are wonderful choices for growing in a perennial container garden. Their fleshy leaves create a striking textural tableau.**

Perennials for containers
Nearly any type of perennial flower can be grown in a container. However, best results come when you select those with a long season of bloom or ones with attractive foliage when blooms fade.

BELLFLOWER
Clusters of violet or white flowers in late spring to midsummer. Full sun to part shade; well-drained soil. Zones 3–10.

BLACK-EYED SUSAN
Drought and heat tolerant with large daisylike blooms in shades of yellow, gold, or mahogany. Full sun, well-drained soil. Zones 5–10.

CORAL BELLS
Evergreen to semi-evergreen foliage in many hues, including burgundy and lime. Full sun to part shade; well-drained soil. Zones 3–10.

COLUMBINE
Pink, blue, white, red, or yellow, spurred blooms in mid- to late spring. Part shade to full sun in rich, moist, well-drained soil. Zones 3–10.

DAYLILY 'STELLA DE ORO'
Cheery yellow flowers open nonstop all season long. Full sun to part shade in moist, fertile, well-drained soil. Zones 3–10.

GRAYLEAF CRANESBILL
Pale purple flowers in spring; fall foliage burnishes red. Full to part shade in moist, well-drained soil. Zones 5–10.

GOLDEN HAKONE GRASS
Gold leaves marked with thin green stripes form a fountainous cascade. Part sun to full shade in rich, well-drained, slightly acid soil. Zones 5–10.

HEART-LEAF BERGENIA
Shiny, leathery evergreen leaves and pink blooms; deer resistant. Part to deep shade; moist soil high in organic matter. Zones 4–10.

HOSTA
Beautiful foliage with variegation or hues; use miniature or small types for pots. Part to full shade; moist soil with plenty of organic matter. Zones 3–9.

NEW ZEALAND FLAX
Variegated or solid leaves in shades of green, cream, yellow, rust, orange, or red. Full sun; fertile, well-drained soil. Zones 8–11.

Perennials in Containers

Planting and tending a potted perennial garden combines

elements of annual container gardening with perennial growing. The result is a garden that boasts all the beauty of a large perennial border in a small growing space.

Getting started

Start with well-drained soil that includes some compost or well-rotted manure to provide a slow-release fertilizer source for plants. For perennials like gayfeather and lavender that require sharp drainage, mix grit or sand into the soil. Adjust the soil pH if you're planting acid-loving perennials, such as barrenwort or lupine.

Cover drainage holes with window screen to prevent soil from washing out. For terra-cotta pots that aren't glazed and permit water evaporation through container sides, blend a water retention polymer into the soil. Before planting, fill the pot with soil and arrange perennials on the soil to confirm placement. Plant perennials following the procedures outlined on pages 126–127.

Keep the soil about 2 inches below the pot rim. Apply mulch after planting to help slow water evaporation from the soil surface. Mulching with chopped oak leaves or pine needles will also slowly acidify soil.

Maintenance

Perennials in containers demand more care than their inground cousins simply because nutrition and water supplies are limited. Water enough to prevent plants from wilting. Each perennial has differing irrigation needs; water your container as needed to provide ideal growing conditions for your plants.

Fertilize containers using compost or rotted manure applied in early spring, before plants poke through soil. Gently scratch fertilizer into the soil. Make a second application in midsummer if leaves appear a lighter shade than normal.

Every year or two, lift the perennials and divide them, replanting the strongest sections. Before replanting, trim the roots of shrubby perennials by one-fourth. Use this opportunity to refresh the soil in the container. Remove and replace at least half the soil.

Opposite: **Perennials dress containers with beautiful changes through the seasons. This blend of purple fountain grass, garden mum, and New Zealand flax stages stunning autumnal interest.**

Winter container care

Before Old Man Winter blusters into town, give your containers the care they need to survive the cold season.

INSULATE Stack straw bales around a container plant, filling any air spaces between pot and bales with loose straw. You can also form screens with chicken wire or burlap and stuff those with several inches of straw, shaping the screen to cradle the pot.

RELOCATE For a tender perennial growing in a frostproof container, plant the perennial in a plastic pot that can be lifted and moved indoors for winter. Another option for preserving marginally hardy perennials is to lift the plants and tuck them into the ground, such as a vegetable garden or annual bed.

USE A DOLLY. A mature plant in a large pot is heavy. Use a dolly to move containers into winter digs, such as a garden shed, basement, or unheated garage.

caring for perennials

Grooming a perennial garden is part technique and part intuition. Daily visits help you learn which plants require attention and which chores can wait.

p.134
WATER & FERTILIZER

Plant growth begins with water and fertilizer. Discover the basic tools and techniques, and decide which methods suit your garden style.

p.140
GROOMING

Most perennial gardens require some primping to keep plants looking their best. Deadheading, pruning, and staking give your garden good looks; they also enhance plant health.

p.152
DIVIDING

As perennials mature, you'll enjoy the excitement of gleaning new plants from existing ones. Explore the techniques and timing for many types of plants.

p.156
SEASONAL CHORES

Seasonal to-do lists eventually echo like a mantra in a gardener's head. Develop a checklist to keep your garden in tip-top condition.

p.160
TROUBLESHOOTING

In some growing seasons, tending perennials involves dodging diseases, pests, and critters. Use this troubleshooting guide to solve garden problems.

Watering and Irrigation

Provide adequate water and your perennial garden will be filled with healthy, beautiful plants.

Water is vital to plant health, moving through plants from roots to leaves. As water moves through a perennial, it carries nutrients from the soil to growing leaves. When water evaporates from leaves, it acts as a cooling mechanism, like sweat on a person.

Irrigation frequency

Watering perennials can be tricky because plants show the same symptoms when they're suffering from overwatering or underwatering. The most accurate way to know if plants need water is to check the soil. If it's wet 3 to 4 inches deep, you don't need to water. Check soil moisture in several locations in the garden because each area may dry out at different rates.

Water perennials infrequently and deeply. This means applying water for a longer period of time than a quick pass with a garden hose.

Morning is the best time of day to water. You can deliver water to your garden using soaker hoses, drip irrigation, an overhead sprinkler, or by hand. Some gardeners prefer to water by hand, using that time to inspect plants. Others like an automated system. If you use automatic irrigation, make sure you can override any programmed settings so plants aren't overwatered during rainy spells.

How much water?

A guideline for watering established perennials is to provide ½ to 1½ inches of water per week in summer, delivered through rainfall or irrigation. During spring and fall, provide that amount of water in a two-week window. In areas where the ground doesn't freeze, 1 to 2 inches per month is sufficient in winter.

Of course, some perennials, such as coneflower, lavender, penstemon, and white gaura are more drought tolerant than others and actually require less water. Newly planted gardens require consistently moist soil, especially for bare-root plants or small starts.

To calibrate automated irrigation, measure how much water you're applying by setting out shallow containers marked in ½-inch increments. Track how long it takes for your irrigation system to deliver the prescribed amount of water and set timers accordingly. In some situations, you may notice that water runs off the bed before 1 inch is delivered to soil. In this case, set the irrigation system to cycle off for 30 minutes after it hits the point of runoff.

How do you know when you have watered enough? Measure the water applied, or for a more accurate gauge, soak the first 8 inches of soil. That's the goal of deep watering, which encourages deep roots. An easy test to see if the soil is soaked is to insert a screwdriver into the planting bed. In moist soil, the blade will slip in easily.

Opposite: **Watering perennials by hand provides an opportunity to inspect plants closely. Hand watering is typically the norm in a small garden or with newly planted perennials.**

TEST GARDEN TIP

Rain water harvest

Tap into free sources of water by installing rain barrels to downspouts. Closed barrels offer many advantages over open ones, including preventing mosquito breeding. Consider connecting several barrels to gather as much rain water as possible. Rain barrels with spouts deliver water via gravity. Elevate barrels to enhance flow or, with a multiple barrel system, explore installing a pump to deliver water to an irrigation system.

Water wisdom

Make the most of water you use in your garden by adopting conservation practices. Here are six simple water-saving techniques.

Apply mulch. A mulch layer slows water evaporation from the soil surface.

Avoid wind. Don't use overhead watering on windy days.

Water early. Water early in the day, when wind speed and temperature are lower, to reduce evaporation losses.

Group like plants. Arrange plants in the garden by water needs. Group perennials that need water during dry periods, and scatter drought-tolerant ones throughout the rest of the garden.

Use microclimates. Plant water-loving perennials near downspouts and hard surfaces, where runoff tends to douse soil.

Water roots. Use soaker hoses or drip irrigation to deliver irrigation directly to roots and eliminate evaporation that can occur during overhead sprinkling.

Fertilizers and Nutrition

Most plants find and absorb adequate nutrients from soil, with the exception of a few key ones:

nitrogen, phosphorus, and potassium. Nitrogen is responsible for vigorous growth and green leaves, phosphorus fuels strong roots, and potassium enhances flower and fruit formation. These are the nutrients most commonly added—in the form of fertilizer—to stimulate plant growth. They are often abbreviated using their chemical symbols: N (nitrogen), P (phosphorus), and K (potassium).

Fertilizer labels indicate the percentage of these three nutrients as a series of numbers, such as 15-30-15, which indicates that 15 percent of the weight of the bag is nitrogen, another 15 percent is potassium, and 30 percent is phosphorus. Those numbers become important when you select a high-nitrogen fertilizer to promote leaf growth or a high-potassium product to increase fruiting.

Types of fertilizer

Understanding fertilizer types can help you choose the product that best suits your garden soil and environmental philosophy. For instance, organic fertilizers, such as manures and compost, have low levels of nutrients but improve soil structure, favor a healthy population of soil microbes and worms, and contribute micronutrients that plants need. Manures are also bulky, vary in nutrient concentration (see the chart on opposite page), and require a large quantity to deliver an adequate amount of nutrients.

Some organic fertilizers are more concentrated, such as blood, bone, or cottonseed meal, so it takes a smaller amount to provide a nutrient boost, which is why they're often priced higher. Most meal fertilizers require microbes to break them down, which means they don't provide readily available nutrients during colder seasons of the year, when microbes are inactive.

Add compost to perennial gardens in spring, placing it directly on the soil near plant stems. Place a 2- to 3-inch layer on an entire planting bed.

Soluble fertilizers, when dissolved in water, deliver a quick nutrient burst to plants. They're easy to handle and often contain a high percentage of nutrients per weight. In a soil with organic matter, nutrients in a soluble fertilizer are retained in soil, but in sandy soil they leach quickly. Spray liquid fertilizers onto plants, however, and leaves absorb the nutrients.

Controlled-release fertilizers discharge nutrients gradually over time. These products can be more expensive, but they provide a steady nutrient source that can feed plants for up to an entire growing season. They don't improve the soil like a manure, but they provide continual nutrition for plant roots.

First-year fertilizer

As you prepared the soil for your perennial garden, you likely mixed in organic matter and possibly other materials recommended by the soil test. These materials will give plants adequate nutrition for their first growing season. If, by chance, you didn't amend the soil with specific nutrients, feed newly planted perennials to encourage plants to send out fresh roots and slow, steady shoot growth.

Nutrient content of fertilizers

Pound for pound, different fertilizers contain varying amounts of nutrients. This chart compares the amount of nutrients that common organic and inorganic fertilizers supply. Actual nutrient content of a fertilizer may vary, depending on the purity of the product, the manufacturer, or whether other materials are blended with the primary item. Nutrient content of various fertilizers are listed in order, left to right, of percentages nitrogen (N), phosphorus (P_2O_5), and potassium (K_2O).

ORGANIC FERTILIZERS	(N)	(P_2O_5)	(K_2O)
Bat guano	0.5	12	0.2
Blood meal	12–15	3	1
Bonemeal (steamed)	0–2	10–28	0–0.2
Chicken litter	1.8	2.8	1.4
Cocoa shells	3	1	3.2
Compost (varies greatly)	0.5	0.3	0.8
Cottonseed meal	6–7	2.5	1.5
Cow manure (dried)	1.5	1.5	1.2
Fish emulsion	5	1	1
Hay (legume)	3	1	2.4
Horse manure (dried)	0.4	0.2	0.3
Mushroom compost	0.7	0.3	0.3
Pine needles	0.5	0.1	0
Rabbit manure (dried)	3.5	1.4	0.6
Sawdust	0.2	0	0.2
Seaweed (dried/meal)	0.7	0.8	5
Sewage sludge (dried municipal)	5	6	0.5
Wood ash	0	2	6

INORGANIC FERTILIZERS*	(N)	(P_2O_5)	(K_2O)
Ammonium nitrate	34	0	0
Muriate of potash	0	0	60
Potassium sulfate	0	0	52
Superphosphate	0	18–20	0.2
Urea ammonium phosphate	25	35	0

Complete inorganic fertilizers are commonly available in various formulations, such as 5-10-5 or 20-5-10.

Fertilizer Application Methods

Hose-end feeders feature premixed fertilizer that doesn't require measuring. A liquid fertilizer is an ideal option to give individual plants a fertilizer boost.

When you fertilize perennials, you'll use one of several methods.

With organic and inorganic fertilizers, you'll scatter the material over the soil surface around plants. Soluble fertilizers are either watered into soil or applied to leaves as a foliar spray. The method depends on the fertilizer you choose. As you fertilize perennials, aim to distribute the material evenly to all plants in the garden.

Liquid blends

With water-soluble fertilizers, use either a watering can or a hose-end sprayer. Make sure the solution is properly and thoroughly mixed. Some liquid fertilizers require periodic agitation during application.

Distribute the mixture directly on the soil around plants. If you're dealing with a foliar

fertilizer, such as kelp or fish emulsion, follow label instructions carefully regarding solution proportions and application techniques and conditions.

Avoid applying liquid fertilizers to soil that's bone dry; the salts in fertilizers can burn roots. Wet the soil first, then pour on the fertilizer. Don't apply liquid fertilizers before forecast rain, which can wash nutrients from the soil.

Granular types

There are two types of granular fertilizer: uncoated and prill. Uncoated granules release nutrients rapidly; they're sometimes called fast-release plant food. Their quick nutrient release is triggered by moisture. Even the moisture from your hands will release the nutrients. If you apply uncoated fast-release granules with bare hands, you'll experience stinging if you have any cuts, and the granules will actually wick moisture from your hands. It's best to wear gloves when applying this kind of fertilizer. Irrigation and rainfall washes these nutrients rapidly from soil. As a result, when using uncoated granular fertilizer, you'll need to reapply the product more frequently.

Prilled granular fertilizers have a specialized coating designed to break down slowly and release nutrients at a constant rate. As the coating becomes wet, it dissolves somewhat,

becoming thinner and releasing nutrients at a greater rate. Some prilled fertilizers contain uniformly sized prills; others include a mix of prill sizes. The differing sizes feature varying thicknesses of coating, which means the fertilizer releases nutrients at different rates. The result with either type is continuous feeding, but the longevity of the fertilizer will vary from one to nine months.

To apply granular fertilizers, scatter the product over the soil surface around plants, sprinkling it in a ring about 6 inches from the outer edge of the broadest point. Scratch the fertilizer into the soil, covering the granules. Take care not to let fertilizer fall into the crown of perennials, touching foliage. This is especially important with fast-release fertilizer granules, which can burn leaves. If fertilizer gets onto leaves, wash it off.

With a bed that's mulched, pull the mulch back, apply the fertilizer, and replace the mulch. Water in the fertilizer after applying or time your application just before rainfall.

Fertilizer cautions

Keep plant food away from water features, such as ponds. Fertilizer that washes into a pond can cause algae blooms that kill fish and other aquatic life. Sweep or wash away any fertilizer you spill on hard surfaces, such as driveways and

TEST GARDEN TIP

Overdoing fertilizer

Avoid applying too much fertilizer to perennials, or you risk burning plants. Take these steps if you accidentally overfertilize.

If you spill granular or prilled plant food, scoop up what you can and spread the rest around the garden.

If you pour too much liquid fertilizer on a plant, use fresh water to wash any from leaves and douse the soil with water to dilute the concentrated nutrients.

Organic fertilizers can burn plants too. Don't overapply these thinking their nature ensures against burning.

It's all about timing

The ideal time to apply fertilizer is just before episodes of active growth.

In wintry regions, fertilize in early spring, as plants are beginning to poke through the soil. Spring rains will keep the soil moist and nutrients available to actively growing roots.

In mildest climes, aim for a late autumn application, so fertilizer is available to roots in moist winter soil.

With container perennials, time applications as indicated above. Or opt to use water-soluble fertilizer applied every two to four weeks during the growing season.

Avoid applying liquid fertilizer to the soil just before rainfall, which can leach nutrients quickly through the soil.

Weeding

Weeds pose one of the most serious threats to your perennial garden because, if left unchecked, they compete with perennials for soil moisture and nutrients. The easiest way to get rid of weeds is to remove them when they're young. You can pull them by hand, or use a tool to make quick work of them. In either case, you'll tackle the task on your knees; invest in a kneeling pad or kneepads.

The best time to tackle weeding is after irrigation or rainfall—when roots slip easily from moist soil. If you can't get to weeding in a timely fashion, don't allow weeds to set seeds. Snip seedheads faithfully until you can remove weeds.

Stock your tool shed with a few choice hand weeders. With a new perennial garden, you'll deal mostly with seedling weeds and an occasional taprooted villain. Some weeding tools are specialized and useful in a specific situation only. Others promise multiple uses, but may prove effective at only one. Look for tool blades that feature metal you can sharpen with a hand file or grinder.

Herbicides

Consider chemicals when weeds are well established or particularly invasive. Preemergence herbicides prevent weed seeds from germinating. These materials need water to become activated. Sprinkle preemergence herbicide granules on soil around perennials prior to rainfall or plan to water after application. Understand that preemergence herbicides interfere with all seed germination. If you're starting annuals from seed in your perennial garden, apply the preemergence herbicide well after seedlings are established or start seeds in a container.

Nonselective herbicides kill leafy weeds. Systemic nonselective herbicides also kill perennials. Spray these chemicals carefully in the garden when the air is calm. Create physical barriers to protect perennials from the chemical and use a hand sprayer with an adjustable nozzle that can direct spray to a specific plant. Choose an herbicide like glyphosate, which lacks a volatile toxic component.

If you treat your lawn for broadleaf weeds using a sprayer or spreader, take care along the edges of perennial beds. Most perennials are broadleaf plants, and the weedkiller can damage or wipe out your plants. If you accidentally apply herbicide to a perennial, wash the chemical from the leaves immediately.

Opposite: **Pulling weeds is easiest after watering or rainfall, when the soil is soft. Hand pull larger weeds, removing them before they set seed.**

Mulch
A 2- to 3-inch layer of mulch can help suppress weeds by interfering with weed seed germination. Learn more about mulch on pages 120–123.

TEST GARDEN TIP

Hand weeders
Here are some tips to help you choose the best weeding tools for your garden.

Cutting and scraping tools. These tools work best for sliding behind and beneath a weed to chop stems from roots. Use angled triangular blades to weed cracks and crevices.

Fish tail weeder. For taprooted weeds like dandelions, this is the weeder of choice. A V-shape tip slips on either side of a weed stem, and the enlarged base gives leverage for prying roots from soil.

Knife. A digging knife is a versatile tool. Use it to dig holes, divide perennials, dig taprooted weeds, and scrape weed seedlings from the soil.

Perennials with weed potential
Some perennials scamper through the garden with gleeful abandon, overtaking less vigorous plants, nudging less mature plants aside, and maybe even launching an assault on nearby turf. Sometimes you can assess a plant's invasive potential by noting certain words or phrases in the plant description, such as "spreading," "vigorous," "robust," or "excellent groundcover." If you spot multiple stems emerging along the sides of a pot at the garden center, that's another clue you're holding a spreader that could be a problem. These perennials have potential to become garden bullies.

BEAR'S BREECHES
A problem on the West Coast for it's spreading roots. Zones 5–10.

BLACKBERRY LILY
Self-sows. Zones 4–10.

CELANDINE POPPY
Self-sows. Zones 4–8.

GARLIC CHIVES
Self-sows. Clip seedheads before capsules burst to release seeds. Zones 4–8.

GOLDENROD
Self-sows and spreads by underground stems. Zones 4–9.

GOUTWEED
Spreads persistently via spreading roots and from any bit of root left in soil. Zones 3–9.

MOUNTAIN BLUET
Self-sows and spreads aggressively via underground shoots. Sprouts readily from any bit of root left in soil. Zones 3–8.

OBEDIENT PLANT
Spreads by underground stems. Zones 4–9.

ROSE CAMPION
Self-sows. Zones 4–10.

SPOTTED DEADNETTLE
Self-sows and spreads aggressively. Zones 3–10.

Grooming and Deadheading

Removing spent flower stalks encourages many perennials to rebloom. For self-sowing bloomers, deadheading prevents plants from setting seeds and overtaking the garden.

Weekly garden maintenance includes grooming and deadheading.

Grooming encompasses many chores, such as deadheading, staking, and restoring washed away mulch. The easiest way to keep your perennial garden looking its best is to tiptoe through the tulips, daily. Quick turns in the garden will alert you to potential problems and uncover issues like invading weeds or edging that needs attention.

Deadheading

Deadheading is the horticultural term for removing spent flowers from plants. When blossoms fade, they don't always fall from plants and politely decompose among the mulch. Some cling to stems, daubing brown splotches into your carefully crafted color scheme. Others droop daintily, looking like damp laundry dangling in the breeze. Either detracts from the garden's appearance.

But removing faded flowers isn't just about keeping up appearances. When flowers die, plants shuttle energy into seed production. Once seeds form, the plant is essentially done for the season and directs energy into overall growth instead of flower production. By snipping dead flowers, you're telling the plant the show isn't over—and another round of bloom is in order. Some perennials oblige and respond to deadheading by forming another set of flowers.

Another reason to deadhead is that spent blooms will rot and may develop botrytis blight, which can easily find a footing on wet foliage and introduce disease to your garden, especially where summer nights are warm and humid. In most gardens, if you deadhead once a week, you'll find the task easy and a wonderful chance to peruse plants.

When not to deadhead

With some perennials, you won't want to remove spent blossoms. Plants like black-eyed susan, blanket flower, coreopsis, and coneflower set seeds that birds favor. If you allow flowers to fade and seeds to form, you'll enjoy hungry birds flitting and feasting through your garden during winter.

Blackberry lily, false indigo, fetid iris, liriope, and woodland peony all bear seeds that earn rave reviews for their eye-catching looks. Perennial gardeners prize ornamental grasses for their seed displays. Anise hyssop, chrysanthemum, euphorbia, 'Autumn Joy' sedum, and yarrow all are attractive in winter.

TEST GARDEN TIP

Tools for deadheading

Keep your garden looking its best by faithfully removing spent blooms. These tools make quick work of the task:

Bypass hand pruners
Small scissors
Hedge or grass shears
Bucket

Maintain your tools with:
Solvent, such as mineral spirits or turpentine
Alcohol
Blade sharpening kit
Penetrating oil

Deadheading with purpose

Deadhead for repeat bloom These perennials stage a subsequent flower show when you remove dead blooms.

BALLOON FLOWER	CATMINT	DELPHINIUM	SALVIA
BELLFLOWER	CENTRANTHUS	FALSE SUNFLOWER	SHASTA DAISY
BLACK-EYED SUSAN	COLUMBINE	HELENIUM	SPIKE SPEEDWELL
BLANKET FLOWER	CONEFLOWER	PINKS	YARROW
CAMPION	COREOPSIS	PINCUSHION FLOWER	

Deadhead to stop seed formation These perennials may take over your garden unless you snip seedheads before they mature.

BLACK-EYED SUSAN	CATMINT	HEART-LEAF	WOODLAND PHLOX
BLOODY CRANESBILL	CUSHION SPURGE	BRUNNERA	YARROW
BUTTERFLY WEED	GARLIC CHIVES	JACOB'S LADDER	YELLOW CORYDALIS
CAMPION	GOLDENROD	MEADOWRUE	
COLUMBINE		MOUNTAIN BLUET	

Deadhead for appearance These perennials look better when you clip past-their-prime posies.

BEE BALM	GOATSBEARD	HOSTA	LUNGWORT
BEARDED IRIS	HARDY HIBISCUS	LADYBELLS	OBEDIENT PLANT
CORAL BELLS	HEART-LEAF	LADY'S MANTLE	RODGERSIA
CLUSTERED BELLFLOWER	BERGENIA	LAMB'S-EARS	SNEEZEWEED
	HEART-LEAF BRUNNERA		

Grooming and Deadheading

Removing spent blooms is as easy as it sounds, but there are some tips you can follow to make the job quicker and more productive. When dealing with perennials that have soft, succulent stems, you can usually snap dead blooms with your fingers. It's often wiser, though, to use a pair of pruning shears or garden snips. Pruners ensure a clean cut and avoid the risk of tearing into plant tissue and leaving a wound that disease or insects can exploit. Over time you'll learn which perennials you can deadhead by hand and which require tools.

Where and when you remove faded flowers depends on the plant's growth habit. With a perennial like hosta, clip the whole flower spike at the base after all buds have opened. The same is true of gayfeather or foxglove, other spike producers. When removing flower spikes, place cuts near the base of the spike within surrounding foliage to allow leaves to hide the stem. For flower spikes, you'll definitely want to use a pair of hand pruners; smaller garden snips may lack the strength to slice stems cleanly.

With perennials such as pinks or coreopsis, where flowers open atop a series of separate stems, grab a pair of grass shears or scissors to snip through the mass of stems at once. Don't worry about getting every single stem; just aim to slice through the vast majority. Use a small perennial rake or your hand to tease out cut dead flowers that drop into foliage. Take care to place your cut above any subsequently developing flower buds.

Some perennials, such as yarrow, joe-pye weed, or fennel open blooms atop branched stems. With this flower structure, either the center buds open first, followed by the side buds, or vice versa. It varies by plant. To deadhead, snip the first opened bud after flowers fade, removing its short support stem, and allow subsequent side shoot flowers to open. Or cut the entire stem after the first flowers open, and skip the smaller, second flowers. The process is purely subjective—do what looks best to your eye.

With plants like garden pinks, which open blooms atop individual stems, snip all the faded blossom stems at once with hand pruners or hedge shears.

Pruning tools

Keep deadheading tools sharp using a simple whetstone or sharpening kit. There's a vast difference between cutting with sharp blades and dull ones. When you sense blades are chewing stems instead of slicing, stop and sharpen. Before sharpening tools, clean the blades with a rag dipped in solvent, such as mineral spirits or turpentine. After sharpening, lubricate the joints using penetrating oil.

It's not necessary to sterilize cutting blades between different perennials, unless you're dealing with a diseased or potentially diseased plant. In that situation, it's worth the effort to pour rubbing alcohol over the blades to prevent spreading disease.

TEST GARDEN TIP

Larger-than-life blooms

With some perennials, you can coax plants to produce flowers that are bigger than normal by removing other flower buds. Good candidates for this treatment include peony, hollyhock, monkshood, and foxglove. When you snip small buds, this causes the plant to put all its energy into the remaining bud, which will create a large bloom. Remove side buds as soon as possible. This minimizes stem wounding and results in a larger overall flower. Use a sharp pair of fine garden shears, cutting close to the stem without damaging it.

Deadheading techniques
The type of deadheading technique to use depends on the perennial. Some are best deadheaded by shearing the entire plant; for others it's best to cut back individual flower stalks. Follow the guide below to discover which techniques work best for the perennials that you grow.

REMOVE STALK
Cut the flower stem just above the ground after flowering has finished to promote growth of a new rosette of foliage.

ASTER
ASTILBE
BEAR'S BREECHES
BELLFLOWER
BERGENIA
COLUMBINE
CONEFLOWER
CORAL BELLS
CROCOSMIA
DELPHINIUM
FOXGLOVE
GAS PLANT
GOATSBEARD
HOLLYHOCK
LUPINE
LUNGWORT
MONKSHOOD
PENSTEMON
SPEEDWELL
TORCH LILY

SHEAR
Shear tiny spent flowers near the top of the plant; this may promote the growth of latent flower buds lower in the plant.

AMSONIA
BEE BALM
BLANKET FLOWER
CENTRANTHUS
COREOPSIS
GERANIUM
PINKS
SHASTA DAISY
WHITE GAURA

REMOVE FLOWERS
Cut the stem just above the first leaf or set of leaves below the spent flower or at the base of the flower stem.

BALLOON FLOWER
BLACK-EYED SUSAN
CHRYSANTHEMUM
LILY
PEONY
PHLOX
POPPY
ROSE TURTLEHEAD
YARROW

PULL STALK
Simply pull up the flower stalk when it has died back enough to come out without effort.

DAYLILY
HOSTA
IRIS

DON'T DEADHEAD
Faded flowers are best left on the plant or deadheading isn't needed.

ARTEMISIA
BLEEDING HEART
BUTTERFLY WEED
JAPANESE ANEMONE
LENTEN ROSE
THRIFT

Pinching and Pruning

Some tasks in the garden must be done on a plant-by-plant basis, using a hands-on approach. Pinching, pruning, staking, and training fall into that category. Over time you'll learn which techniques you need to use on the perennials in your garden. You'll find some guidance for pinching and pruning in the Perennial Encyclopedia (page 174) in the individual plant entries. Learn other tips in next few pages.

Pinching

When you pinch a perennial, especially when you remove the growing tip, that act of removal stimulates the plant to produce hormones that cause the lower buds on the stem to sprout. That's why, when you pinch, you end up with a bushier, fuller plant.

In early spring, as perennials emerge and send shoots skyward, pinch midsummer bloomers to

When spring bloomers fade, removing faded flowers can rejuvenate the plant, causing it to produce fresh foliage growth and flower buds.

encourage a bigger crop of blooms. Remove the growing tip and the stem underneath, allowing only two to six sets of leaves to remain. This method spurs buds along the lower branches to sprout, and you'll be rewarded with a bushy plant filled with blooming shoots. Don't pinch too high, or every bud along the stem will sprout, producing spindly side shoots that may not bloom because the plant doesn't have enough energy to support so many shoots. This technique works well with perennials like anise hyssop, bee balm, centranthus, heliopsis, and false sunflower.

Pinch early in the growing season. If you pinch up to a month after growth has started, you'll remove a large proportion of the plant and effectively reduce final plant size. If you pinch too late, you may interfere with flower bud formation and will substantially reduce the number of blossoms.

Spring bloomers
Many spring perennials experience a crash by late June, when foliage fades and plants appear spent and worn. Prune these performers shortly after flowering and you'll savor a fresh flush of foliage by summer's end that will linger lushly into fall. Spring showstoppers that benefit from a summer trim include cranesbill geranium,

lupine, moss phlox, and penstemon. Cut cranesbill geranium to just above the ground, leaving the new developing foliage intact in the center of the plant.

In the South and West, balloon flower benefits from a midsummer cutting back. Mature specimens of threadleaf coreopsis and pink coreopsis also perform better when they're pruned back by half in late summer.

Foliage favorites
With perennials prized for their foliage, such as artemisia or lamb's-ears, faithfully clip flower shoots as they form to prevent plants from blooming. When these plants flower, the plants appear ratty and spent. Prune 'Valerie Finnis' and 'Silver King' artemisia back by half in early summer. Cut silvermound artemisia plants to 2 inches tall as soon as flowers appear in mid- to late June.

Fall color
Prune tall fall bloomers to reduce final plant height and eliminate the flopping that typically occurs among autumn perennials. Prune these plants by mid-July at the latest to avoid hampering the flower show. For a foolproof guide, prune by the Fourth of July, cutting plants back by one-half to two-thirds.

TEST GARDEN TIP
Maximize mums

You'll get more chrysanthemum blooms in the fall if you pay attention to plants in early summer. When plants are 6 inches tall, use scissors or shears to remove ½ to 1 inch of stem. Cut back to just above a leaf. Many new branches will emerge. When new growth is 6 to 8 inches long, snip off ½ to 1 inch of stem. Cut back to just above a leaf. The cuts may seem drastic and look shocking in the garden, but come fall you'll have a well-branched mum full of flower buds.

Prune to reduce height
Help some tall perennials stand straight without staking. By mid-July, cut back stems on these towering beauties. Remove up to two-thirds of stem length. The result will be shorter plants with more branches—and more blooms.

ASTER	GARDEN PHLOX	JOE-PYE WEED
BALLOON FLOWER	GOATSBEARD	RUSSIAN SAGE
BEE BALM	GOLDENROD	SEDUM 'AUTUMN
BOLTONIA	HELENIUM	JOY'

Revival pruning
Some perennials benefit from a trim after flowering to encourage them to produce fresh foliage. Cut plants back by one-fourth to one-half.

CATMINT	HEART-LEAF	SIBERIAN IRIS
CRANESBILL	BERGENIA	SPIDERWORT
GERANIUM	MEADOW SAGE	
DEADNETTLE	SHASTA DAISY	

Staking and Training

Plants like Oriental lilies require individual stakes for individual stems. Metal spiral stakes outfit functional garden gear with artistic style.

The beauty of a perennial garden lies largely unseen.

Showy bloomers and striking foliage command attention, but it's well-amended soil, compost, mulch, and nutrients in the soil that invisibly fuel the show. In the same way, stakes and supports create a hidden infrastructure that keeps a garden looking its best.

The case for stakes

Perennials lean, topple, and flop for a variety of reasons. Sometimes an otherwise sturdy stem tumbles when rain and wind conspire with weighty blooms to bend stems to the ground. In other cases, stems grow lush and weak due to overfertilizing. Most established perennials thrive on limited fertilizer. A mulch of compost in spring or an annual addition of an organic fertilizer scratched into soil will power plentiful growth without creating weak stems.

Sun-loving plants in part shade tend to stretch for the sun and frequently require staking. Other perennials are simply flop prone by virtue of large flowerheads or lanky stems.

In their natural habitat, many perennials don't require staking because they grow among—and lean on—taller, stronger plants, such as grasses, shrubs, or bushy perennials. Tackle leaning and falling stems by emulating nature's planting schemes in your own garden or craft your own system of stakes and supports.

Stake 'em up

Typically, staking falls into two categories: preventive and remedial. Preventive staking involves thoughtful planning and action before any stems collapse. It's what you do for the known floppers in your garden, such as peonies, meadow rue, and yarrow.

Choose from a variety of stakes to support perennials. Grow-through supports work well with plants that tend to flop just before bloom, like aster, boltonia, garden phlox, and goldenrod. Select plastic-coated wire cages, tomato cages, or grids for grow-through supports. Grid stakes offer sturdy support for heavy-headed bloomers and multistemmed perennials, like peony, false indigo, Russian sage, and tall daisies. You can also use tree and shrub prunings, branches that blow down from trees, or even boughs cut from discarded Christmas trees (after needles fall off).

With preventive staking, insert supports in spring, when plants are emerging from soil. This is vitally important for grow-through and grid stakes. As plants grow, stems weave through stakes, effectively absorbing them into the clump and hiding them from view.

Remedial staking is reactive, inserting supports after perennials fall over due to high winds, strong summer downpours, or other interference. Keep a variety of materials on hand to make supports—twine, plant ties, bamboo stakes, single stakes, and branched twigs.

TEST GARDEN TIP

To stake or not to stake?

With some perennials like peonies or Oriental lilies, it's obvious that staking is needed when plants flower and stems flop under the weight of the blooms. Over time you'll learn which plants perform better with staking. In general, tall, single-stem beauties can often use a little support, as can shrubby bloomers that tend to sprawl.

Plants that need staking No matter how perfect your growing conditions, some perennials just grow on the leaning side and benefit from a little extra support.

ASTER
Grid, grow-through, tomato cage

BALLOON FLOWER
Grid, grow-through, tomato cage, twig stake

BOLTONIA
Grow-through, tomato cage, twig stake

CENTRANTHUS
Grow-through, tomato cage, twig stake

DELPHINIUM
Single

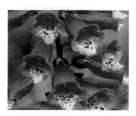

FOXGLOVE
Single

GAYFEATHER
Hoop, tomato cage, twig stake

GOLDENROD
Grow-through, tomato cage

HELENIUM
Grow-through, tomato cage

PEONY
Grid, grow-through, tomato cage

In general, when you stake, you want the support to fall somewhere between the midpoint of plant height and the peak growing point. That's easy to judge with remedial staking. With preventive staking, choose supports based on final plant height as noted in the Perennial Encyclopedia (page 174).

Unleash your creative instincts and invent your own staking system using straight stakes, string, linking stakes, tomato cages, chicken wire, twine—whatever you have on hand. Approach your own staking ideas with a trial-and-error approach. If something doesn't work for one perennial, it may for another. You'll find the best solution as you continue crafting.

Tomato cages

Versatile and inexpensive, tomato cages can fill many roles in the perennial garden. Press extra-large ones (3 to 4 feet tall) into service supporting tall, bushy bloomers like joe-pye weed, hollyhock, and meadow rue. Medium-size cages (2 to 3 feet) graciously corral mid-range perennials such as peach-leaf bellflower, purple coneflower, and Siberian iris. Transform a tomato cage into a grow-though support by wrapping and weaving twine across the horizontal support wires to form a loose grid.

Use bolt cutters to transform cages into cut-to-size supports. Snip tomato cage legs just above hoops to form stakes of varying heights. For perennials growing along a fence or wall, clip cages at one spot along the hoop on each horizontal circle and open the cage to form a half-circle support.

Bamboo and twine

Combine stakes and twine to craft custom supports that you adapt and complete during the growing season. Insert stakes in early spring before plants need them. Drive them deep into the soil to anchor them.

As perennial stems emerge, tie twine around one stake and string it the next stake, looping it around that stake a few times before continuing to the next stake. Add string layers throughout the growing season as stems continue to soar skyward. Keep the string tight enough to support leaning stems, but loose enough to prevent a trussed-up look.

At the end of the growing season, remove this support when you clean up the garden. Wooden and bamboo stakes slowly rot over time, so it's wise to remove them from the soil over winter. Dipping the ends of wooden supports in wax can help slow the deterioration process.

Chicken wire

Form chicken wire into a cage that's slightly narrower than the mature width of the floppy perennial you want to coax upright. Place the wire cylinder against soil, and anchor it by weaving bamboo stakes through the wire into the soil. This is a wonderful choice for bushlike perennials that have thin stems, such as asters, baby's breath, helenium, or plants that rabbits tend to nibble.

Staking supplies Stock your toolshed with a variety of plant stakes and materials that you can cobble together to create plant supports. Use this list to get started.

STAKING GEAR
Bamboo straight stakes
Bamboo U-stakes
Bolt cutters
Chicken wire
Cotton string
Grid stakes
Grow-through stakes
Padded wire
Plant ties
Tomato cages
Twine

Ways to support plants

There are as many ways to support plants as there are creative gardeners. Shown here are a collection of some favorite kinds that are commercially available, as well as some traditional techniques.

GRID
Flat, circular grid with three or four legs; push legs into soil first, then snap ring in place; stems grow through grid.

USE WITH clump-forming perennials, such as peony, garden phlox, sea holly, monkshood.

GROW-THROUGH
Flat, circular support with concentric circles; three or four legs push into soil; stems grow through circles.

USE WITH multistemmed upright plants with thin stems, such as balloon flower, blanket flower, bugbane, helenium.

LINKING
Upright pieces with arms that link and form joints you can bend.

USE WITH any perennial that has flopped, is overtaking less vigorous plants, or leaning into a path. Examples are centranthus, crocosmia, pincushion flower, ladybells, Shasta daisy.

MESH CAGE
Form a cylinder of chicken wire slightly narrower than the mature width of the plant you're staking; place it over the perennial early in the season; thread a few stakes through the mesh and sink into soil for added support.

USE WITH sprawling perennials such as aster, blackberry lily, obedient plant, yarrow.

OTHER PLANTS
Position floppy perennials near stronger perennial or shrub neighbors and let stems lean on other plants for support.

USE WITH all perennials.

SINGLE STAKE
Use twine, hook-and-loop plant ties, or padded wire to bind stems to bamboo or wood stakes; look for single-stem stakes at garden centers.

USE WITH tall perennials topped with heavy flower spikes, such as delphinium, foxglove, hollyhock, lily.

TOMATO CAGE
Sink a tomato cage into soil; thread a few stakes through cage sides and sink into soil for added support.

USE WITH clump-forming perennials, such as helenium, salvia, showy sedum.

TWIG STAKE
Insert sturdy, branched twigs into soil near floppy plants for support.

USE WITH clump-forming perennials, such as false sunflower, meadow sage, spotted bellflower.

Dividing and Transplanting Perennials

As your perennial garden matures, you'll experience the excitement of watching clumps increase in size and flower number. At some point, you'll need to tackle dividing plants to renew vigor. Most perennials require renovation every two to five years. Some, like garden mums, need digging every year, while others, such as peonies, torch lily, and Siberian iris, rarely need division.

Candidates for division

Perennials send out signals that they need renovation. A plant may not flower as heavily as normal because too many stems are competing for nutrients. This is a typical clue for dividing bearded iris. A crowded clump can also lead to smaller flowers than normal.

You may also notice dead spots in the plant base. This frequently occurs with showy sedum and garden mums. Division provides an excellent means to corral invasive perennials. You can divide entire clumps every few years and effectively rein in wandering stems. Division also provides an inexpensive way to increase the number of plants in your garden.

Time it right

The ideal time to divide plants depends on where you garden and what you're growing. Many gardeners prefer to divide in fall, when the growing season is winding down. Tackle fall

After digging a perennial and lifting it from the soil, you can often pull the clump apart to create divisions. With many perennials, compost the older, central part of the clump.

division at least one month before the average frost date to give plants sufficient time to develop roots before the ground freezes.

In cold climates, dividing plants in early spring often proves most successful, primarily because spring rains and warming soil enhance root growth. Many gardeners base division on bloom time, dividing fall-flowering perennials in spring and spring bloomers in fall. A few perennials have rigid division timing requirements. Divide bearded iris from July through September, Oriental poppies in August, peonies in fall, and lilies from mid- to late autumn.

Techniques for dividing

To divide, use a shovel, spade, or digging fork to dig around the perennial in a circle. Insert the shovel 6 to 12 inches away from the crown— you aim to dig the bulk of the roots. Once you've circled the plant with digging, pry it from the soil.

When the plant breaks free from the soil, lift it (if it's a large clump, lift one side at a time) and gently knock away soil clinging to outer roots. With small perennials, parts of the plant may break away easily from the crown. For large plants, you'll need to chop the clump apart. Shift large plants onto a tarp to make them easier to move or to catch soil.

Use your shovel to push through the crown, or use a tool like a perennial divider. This short-handle tool is easy to sharpen and drive into the heart of a perennial. A sharp garden or kitchen knife slices neatly through small crowns. Some perennial roots will prove challenging to cut. Plants like goatsbeard or astilbe can develop massive, thick roots that require an axe or machete to slice through them.

If you can't replant divisions immediately, place them in a shady spot and keep the rootballs covered with a sheet, tarp, or newspaper. Spray divisions daily with water to keep the rootballs moist. Cut the clump apart into divisions before planting.

Final steps

Amend the soil while it's perennial free, mixing a few inches of compost in and around the planting hole. Dig it in to a depth of one shovel blade, turning it over. Don't worry about cutting the roots of surrounding perennials; they'll recover. Mix some fertilizer into the planting hole.

Trim the foliage on divisions by one-half to three-fourths before planting. Replace mulch and then water the plants. Keep newly planted divisions moist. If dividing in the fall, continue to water perennials until the ground freezes.

TEST GARDEN TIP

Tools for division

Stock your toolshed with just a few tools, and you'll be set to divide perennials.

Digging fork
Hand pruners
Knife
Perennial divider
Shovel
Transplant spade

Types of perennial roots
Understanding what kind of root system you're dealing with helps you anticipate how you'll divide the plant once you dig it.

OFFSET Some perennials form offsets—small plants connected to the main clump by a root. Cut through the root to free the offset; transplant it as a division.

EYE Multiple eyes or buds form on tubers or rhizomes each year at the base of the previous season's stems. Each eye will eventually produce an entire plant. Dig tubers and cleanly slice between eyes. Aim for three to seven eyes per division.

TAPROOT Some perennials form one or more taproots that grow straight down from the crown. To obtain divisions from a taproot with a single crown, slice off an eye, catching some of the root with it.

FIBROUS Clumps of stems extend many roots in soil. Some are fleshy and some are fine. Split the clump so you have roots and shoots in each division.

RUNNERS Underground stems (rhizomes) or aboveground stems (stolons) spread from the original plant. Buds on stems grow into a new plant some distance from the original plant. Slice the runner to liberate the plant and obtain a division.

Dividing bearded iris
They grace the late spring garden with blooms, but when clumps are overcrowded, flowering dwindles. Divide these and similar perennials like this.

1 LIFT
Bearded iris (shown), heart-leaf bergenia, and some bamboos form thick stems or rhizomes. When dividing, dig the rhizomes from the soil, lifting them free. Use a digging fork, inserting it well away from any visible rhizomes. Dig carefully to avoid spearing rhizomes.

2 BREAK
Shake the clump to allow loose soil to fall away. Break rhizomes into pieces you can easily handle. Some clumps will break apart naturally at joints located along the rhizome. Break off any old, rotted rhizomes and discard. If you have battled rotting rhizomes in your iris bed, dip cut ends of healthy rhizomes into powdered fungicide.

3 CUT
If you can't break rhizomes apart, use a sharp knife to slice through them. Place cuts so that each rhizome has a growing point associated with it.

4 REPLANT
Before planting, trim leaves to form a mitered point. Cut leaves to 6 inches so strong winds can't rock newly planted rhizomes loose in soil. Arrange rhizomes 5 inches apart with growing points facing the same direction. You can also dig a shallow trench and place rhizomes side by side in it. Don't bury rhizomes more than 1 to 2 inches deep or they will be more likely to rot.

Dividing fibrous-rooted perennials
Many perennials, including daylilies and hosta, have a fibrous root system. Lift clumps and break them apart to create divisions.

1 DIG
Dig all around the plant about 6 to 12 inches from the crown. Be sure to dig on all sides before trying to pry the plant from the soil or you risk damaging the clump or your digging tool. With perennials like hosta, you won't divide that often unless you want extra plants, so you'll likely be dealing with a large plant.

2 LIFT
Slide a digging tool under the clump to help free it from the soil. A sharp perennial divider or spade works well for this task. Lift the plant free. Slide it onto a tarp, burlap, or potting soil bag if you're working near lawn and want to save soil to return it to the bed.

3 CUT
Decide how large you want each division, then plunge a sharp tool into the clump to begin carving out divisions. With a plant like hosta, the clump is essentially a grouping of small plants with individual crowns, which separate easily. Perennials like goatsbeard have thick roots that may require serious cutting tools to separate divisions.

4 PLANT
Discard parts of the plant that look old or are unhealthy. Often the center of a clump will be old and should be discarded. Toss discarded plant parts into the compost pile. Replant the divisions you want and give extras away.

Get digging Some perennials need more frequent division than others. Digging and dividing perennials is probably the heaviest chore in maintaining the garden. To reduce the backbreaking labor, fill your garden with these perennials that don't need frequent division.

Do not disturb

These perennials resent division and are best left undisturbed.

Astilbe
Balloon flower
Butterfly weed
Clematis
False indigo
Lenten rose
Lupine
Oriental poppy
Peony
Torch lily

BLACK-EYED SUSAN

DAYLILY

CHRYSANTHEMUM

CONEFLOWER

YARROW

SPIDERWORT

Divide every 2 to 3 years

ASTER
BEARDED IRIS
BEE BALM
CARDINAL FLOWER
CHRYSANTHEMUM
COREOPSIS
FALSE SUNFLOWER
OBEDIENT PLANT
PINCUSHION FLOWER
PINKS
SHASTA DAISY
YARROW

Divide every 4 to 5 years

ANEMONE
BLACK-EYED SUSAN
BLEEDING HEART
COLUMBINE
CONEFLOWER
DAYLILY
GAYFEATHER
MEADOW RUE
MONKSHOOD
PENSTEMON
SEDUM, CREEPING TYPES
SPIDERWORT

Preparing for Winter

As autumn's golden light begins to slant through the garden, perennial growth may start to slow, leaves may explode in a burst of fall color, or seedpods may outnumber flowers. Before cold winds whistle, tuck in your perennial garden for a long winter's nap.

Begin fall cleanup by emptying the compost bin, then quickly fill it with falling leaves and garden waste. Add compost around perennials with big appetites: astilbe, clematis, and delphinium. Roses, raspberries, and garlic planting beds also always benefit from extra compost. Stash excess compost in a separate bin or in an old, half-buried, plastic trash can with holes drilled in the bottom and lower sides.

After the first frost, start cutting stems of perennials that have browned. In spring, all stems will need to be removed, so it's wise to deal with a portion of them in fall. Leave any stems that weave winter interest into the garden, such as ornamental grasses, 'Autumn Joy' sedum, and blackberry lily. Some perennials form seeds that birds feast on through winter: purple coneflower, black-eyed susan, and prairie dropseed grass. Allow these stems and seedheads to remain in place.

Some perennials, such as hollyhock, should be cut down and prunings destroyed because leaves and stems can harbor pests or diseases. Gather and destroy any fallen foliage underneath these plants as well. Evergreen perennials, like Lenten rose, pinks, spurge, or liriope, can remain in place through winter. In climates where snow covers plants, remove foliage in spring.

As you clean up perennials, pull any bamboo stakes to prevent them from freezing and rotting over winter. You may or may not want to gather metal stakes; it's your call.

Irrigation

Don't forget to water perennials in fall. Many perennials make most of their root growth in fall, and moisture helps fuel that process. Healthy roots are key to a strong flower performance next year. Strong root systems can also help anchor plants through winter freeze-thaw cycles that can heave perennials from the soil.

Look for deals

Sometimes you'll discover bargains at nurseries and garden centers this time of year. Shrubs and perennials may be discounted; buy any on your wish list. If you don't have a place prepared for them, stash them in the ground over winter in a corner of a planting bed, mulching them after the ground freezes.

Look for discounts on bagged mulch. Add mulch to beds this fall, or stockpile bags in a corner until spring. If you had a problem with slugs or snails this season, wait a week or two after you clean up the garden before applying fall mulch. Allowing the sun to saturate exposed soil can help reduce the pest population.

Winter blanket

After the ground freezes, mulch any newly planted perennials, garden mums, and borderline hardy plants. Mulch with chopped leaves or straw. A layer that's 6 inches deep will protect plants from severe cold. If snow typically covers your garden all winter, don't worry about additional mulch protection. It's most vital in areas where snow cover is lacking or comes and goes.

Opposite: **In regions with cold winters, mulch perennials using a loose material that traps air to insulate the plant crown. Straw, evergreen boughs, or shredded fall leaves provide effective protection.**

TEST GARDEN TIP

Snowbelt perennials

If you garden in an area with heavy snow or your planting bed receives snow courtesy of local plows, plan your perennial garden for winter survival.

Protect plants. Prevent snow from being heaped on plants or an entire bed by creating a barrier. Build a framework with snow fence sections, lumber, wire, and/or burlap. You can also arrange hay bales around a perennial or along a bed edge.

Cut stems. Prune stems to within 6 to 8 inches of the soil to prevent them from breaking beneath the weight of heavy snow. For an extra layer of protection, after the holidays, gather discarded Christmas trees, cut off boughs, and lay them over perennials.

Design accordingly. Create your garden with heavy snow in mind, choosing perennials that melt away or must be cut after frost, such as hosta, variegated solomon's seal, or ferns for shade, and peony, hollyhock, or daylily for sunny spots.

When to cut back perennial stalks

Perennials to cut back in fall: Compost prunings

ANEMONE	EVENING PRIMROSE
BEE BALM	GARDEN PHLOX
BELLFLOWER	LADY'S MANTLE
BLEEDING HEART	MOUNTAIN BLUET
CAMPION	SPIKE SPEEDWELL
CATMINT	SPURGE
DELPHINIUM	

Perennials to cut back in fall: Destroy prunings

ASIATIC LILY	FALSE SUNFLOWER
BEARDED IRIS	HELENIUM
(remove dead	HOLLYHOCK
leaves only)	ORIENTAL LILY
COLUMBINE	PEONY
DAYLILY	

Cut to 6 inches in spring: Compost prunings

BUTTERFLY BUSH	RUSSIAN SAGE
CARYOPTERIS	TREE MALLOW
LAVENDER COTTON	

Seasonal maintenance calendar
Perennial gardens require care through the year. Over time you'll learn what your garden needs. Use a checklist like this one until then.

JANUARY
KICK OFF THE NEW YEAR by recycling discarded Christmas trees. Clip boughs and lay them over perennial beds for insulation and winter color. In spring use well-branched, needleless boughs as stakes.

SCOUR PLANT CATALOGS for new perennial introductions. Order early; supplies are usually limited.

INSPECT STORED TUBERS OR BULBS; discard anything that's moldy or rotten.

IN THE SOUTH AND WEST, cut back grasses before new growth emerges.

PLANT container-grown and bare-root perennials.

FEBRUARY
INVENTORY AND INSPECT garden tools. Make necessary repairs and sharpen and oil blades.

START PERENNIAL SEEDS this month. Purchase a grow light to provide ample light in northern climes.

IN THE SOUTH, deal with winter annual weeds before they set seeds. Clean the perennial garden, removing winter-damaged leaves.

ON THE WEST COAST, watch for aphids on new growth; remove them with a blast of water from the hose. Keep an eye out for slugs and snails. Weed beds frequently.

MARCH
CONTINUE SEED STARTING. At this point in the year, a bright window provides sufficient light for seedlings.

CLIP remaining foliage and stems on perennials.

RESIST THE TEMPTATION to remove mulch too soon. Temperatures below 20°F at night can damage perennials.

IN THE SOUTH AND WEST, divide summer- and fall-flowering perennials, such as coreopsis, garden phlox, and chrysanthemums, after new growth emerges. Keep on top of weeds. Plant perennials.

APRIL
REMOVE any remaining winter protection around plants. Gardeners in the Upper Midwest and New England should leave winter mulch in place until May.

ADD COMPOST or slow-release fertilizer around perennials, scratching it into the soil.

DON'T WORK SOIL while it's too wet (see Just-Right Soil, page 119.

START INSERTING STAKES for top-heavy or tall perennials.

WEED FAITHFULLY, removing offenders as soon as you spot them.

IN THE SOUTH AND WEST, continue weeding and dividing perennials. Buy and plant summer bulbs.

MAY
RENEW MULCH around perennials as needed to maintain a 2-inch layer. Consider using compost as mulch; it will fertilize plants as it breaks down. Don't bury late risers, such as butterfly weed or balloon flower.

PINCH chrysanthemums, garden phlox, asters, hyssop, and bee balm. Cut stems back to two sets of leaves.

IN THE SOUTH, remove dying daffodil and Dutch iris foliage. Keep up with weeds and pests.

ON THE WEST COAST, divide Oriental poppies, irises, and daylilies after bloom.

JUNE
DIVIDE SPRING BLOOMERS after flowers fade. This includes bearded irises and Oriental poppies.

DEADHEAD perennials to keep the garden tidy and limit disease outbreaks.

PERENNIALS NEED 1 INCH OF WATER per week right now. Water if rainfall is scarce. Check container perennials frequently to assess water needs.

PINCH asters and chrysanthemums one last time before July Fourth.

ON THE WEST COAST, order spring bulbs now for fall planting.

PLANT fall-flowering perennials.

JULY

EVALUATE the garden for gaps in the flower show. Visit a garden center to see what's blooming that you can add.

RENEW MULCH as needed to maintain a 2-inch layer.

NOTE CROWDED PERENNIAL CLUMPS that need division. Divide daylilies after bloom so roots have time to establish before fall.

WEED, WATER, AND WATCH FOR PESTS. Handpick Japanese beetles; treat for grubs.

IN THE SOUTH AND WEST, think fall. Set out chrysanthemums for fall flowering.

AUGUST

WATER the garden regularly if rains fail. Extra water to fall-flowering perennials fuels a beautiful show.

CLEAN UP the garden by deadheading and clipping brown leaves. Snip remaining flowering stems of perennials like bearded iris, daylily, and hosta. Divide irises if you haven't already.

ORDER PERENNIALS now for fall planting.

SEPTEMBER

BUY fall chrysanthemums and spring-flowering bulbs. Tuck flowering kale or pansies in planting beds or containers. In mild climates, these annuals provide winter-long color.

PLANT potted asters and chrysanthemums in the garden to punch up late-season color. Insulate these plants after the ground freezes to boost winter survival.

CHECK OUT perennials in bloom at local public gardens or garden center displays. Plan to add these to your yard next spring.

OCTOBER

PLANT spring-flowering bulbs in all but the Deep South.

WATER PERENNIALS until they go dormant, then clean up the garden, composting plant debris you remove.

TEST SOIL pH; add lime if needed if it is too acidic; sulfur if it is too alkaline.

DIG AND STORE tender bulbs that won't overwinter, such as caladium, agapanthus, dahlia, or elephant's ear.

IN THE SOUTH AND WEST, plant perennials.

NOVEMBER

MULCH the garden after the ground freezes.

ADD ROTTED manure, compost, or chopped leaves to the perennial garden.

IN COLD CLIMES, prepare container gardens for overwintering.

DRAIN AND STORE HOSES if you live where winters are cold.

GATHER STAKES, discarding any that are rotten.

IN THE SOUTH, keep the compost pile moist when rainfall is scarce. Plant spring-flowering bulbs and peonies.

DECEMBER

OBSERVE your garden for winter scenery. Note which perennials offer greatest interest and which areas of the garden lack off-season pizzazz. Plan now to add perennials in the coming year.

INVENTORY and order seeds.

ORGANIZE your garden storage area.

ON THE WEST COAST, plant summer bulbs and divide established perennials.

Troubleshooting

When you plant a perennial garden, you cultivate an ecosystem.
Shortly after planting, you'll notice insects active in and around plants. You might see butterflies, ladybugs, caterpillars, ants, and bees. You may also spot beetles, hoverflies, lacewings, dragonflies, and sphinx moths. A perennial garden provides a perfect habitat for all kinds of wildlife, including insects.

The garden is also an ideal place for microbes—both beneficial and harmful organisms. While your desire may be to keep your garden pristine, picture perfect, and pest and disease free, the natural world will invade and set up housekeeping. Your job as gardener is to tend not only the plants but also the entire system in such a way that organisms coexist. As you do, beauty will prevail.

Cultural practices matter
Planting diverse species is one of the most important things you can do to grow a healthy garden. Insects and diseases tend to prey upon a particular plant group. If your garden is filled with plants that form an integral link in a pest's life cycle, you'll likely have that pest living happily in your garden.

Along with diversity, it's also wise to choose plants suited for your garden's growing conditions. Healthy plants start with the right growing conditions—and healthy plants can naturally overcome many pest and disease attacks.

More is not always better in perennial gardening. More water, more fertilizer, and more mulch can all lead to disease and pest problems. Overcome the temptation to overdo in watering or fertilizing, and you'll

As you spend time in your perennial garden, tending plants and observing them, you'll be able to spot problems as they start and be able to treat them before they become entrenched.

avoid lush growth that succumbs more readily to pest and disease attack. Too much mulch also creates conditions for pests and diseases to take hold.

While it may seem ideal to use preventive pesticides, that approach will also kill beneficial insects that prey on harmful ones. Learn to tolerate a certain level of insects—including pests—in your garden.

Scouting and counting

The easiest way to learn about your garden is to wander through it, taking time to observe. Once every 7 to 14 days, spend time in the garden noting its progress, flipping over leaves, and generally inspecting plants. With a large garden, study the garden in sections. These frequent inspections will uncover what's happening in the garden and provide you with a greater understanding of what's normal.

You'll typically spot a pest problem by the damage the insects create or by their vast numbers. If you suspect a pest problem but don't see clear evidence of symptoms, it's a good idea to conduct a "beat" test (see below). If you count 10 to 20 pests per test, that's typically a background amount and doesn't require treatment.

With more than 20 pests, consider the plant's appearance before treating. If up to 10 percent of the plant shows damage, wait before taking action. Predatory insects that feast on the problem pests may be at work in the garden; give them a chance to act before wiping out their food source. To learn more about beneficial insects, see page 165.

As you scout your perennial garden for pests, keep in mind that in a few days this voracious caterpillar will turn into a beautiful swallowtail butterfly.

The beat test Looking for damaged plants is one way to stay on top of pest and disease problems, and you can quickly determine the pests and their numbers with this simple monitoring technique. Use the beat test to find small insects such as aphids that blend in with the foliage of your perennials and tiny mites that are too small to see.

1 ATTACH
Attach a white sheet of paper to a clipboard. Hold the clipboard under the foliage of a plant you're checking. Gently tap the foliage to dislodge any pests that may be present onto the clipboard.

2 LOOK
Look at the paper to see if aphids, mites, or thrips are crawling across it. If dust and debris also drop on the paper making it hard to see the pests, gently blow on the paper. Insects and mites will stay put because they have hooks on their feet to help them grasp the paper fibers while the debris blows off. Watch for tiny moving specks or use a magnifier or a jeweler's loupe to get a closer look at the pests. If your plants are showing signs of damage and you see many specks, you have the evidence you need to know it's time to start treating for the pests.

Common pests

Various bugs will visit or stay in your garden throughout the gardening season. Most you won't notice, but some you'll quickly spot because of their size or damage they cause. Focus on these common pests and what it takes to control them.

Aphids
Soft-bodied insects that suck plant sap, aphids cluster along tips of new growth. Look for white or greenish shed skins along with the insects. Aphids spread plant viruses, which makes them doubly infectious. Most active in cool weather, aphids tend to disappear as summer heat builds and predators and parasites that destroy aphids multiply.

DAMAGE
New growth may be distorted. Aphids secrete sugary honeydew, a sticky, shiny substance that may speckle leaves. Black sooty mold grows in honeydew and remains until rain washes it off. In severe infestations, ants will scurry along infested plant stems, feeding on honeydew.

CONTROL
Use a jet of water from the hose to dislodge aphids, or insecticidal soap to kill them. Avoid overfertilizing and overwatering, which promote the lush growth aphids favor. Ladybugs, syrphid flies, and aphidiid wasps control aphids, but you must allow aphids to increase to 10 to 20 per shoot tip for beneficial insects to lay eggs and counteract the pest.

Caterpillars
Assorted caterpillars feed on perennial leaves. You may spot monarch butterfly larvae, a beautiful black, gold, and white striped caterpillar (above), feasting on butterfly weed. Painted lady butterfly larvae feed on lupines; common hairstreak larvae, the immature stage of a California butterfly, feed on false indigo. Other caterpillars, such as cutworms, are more destructive.

DAMAGE
Feeding destroys foliage to varying degrees—from a few holes to total decimation.

CONTROL
If caterpillars are destructive pests, handpick them or treat plants with *Bacillus thuringiensis* (*Bt*). Horticultural oil and insecticidal soap also control young caterpillars.

Sawfly larvae look like little bluish caterpillars and infest hardy hibiscus and loosestrife species. They can't be controlled with *Bt*. Use horticultural oil or spinosad.

Iris Borer
A pest that feeds inside plant stems, roots, or rhizomes is called a borer. The iris borer is the caterpillar stage of a moth that lays eggs on iris foliage in fall. Eggs hatch the following spring, and the caterpillar bores downward as it feeds through leaves, growing much larger when it reaches rhizomes.

DAMAGE
Central leaves emerge with ragged edges due to borer feeding inside the base of leaves. In a severe infestation, the central leaf may yellow and easily pull free. The iris borer also carries a bacterial disease that rots rhizomes, transforming them into smelly mush.

CONTROL
Remove any brown or ragged leaves or diseased rhizomes as soon as you spot them. Don't cover iris rhizomes with mulch, and keep the top of the rhizome at or slightly above soil level. Cut down and clean up all iris foliage in fall, removing it from your property.

Grasshopper
Grasshoppers typically become a problem in perennial gardens in hot, dry regions. Adult females may have laid eggs in garden soil, or grasshoppers may move in from nearby farm fields.

DAMAGE

Leaf margins become chewed. A large grasshopper population can defoliate plants.

CONTROL

Once you spot large adult grasshoppers, it's too late to do anything but handpick them. If you've had grasshopper infestations in the past, keep areas near your perennial garden mowed and cleared of weeds. If grasshoppers become a problem in your garden, apply a naturally occurring microbe, *Nosema locustae*, over garden soil. Birds, snakes, lizards, and toads eat grasshoppers; maintain a wildlife-friendly garden to attract these grasshopper predators.

Japanese Beetle
The adult Japanese beetle feeds on flowers and leaves of various perennials, such as hollyhock, tree mallow, daylily, and blanket flower. When the beetles find a food source, they release a scent that attracts more beetles. Females lay eggs in the ground, which hatch into grubs, a major lawn pest.

DAMAGE

Japanese beetles eat leaf tissue between the veins, creating a skeletonized effect. They may also eat large holes in flower petals.

CONTROL

Control grubs in your lawn and you'll reduce the number of Japanese beetles (unless your neighbor doesn't control grubs, in which case beetles will invade your garden). A fungus called milky spore controls grubs but may take a few years to build up an effective concentration. Knock beetles from plants into a container of soapy water. Adult beetle traps may lure more beetles than you already have in your garden.

Leafhopper
Cousins to aphids, leafhoppers hop away from the plant they're feeding on when disturbed. As they feed, these springy critters spread an incurable disease known as yellows or aster yellows. They cause the greatest damage in hot microclimates, such as planting areas by driveways and sidewalks, where heat is reflected, radiated, and concentrated.

DAMAGE

Feeding on leaf undersides creates a coarse yellow stippling on the upper surfaces.

CONTROL

Pesticides that act by touching the pests are ineffective against leafhoppers—they just hop away when you spray. Use a pesticide containing acephate for successful control.

Leaf Miner
The larvae of small flies, leaf miners feed between upper and lower layers of leaves. Various leaf miner species infest different perennials at certain points in the growing season. Commonly affected plants include columbine, hollyhock, and chrysanthemum.

DAMAGE
Leaf miner feeding creates light green or yellow tunnels on leaf surfaces.

CONTROL
Removing infested leaves or cutting plants to soil level and destroying clippings typically eliminates the problem. Leaf miners tend to gravitate to weedy areas; keep the garden cleaned up to help eradicate these pests.

Mites
Typically clustered along leaf undersides, mites are actually a type of spider. In a heavy infestation you'll see webbing under leaves and where leaves join stems. In the webbing will be pinhead-size specks—mites. Mites suck sap from leaves, creating a stippling effect. They usually arrive courtesy of breezes or hitchhike on new plants. These sapsuckers thrive when temperatures soar and dry conditions prevail. They're a classic pest of peak summer, but often multiply quickly if June's cooler days are punctuated by a blast of August-style heat.

DAMAGE
Look for fine, pale stippling on upper leaf surfaces.

CONTROL
Use a jet of water from the hose to dislodge small populations of mites. Spray horticultural oil in severe infestations, coating both upper and lower leaf surfaces. If mites infest spring bloomers in summer, cut heavily infested foliage and allow plants to resprout. Predatory mites prey on mites. Use the beat test (page 161) to determine if mites are present on plants.

Slugs and Snails
Slugs are snails without shells. Slugs and snails feed on a variety of perennials, leaving ragged holes in leaves. Common in shade gardens, slugs and snails prefer damp areas and often wreak havoc on hosta.

DAMAGE
These mollusks chew through leaves with rasping mouthparts, which create jagged holes.

CONTROL
Slugs and snails hide beneath plant debris and in mulch. Keep a clean garden and use mulch like pine straw to help eliminate hiding places for these pests. Toads prey on snails and slugs; install a small pond to attract these amphibians. Iron phosphate baits control slugs and snails and won't harm pets. Or trap the pests in shallow saucers filled with beer or a yeast solution. Dispose of captured pests and renew the solution daily until slugs and snails are under control. These pests won't cross a copper barrier because copper reacts with their slime to form toxic compounds. Use copper flashing to make collars to surround susceptible plants.

Gallery of Good Bugs Every gardener is familiar with a few beneficial insects such as ladybugs. Few are aware of what the life stages of these insects look like and that mites, true bugs, and wasps are important biological control agents in the garden.

Thrips
Tiny cigar-shape insects, thrips typically feed inside flowers but also eat leaves. They arrive in the garden on southerly breezes or overwinter in the soil under host plants. Some thrips carry viruses, transmitting them as they feed.

DAMAGE
With mouthparts that scrape as they feed, thrips create white streaks in affected flowers and leaves.

CONTROL
In the longest days of summer, a beneficial insect, minute pirate bug, appears and feasts on thrips, bringing the population under control. Some beetle and mite species also prey on thrips. Alternatively, control thrips with a pesticide containing spinosad.

1 LADYBUGS
Everyone knows what a ladybug looks like, but few recognize the eggs, larvae, or pupal cases that precede the adult stage of the insect. Several species are found in North America. The imported Asian ladybug especially has become common in recent years.

Adult ladybugs are often sold in garden centers or by mail order. They are collected from locations where they gather to wait out the hottest part of summer and are kept under refrigeration until sold. They arrive at the retail outlet or your doorstep ready to fly long distances to get back to their breeding areas from which they were collected, so it is difficult to keep them in the garden in which they are released. It's better to rely on local populations of ladybugs.

2 PREDATORY MITE
Not all mites are pests. Some, such as the predatory mite, may be present in the garden without you knowing it. When you are doing a beat test to detect mites and small insects on your plants, you might see a few predatory mites moving rapidly across the paper. They are more translucent than pest mites and have longer legs that allow them to move faster than their prey.

3 SYRPHID FLY
Also known as flower flies and hover flies, syrphid flies are important predators of aphids and mites. They look like bees or wasps, but their large eyes and single set of wings set them apart from the bees and wasps they mimic. Syrphid flies can usually be found hovering near daisy or carrot family flowers. Larvae (shown at left) devour aphids and other pests.

4 APHIDIID WASP
An important parasite of aphids and scale insects, this wasp is a gnat-size insect too small to harm people. It lays eggs inside pest insects; the eggs hatch and develop inside the pest, killing it.

5 PRAYING MANTIS
Often thought to be beneficial, praying mantids actually are not effective predators of common garden pests. They are territorial and never exist in numbers high enough to have much impact on pests. Often their diet consists of bees and butterflies, and so they can be considered pests in a butterfly garden.

Common Critters

Most four-legged creatures add ambience and interest to a perennial garden; others wreak havoc with plants as they tunnel, munch, and peck their way through cherished perennials. Here's how five common animals damage plants and the best ways to cope.

Voles
Tunneling rodents can damage plant roots, and some feed on plant parts. They may also create aboveground trails, especially under snow cover or mulch.

DAMAGE

Wilting foliage and plants that easily pull from soil signal potential vole, gopher, or other underground rodent activity.

CONTROL

Try trapping or barriers, such as lining a planting hole or raised bed with hardware cloth, crushed shells, or sharp-edge stones. Staple chicken wire to the bottom board of a raised bed to prevent burrowing.

Gophers and Moles
Tunneling rodents can damage plant roots, and some feed on plant parts.

DAMAGE

Wilting foliage and plants that easily pull from soil signal potential vole, gopher, or other underground rodent activity.

CONTROL

Try trapping or barriers, such as lining a planting hole or raised bed with hardware cloth. Staple chicken wire to the bottom board of a raised bed to prevent burrowing.

Birds
Many types of birds feed on seeds, seedlings, fruits, and berries in the garden.

DAMAGE

Birds scratch away at soft soil to unearth newly planted seeds. They peck at seedlings and young leaves.

CONTROL

Once birds develop the habit of feeding in your garden, you'll probably have to exclude them with wire or fabric cages. If birds have not yet developed the habit, you may be able to repel them. Set up stakes around the plantings you wish to protect and tie crisscrossing strings between the stakes. Attach strips of aluminum foil to the strings. Birds will not readily fly through the crossing string and will avoid the shiny aluminum. To prevent birds from digging up seeds, lay hardware cloth (¼-inch mesh) over the seedbed. It must be removed before the plants are too large to slip through the mesh.

Rabbits
Rabbits habitually feed on the same plants in the garden, making it nearly impossible to grow certain perennials. They may tend to favor one part of the garden, which is likely located near shelter.

DAMAGE
Early spring is usually the most troublesome time with rabbits, which prefer succulent, new foliage and feed on emerging perennial shoots.

CONTROL
A low, 24- to 36-inch fence of poultry mesh excludes rabbits if it's buried about 8 inches below the soil surface. Blood meal repels for a time but needs to be refreshed for continuous control. Distasteful or scented spray repellents may prove effective for a time, but change products often because individual rabbits differ in their response. Dogs and cats can also help limit rabbits. Plant rabbit-resistant perennials.

Deer
The most rapidly growing urban pest is deer. Look for hoofprints in soil to determine if your disappearing perennials are victims of deer browsing.

DAMAGE
Leaves appear roughly clipped; blossoms disappear as soon as they form.

CONTROL
Bait an electric fence with peanut butter, or anchor a plastic mesh fence, which farsighted deer won't see. Effective fences must be at least 8 feet tall and firmly anchored. Liquid repellents work for short periods. Change them often, because deer get used to the scent of nearly any product. Plant deer-resistant perennials.

Deer- and rabbit-proof perennials
One way to combat the attack of nibbling deer and rabbits is to plant perennials they dislike. Use these perennials exclusively to create a garden that's less palatable to these critters or place them strategically around plants these animals favor. Even resistant plants will often suffer damage; they're resistant, not foolproof.

Anemone
Artemisia
Astilbe Bugbane
Bear's breeches
Bee balm
Black-eyed Susan
Blanket flower
Bleeding heart
Butterfly weed
Catmint Lenten rose
Coral bells
Coreopsis
Cushion spurge
Evening primrose
False indigo
Globe thistle
Monkshood
Oriental poppy
Pincushion flower
Purple coneflower
Queen-of-the-meadow
Yarrow

Common Diseases

Wilted leaves, yellow foliage, moldy flower buds, buds that fail to open; speckles, spots, and raised bumps—the symptoms of plant diseases are many. Review these common diseases and learn to spot the signs of trouble.

Leaf Spots
Fungi, bacteria, and viruses cause leaf spots on leaves, but fungi are the most common source. Yellow, red, or purple borders typically surround brown or tan tissue. When the weather is conducive to new infections, leaf spots can expand or even coalesce to kill leaves and stems. Severe leaf spot infections cause foliage drop.

Bacterial leaf spots are usually irregular; fungi create round or oval spots. Virus-generated spots have purple borders and plant growth is often stunted.

CONTROL

Gathering fallen leaves in early spring can help prevent leaf spots by destroying infectious spores that overwintered on foliage. Avoid overhead watering, especially if you have battled leaf spot in the past.

To treat leaf spot, use a fungicide labeled for leaf spots and the plant you want to treat, or try a copper-based fungicide, which is one of the few materials effective against bacterial diseases. If a virus is the culprit behind your leaf spot, your only course of action is to clip and remove affected foliage.

Botrytis Blight
Also known as gray mold, botrytis blight occurs most frequently on faded blooms. Poor air circulation and high humidity favor botrytis formation, as do long periods of rainy, cloudy weather. The fuzz that appears on afflicted plant parts is the spore of the fungus behind the blight. Peony is a frequent target of the fungus.

CONTROL

Thin perennials to increase air circulation. Water only in the morning, and avoid overhead irrigation. Deadhead frequently to prevent the fungus from attacking dead blooms. For chemical control, choose a fungicide labeled for botrytis and the plant you want to treat.

Nematodes
Tiny roundworms in soil called nematodes play a significant role in soil ecology as beneficial microorganisms. Other nematodes cause plant disease by feeding on roots and leaves.

Plants suffering from root-feeding nematodes become stunted and turn yellow because roots cannot take up nutrients effectively. Infected roots develop round or spindle-shape galls. Leaf nematodes feed on new foliage as it emerges in spring, causing areas between major veins to turn brown and die. Many perennials are affected by nematodes, but hosta and Japanese anemone are frequently attacked.

CONTROL

Nematodes can't withstand heat; use soil solarization to destroy them in planting beds (see page 116–117). Control foliar nematodes by cleaning up leafy debris by early winter. If you have an infected perennial, dig and divide it. Dip divisions in hot water (120 to 140°F) for 10 minutes to kill nematodes. After the hot water bath, dip the divisions in cool water and plant. Site divisions in a location away from where the original, infected plant grew.

Powdery Mildew
Powdery mildew forms a white coating on leaf and flower surfaces during dry, cloudy weather with high humidity. Leaves may become distorted. Unlike most fungal diseases, powdery mildew spores are actually killed by prolonged exposure to water.

CONTROL
Washing leaves with water can kill spores on the leaf surface but may activate other fungal problems. Cut and destroy infested foliage. Sprays containing neem oil or horticultural oil provide good control after infestation occurs.

Weekly sprays using a sodium bicarbonate (baking soda) and liquid soap solution prevent powdery mildew, but can burn leaves of some plants. The best way to overcome powdery mildew is to plant resistant varieties of perennials. 'David' and 'Andre' garden phlox, 'Spilled Milk' lungwort, 'Tiger Eye' rudbeckia, and 'Marshall's Delight' bee balm are among common perennials that are resistant to powdery mildew.

Root Rots
Water molds are the culprits behind the common *Pythium*, *Phytophthora*, and *Rhizoctonia* root rots. These diseases commonly attack perennials, developing where poor drainage and saturated soil reign. These diseases can be tough to identify because the soil is moist but plants wilt. Often the entire plant wilts suddenly, the result of the root system collapsing. Upon digging, you'll notice dead roots are brown and shriveled. There's often a sewer gas odor when you turn the soil over, and the outer portion of the root ball pulls away easily.

CONTROL
Ensure that the soil drains well, and avoid overwatering, which creates soggy soil. Two conditions predispose plants to root rots: alternating extremes of drought and saturated soil, and high salt content in soil, often due to salty irrigation water or overfertilization. You can use fungicides as a soil drench to prevent new infections, but they won't cure existing conditions. If your soil tends to be soggy, create a garden using plants that tolerate those conditions (see page 29).

Rust
When you see orange, gold, or reddish spots rupturing leaf surfaces, you're dealing with rust. While it rarely kills perennials, rust fungus makes leaves unsightly and weakens the plant by interfering with photosynthesis, the process a plant uses to make food. Each plant species hosts particular rust species that may vary from one another in appearance.

CONTROL
Avoid wetting leaves. Clean up and destroy all remnants of the previous year's growth before new plant growth emerges in spring. Commonly affected perennials include hollyhock, goldenrod, and daylily. Look for rust-resistant varieties of each.

Southern Blight Hot
and humid weather favor the onset of
Southern blight. This fungal disease kills
most perennials quickly, and rot is typically
present in the crown of the plant. Dead
stems near the soil surface often bear white
fungal strands, and yellow spores appear
near the crown. Southern blight occurs
when frequent watering, acid soil pH, and
mulch touching or covering a crown prevail.
Some perennials, like lamb's-ears, may
recover from this disease, but most die.

CONTROL
Culturally, water deeply but infrequently
and keep mulch away from plant crowns.
A deep tilling before planting buries
any fungal spores, which can persist
in soil for years. Solarizing soil (see
page 116–117) also destroys spores.
Use a fungicide drench as a preventive
treatment.

Yellows Incurable, yellows disease
turns normally healthy green leaves yellow.
It's caused by a parasitic microorganism
known as phytoplasma that's spread from
plant to plant by aster leafhoppers. Yellows
also distorts flowers, creating small, green,
leafy-looking blooms. All plants in the aster
family are susceptible, paticularly black-eyed
susan, chrysanthemum, and coneflower.
Delphinium is also susceptible.

CONTROL
Yellows is incurable; dig and destroy
infected perennials. Control leafhoppers
(see page 163) to prevent disease spread.
Yellows is often present in common
weeds, such as dandelion and plantain.
Keep these plants out of perennial
gardens and nearby lawns.

Viruses Many plants carry viruses,
some of which cause few noticeable
symptoms. Other viruses may produce
yellow or mottled leaves, stunt plant
growth, or reduce flower number. Viruses
spread through various means. Infected
plants may be used for taking cuttings or
divisions. Feeding insects, such as aphids,
leafhoppers, and thrips, can spread disease
organisms from one plant to another.

CONTROL
If you spot severe damage to a perennial,
such as stunting, and you suspect it's
caused by a virus, dig and destroy the
plant. Controlling insects that spread
viruses is the most effective way to
reduce virus spread in the garden.

 ASK THE GARDEN DOCTOR

Which pest, or pests, are attacking your perennials? Often multiple pests are at work on a single plant, and the plant may show several symptoms. These are some of the most prominent garden pests.

1 IS THE PLANT WILTING?
Yes. Go to number 8.
No. Continue to number 2.

2 DOES THE FOLIAGE APPEAR TO HAVE BEEN EATEN OR CHEWED?
Yes. Go to number 10.
No. Continue to number 3.

3 DO THE LEAVES HAVE A STIPPLED APPEARANCE OR DO THEY APPEAR TO HAVE TUNNELS?
Yes. Go to number 11.
No. Continue to number 4.

4 ARE THE FLOWERS DAMAGED?
Yes. See thrips (page 165), Japanese beetle (page 163), and botrytis blight (page 168).
No. Continue to number 5.

5 ARE THE ROOTS DAMAGED?
Yes. Go to number 9.
No. Continue to number 6.

6 ARE LEAVES MARRED WITH COLORED SPOTS OR A FUZZY OR RUSTY COVERING?
Yes. Go to number 12.
No. Continue to number 7.

7 DOES THE PLANT HAVE UNUSUAL LEAVES, STEMS, OR FLOWERS?
Yes. Go to number 13.
No. Continue to number 8.

8 CAREFULLY EXAMINE A PORTION OF THE ROOTS OF THE WILTING PLANT. DO THEY APPEAR TO BE HEALTHY?
Yes. See root rots (page 169).
No. Go to number 9.

9 EXAMINE THE DAMAGED ROOTS. WHICH DESCRIPTION BELOW BEST DESCRIBES THE DAMAGE?
Roots are severed a few inches below the crown of the plant. See voles, gophers, and moles (page 166).

The roots have pronounced round galls or growths. See nematodes (page 168).

The roots are mushy and decaying, or the growth near the crown of the plant is decaying. See borers (page 162), root rots (page 169), and Southern blight (page 170).

10 EXAMINE THE LEAF DAMAGE. WHICH DESCRIPTION BEST DESCRIBES THE DAMAGE?
Large sections of leaves are missing, primarily on the uppermost part of the plant. See deer (page 167).

Large sections of leaves are missing, primarily on the bottom part of the plant. See rabbits (page 167).

Ragged roundish holes mar several leaves. See slugs and snails (page 164) and caterpillars (page 162).

Many leaves are damaged and large portions of the plant may be defoliated. See Japanese beetle (page 163) and grasshoppers (page 163).

11 EXAMINE THE LEAVES CLOSELY. WHICH DESCRIPTION BEST DESCRIBES THE DAMAGE?
The stippling or raised surface is pale yellow. See mites (page 164) and leafhoppers (page 163).

The surface of the leaf is smooth, but light green or yellow tunnels are visible. See leaf miners (page 164).

12 EXAMINE THE SPOTS CLOSELY. WHICH DESCRIPTION BEST DESCRIBES THE SPOTS?
The discoloration is rust color. See rust (page 169).

The leaves appear to be covered with a powdery white substance. See powdery mildew (page 169).

The spots are shiny or appear to be a black sooty substance. See aphids (page 162).

The spot is bordered with a purple, brown, red, or yellow ring. The interior of the spot may be tan or brown, dead tissue. See leaf spots (page 168).

13 EXAMINE THE UNUSUAL GROWTH. WHICH OF THE FOLLOWING BEST DESCRIBES THE GROWTH?
There's general yellowing of the foliage along with a possible proliferation of green and leafy flowers. See yellows (page 170).

Leaves are mottled or variegated and may be distorted (twisted). Plant growth is stunted and flowering is reduced. See viruses (page 170).

Pest Control Methods

In the past, the standard approach to controlling pests and diseases was to reach

for a chemical. In today's environmentally aware world, many perennial gardeners don't want to use chemicals. Alternative pest control solutions exist, and an earth-friendly approach is to combine various control tactics as a strategy for maintaining a healthy garden.

Physical and mechanical control

This method transforms daily strolls in the garden into pest-fighting missions. If you spot a troublesome insect or pest eggs, squash them. If you notice Japanese beetles are feasting on hollyhocks, grab a can, fill it with soapy water, and bump those beetles into sudsy oblivion. Make sure that you're killing pests and not beneficial insects.

Another simple physical control technique is to clean up the garden in fall, gathering fallen leaves and stems. This eliminates winter hiding places for pest and disease organisms. Physical barriers, such as rodent- or deer-excluding fences, copper edging, and floating row covers are other barrier methods.

Cultural control

Cultural controls manipulate growing conditions to favor healthy plants and limit pests and diseases. For example, go easy on fertilizer so you don't promote the lush growth that aphids favor. Water with soaker hoses or limit overhead watering to morning hours to curb the spread of fungal diseases; doing so will keep leaves dry or restrict the amount of time they're wet.

Biological control

Releasing beneficial insects or spraying predatory nematodes on soil provides biological control in the garden. Planting a diverse range of plants and limiting chemical use will help cultivate healthy beneficial insect populations in your garden. Include perennials known for nectar production, such as joe-pye weed or bee balm, to lure predatory wasps, mites, beetles, and other beneficial insects to your garden. Biological controls target specific pests and won't wipe out other insects.

Chemical control

Chemicals can keep pests in check, and if you select ones with low environmental impact, you won't be releasing highly toxic materials. Horticultural oil and insecticidal soap are reduced-risk pest controls that kill insects physically. The oil smothers insects' breathing tubes, while the soap burns the bodies of soft-bodied insects, such as aphids. Pests can't develop resistance to physical controls.

With systemic chemical controls, you apply the chemical to the soil, and plant roots absorb it, moving it throughout the plant. Insects that feed on leaves ingest the chemical and die. Systemic controls provide protection against pests for a few days to a full season—or longer. Newer botanical chemicals developed from plants provide effective pest control without harmful side effects to the environment.

When choosing chemicals, read the label carefully and follow directions exactly. Some chemicals are blanket killers, affecting bees and other beneficial insects, as well as the target pest.

Resistant plants

Choose disease- or pest-resistant perennials whenever possible. While resistance isn't immunity, these plants stand up to pest attacks without the need for chemical intervention.

Above left: **When you need to apply a chemical, select one that's environmentally friendly, such as a botanical extract, horticultural oil, or a soap-based solution.**

Above center: **When possible, plant disease-resistant cultivars, like Fireworks goldenrod, which is resistant to rust.**

Above: **For aphids, a spray of water from a garden hose disperses and destroys insects.**

Opposite: **To exclude destructive wildlife, build a tasteful fence that's as easy on the eyes as it is impenetrable by deer and rabbits.**

perennial encyclopedia

Planning a perennial garden begins with research. Whether you favor romantic delphinium, playful daisies, or pollinator-friendly joe-pye weed, these pages will help you discover which plants are best suited for your garden.

DYNAMIC

Perennials create a dynamic landscape that's alive with beauty. Seasons script changing scenery, from early spring shoots to the blooms of high summer, and on autumn's foliage and seedheads.

VERSATILE

Privacy screening, wildlife attracting, droughty soil, flowers for bouquets, deep shade—no matter your garden situation or landscape need, you can find a perennial that will thrive.

RELIABLE

Once you tuck a perennial into soil, you embark on a journey featuring reliable color that comes back year after year. Some perennials grace a garden with beauty for decades.

Agapanthus
(*Agapanthus*)

Wandlike flower stems explode with floral fireworks on this South African native. Blossoms in blue, lavender, purple, or white open from late spring to early fall. Clumps of glossy, drought-tolerant, evergreen leaves are showy when flowers aren't in bloom.

Best site
Plant in full sun or light shade in well-drained soil. In northern regions, give plants as much light and heat as possible. Zones 7–11.

Growing
Agapanthus grows 6 to 30 inches tall; with flowers, 12 inches to 5 feet tall. Divide plants every two or three years in early spring. Let container plants become rootbound before dividing, roughly every four to five years. Deadhead spent flowers, snipping the whole stem. Grow plants indoors in winter in a bright window. Keep the soil barely moist.

Design ideas
Grow in perennial beds or containers. Add potted plants to beds for a tropical touch. Cut flowers last five to seven days.

variety:

❶ 'BLUE HEAVEN' Violet-blue blooms on plants 18 to 24 inches tall.

Anemone
(*Anemone* × *hybrida*)

Punctuate the late summer to early fall garden with the pastel blooms of anemone. Cupped, 2-inch-wide flowers soar above foliage. Single or double blossoms in white or pink feature a ring of gold stamens that sparkles against delicate hue petals.

Best site
Plant in part shade to full sun in moist, fertile, well-drained soil. In Southern climes, give plants part shade. Zones 3–10.

Growing
Japanese anemone grows 12 to 36 inches tall and 24 to 36 inches wide. Plant in spring. Cut plants back in late fall after frost. Apply heavy mulch post-frost, and they will survive in Zone 4. Plants spread aggressively. When planting divisions, clip foliage back by half. Keep rhizomes moist until new leaves appear.

Design ideas
Plant hybrid anemones where surrounding perennials mask their bloom height, lending vertical interest. Crinkled leaves complement Siberian iris and Little Bunny fountain grass.

species:

❶ SNOWDROP ANEMONE (*A. sylvestris*) Spring-blooming, spreading groundcover, 6 inches tall and 12 inches wide, with deeply lobed leaves. Fragrant white blossoms top leaves. Zones 3–8.

Artemisia
(Artemisia)

Prized for silvery foliage, with neutral tones that blend and soften clashing colors, artemisia is one great negotiator in the perennial garden. Drought tolerance, deer resistance, and (mostly) a polite personality earn artemisia a place in the garden.

Best site

Like many silver-leaf plants, artemisia thrives in full sun and infertile to average sandy soil. Roots rot in wet soil, and plants growing in poorly drained soil are least likely to survive winter, even in areas where they're hardy. Air circulation is key to best foliage. Prolonged high humidity can damage foliage. Zones 4–10.

Growing

Artemisias grow 12 to 36 inches tall, depending on species. Form varies and includes mounded, upright, and spreading. Plant in spring or fall, watering regularly until roots are established.

Most artemisias have woody stems. Prune in spring after leaves emerge. Cut soft-stemmed species to the ground in fall. Prune plants that become floppy or open in the center, removing one-third to one-half of growth.

Design ideas

Pair silvery artemisia with dark-tone blossoms or foliage. Planting partners include 'Rubrum' fountain grass, burgundy cannas, and 'Sapphire' blue oat grass. Use artemisia as a backdrop for dark-blossomed perennials, such as meadow sage, ladybells, or deep purple dwarf 'Junior Dream' garden phlox. The silver tones of artemisia also sparkle when matched with pink blooms or dark green leaves.

species and varieties:

❶ BEACH WORMWOOD (*A. stelleriana*) Broad-lobed leaves and tiny yellow blossoms; 12 to 24 inches tall and 24 to 36 inches wide. 'Boughton Silver', 6 to 8 inches tall and 12 inches wide. Zones 3–8.

❷ 'POWIS CASTLE' HYBRID ARTEMISIA 24 to 36 inches tall and wide, larger in the West. Forms an upright mound of lacy silver leaves. Zones 6–8.

❸ SILVERMOUND ARTEMISIA (*A. schmidtiana*) Tidy, 12- to 24-inch-tall mound of soft, finely textured silver foliage. Best in cool climates and infertile soil. Zones 3–9.

❹ WHITE SAGE (*A. ludoviciana*) Rampant grower, forming upright spreading mass of 24- to 36-inch-tall stems covered with aromatic silver leaves. Spreads into surrounding soil, making it a great choice for hillside erosion control. Zones 4–9. 'Silver King' and 'Silver Queen' (aggressive spreaders). 'Valerie Finnis' (hardier, more moderate spreader; 18 inches tall by 18 to 24 inches wide. Zones 3–8).

YOU SHOULD KNOW

Count on artemisia to play a starring role in an evening garden, where its silvery leaves will reflect available light and lend a luminous glow. Also known as wormwood and mugwort, some artemisias are valued for their herbal medicinal qualities.

Aster
(*Aster*)

Fill the late summer and fall garden with the breathtaking beauty of asters. Their daisy flowers open in white or shades of pink or purple. Flower size varies from ½ to 2 inches in diameter. Asters blend charm with adaptability, growing well in containers and beds.

Best site

Plant asters in well-drained soil in a spot with good air circulation. Most asters flower strongest in full sun. Two exceptions are white wood aster, which blossoms in part shade, and asters in the South. Southern heat and humidity make asters short lived; provide afternoon shade and they'll survive longer. Zones 4–10.

Growing

Plant size varies from 18 inches to 5 feet tall, depending on species. If shade splashes through your aster bed, plants can grow lanky. Insert grow-through supports early in the season to keep stems from flopping.

Deadhead plants frequently to prolong bloom and limit self-sowing. After plants finish flowering in late fall, cut them back. Divide clumps every two to three years in spring to corral spreading stems and renew the clump. Discard the oldest central section of the clump

Design ideas

Pair these autumn stars with other fall favorites, such as ornamental grasses, 'Autumn Joy' sedum, Russian sage, or monkshood. Purple-blossomed types look striking planted with yellow mums or false sunflower. Plant shade-tolerant asters with bugbane for a lovely autumn combination.

species and varieties:

❶ **CALICO ASTER** (*A. lateriflorus*) 'Lady in Black' (purple foliage; white flowers). 'Prince' (white blooms with pink centers over purple leaves). Zones 5–8.

❷ **FRIKART'S ASTER** (*A. × frikartii*) Disease-resistant summer bloomer. 'Monch' (24 inches tall with lavender semidouble blooms). 'Wonder of Staffa' (flowers light blue). Zones 5–9.

❸ **NEW ENGLAND ASTER** (*A. novae-angliae*) 'Purple Dome' (purple flowers on 18-inch-tall plants). 'Alma Potschke' (red-violet daisies on 4-foot-tall plants from August to frost). Zones 4–10.

❹ **NEW YORK ASTER** (*A. novii-belgii*) Also known as Michaelmas daisy. Grows 12 inches to 6 feet tall and 36 inches wide, opening violet daisies late summer to fall. Zones 3–8.

❺ **SMOOTH ASTER** (*A. laevis*) Yellow-centered blue daisies on plants 3 to 4 feet tall. 'Blue Bird' (mildew resistant). Zones 3–8.

Astilbe
(*Astilbe*)

Brighten shady spots with sparkling astilbe plumes. These exotic-looking bloomers unfurl feathery flowers in white and pink, red, or lavender in summer. Flower form varies from a loose, drooping plume to a compact steeple. Foliage may be red-bronze or bright or deep green.

Best site
Plant astilbe in part to full shade. It demands consistently moist, well-drained soil. Zones 4–8.

Growing
Astilbe forms a mounded clump of fernlike foliage 6 to 36 inches tall. Flowers add another 12 to 24 inches. It has few pests but is intolerant of drought. When moisture is lacking, leaves dry and turn brown. Mix organic matter into the soil to enhance water retention, and mulch.

Deadhead early-flowering species to encourage repeat bloom. Cut plants back in late fall or early spring before new growth emerges. Astilbe rarely requires division; if you need to divide plants, do so in fall. Roots on established plants can be massive; you may need a hatchet to chop through them.

Design ideas
Use astilbes for color in shady borders. Mass plants for a deer-resistant groundcover in a woodland setting or tuck near a pond or stream. In beds, group astilbe toward the rear for a color show.

Astilbe pairs with hosta, especially blue-tone types, golden hakone grass, or Japanese painted fern. Stage a sequence of bloom by mixing astilbes that flower at different times.

species and varieties:

❶ CHINESE ASTILBE (*A. chinensis*) Flowers late summer. More drought tolerant than other astilbes. 'Pumila' (compact; excellent groundcover. To 10 inches tall in bloom, 6 inches without flowers, and 12 inches wide; lavender-pink blooms contrast with dark bronzy green leaves). 'Superba' (4 feet tall with magenta flowers and shiny dark green leaves). 'Visions in Pink' (fluffy pale pink blooms atop bluish green leaves on a 24-inch-tall plant).

❷ HYBRID ASTILBES 'Sprite' (12 to 18 inches tall; pale pink mid- to late summer blooms with reddish brown seedheads). 'Deutschland' (ivory flowers in late spring to early summer on plants 24 to 30 inches tall). 'Rheinland' (clear pink flowers in early summer on plant 24 to 30 inches tall and wide). 'Fanal' (midsummer burgundy blooms above red-bronze leaves on 24-inch-tall and 18-inch-wide plants). 'Color Flash' (foliage steals the show, emerging bright green, turning burgundy in summer, and fading to gold in fall. Pale pink blooms top 10-inch-tall and 18-inch-wide plants in late spring to early summer.

STAR ASTILBE (*A. simplicifolia*) Dwarf, mounding habit to 18 inches tall. 'Hennie Graafland' has rose pink flowers that last for many weeks. 'Snowdrift' has white flowers.

YOU SHOULD KNOW
Astilbe forms an easy-care groundcover thanks to its ability to self-seed. If you want to cultivate a thick stand of astilbe, don't deadhead; allow blooms to set seed.

Balloon Flower
(Platycodon grandiflorus)

When you plant balloon flower, you're adding a little magic to the garden. Starting in early summer, round, puffy buds swell and burst open to reveal star-shape blooms. Flowers shine in white or shades of blue-violet, or pink atop strong stems that easily support blossoms.

Best site
Plant in full sun to part shade in well-drained soil. Zones 3–10.

Growing
Plants, which grow up to 36 inches tall by 12 inches wide, are pest and disease free. Stake plants and deadhead each blossom; stems exude a milky sap that isn't harmful. Plants are slow to emerge in spring. They self-sow, seedlings of taller types outcompete smaller varieties. Moving established plants is difficult.

Design ideas
Place balloon flower near the front of the garden, partnering it with fine-textured and mounded plants, such as blanket flower, butterfly weed, catmint, or centranthus. Use low varieties in rock as edging. The blossoms last long as cut flowers.

variety:

① 'SENTIMENTAL BLUE' Long-lasting, 3-inch-wide blue flowers on 6- to 8-inch-tall plants.

Barrenwort
(Epimedium)

Graceful and elegant, barrenwort forms a dense groundcover in shady conditions. Petite, spurred flowers in white, pink, red, or purple dangle above heart-shape leaflets in early to midspring.

Best site
Barrenwort thrives in part to full shade in soils that are fertile, rich in organic matter, moist, well drained, or dry. This perennial groundcover even grows in the dry shade beneath mature trees. Zones 4–8.

Growing
Plants grow 4 to 12 inches tall and 12 to 18 inches wide. Flower stems add another 2 inches to plant height. New leaves open bronze, then turn green. Provide consistent moisture the first season to help plants establish.

Design ideas
Tuck barrenwort beneath the shade of trees or shrubs, where it will thrive in all but the darkest corners. This groundcover fits naturally into woodland settings, blending prettily with small hostas, ferns, or bugleweed.

species:

① RED BARRENWORT (*E. × rubrum*) Red and yellow blooms ¾-inch wide. Red-edged leaves with rosy undertones. Plant under deciduous trees where it will receive ample light in early spring.

Bee Balm
(*Monarda didyma*)

Beckon butterflies, bees, and hummingbirds with the bright, shaggy blooms of bee balm. Tubular red, pink, purple, or white flowers open in early to midsummer in 1- to 2-inch-diameter whorls. A mint relative, bee balm spreads, creating an ever-enlarging clump.

Best site

Give bee balms sun to part shade with some open space around plants to provide good air circulation. This deer-resistant native tolerates most soils but thrives in moist, well-drained soil with organic matter. Plants may need staking in rich soils and don't excel in drought or high humidity. Zones 3–9.

Growing

Bee balm grows 24 to 36 inches tall and 3 to 4 feet wide, although some cultivars reach 5 feet. Tall types or those grown in shady sites may require staking; use a grow-through support or tomato cage to hoist stems upright.

The first flowering on bee balm is the strongest and showiest of the season. You'll get rebloom if you shear plants after flowering, but subsequent blooms will be significantly smaller.

The main pest of bee balm is powdery mildew, which assails plants later in the growing season. The solution is to grow mildew-resistant varieties. If mildew affects plants, cut down old stems, leaving fresh growth. Discard diseased parts. Divide bee balm when the plant's center dies out, approximately every two to three years.

Design ideas

Because bee balm wanders in the garden, with stems creeping out of an assigned growing spot, it's best suited to the middle of a naturalized border, where stems can form a casual drift. In a formal garden, plant bee balm in the middle of a bed. Dig or pull spreading stems, discarding or sharing divisions.

varieties:

1. **'BLUE STOCKING'** Violet-blue flowers on 2- to 4-foot-tall stems. Zones 3–9.
2. **'GARDENVIEW SCARLET'** Carmine red flowers on 2- to 4-foot-tall stems. Zones 4–9.
3. **'JACOB CLINE'** Stems can reach 5 feet. Large red blossoms. Zones 4–9.
4. **'MARSHALL'S DELIGHT'** Long bloom time, from July to September, with rose-pink flowers. 4 feet tall. Mildew resistant. Zones 4–9.
5. **'PETITE DELIGHT'** Grows only 15 to 18 inches tall. Bright lavender-pink flowers. Mildew resistant. Zones 4–8.

Bellflower
(*Campanula*)

Celebrate variety with bellflowers, a perennial that comes in multiple forms—ground huggers, clumpformers, casual spreaders, and stately upright spires. All unfurl bell-shape blooms. Flowers face up or down in white or tones of blue, pink, red, or violet.

YOU SHOULD KNOW

When you plant bellflower, you'll never want for divisions. Some types wander through the garden by spreading aboveground and underground stems. Others self-seed, with seedlings often coming true to the mother plant.

Best site

Bellflower thrives in full sun to part shade in neutral to slightly alkaline, well-drained soil. Average fertility is sufficient for good garden performance. Plants don't tolerate drought, full shade, wet soil, or hot summer nights. Zones 3–10.

Growing

Plants range anywhere from 9 to 36 inches tall and wide, depending on species. Few pests bother bellflower. Tall species and cultivars require staking. Try grow-through supports for a low-maintenance staking option. Deadhead to extend flowering.

Divide plants every three to five years or when clumps weaken. Divisions transplant easily. For cut flowers, harvest stems just before buds open.

Design ideas

Tuck small species in the front of the garden, tall types in the middle. Plants tend to self-sow and spread, which makes them well suited to cottage or informal garden styles. Bellflower makes a long-lasting cut flower; plant enough so the garden can spare some stems for bouquets.

Names to watch for

Carpathian bellflower (*C. carpatica*) Dense, spreading clumps dotted with 1-inch flowers. Ideal for rock gardens and edging. 'Blue Clips' (blue blooms), 'White Clips' (white), and 'Pearl Blue' (vivid blue-violet). Zones 3–9.

Peach-leaf bellflower (*C. persicifolia*) Very fine foliage on plants 12 inches tall and wide. In early to midsummer, short spires rise above the plant on stems that frequently need staking. 'La Belle' (double sky blue; 24-inch stems). 'Chettle Charm' (white edged in lavender; 30- to 36-inch stems). 'Telham Beauty' (lavender blue; 30-inch stems). Zones 3–7.

species and varieties:

❶ CLUSTERED BELLFLOWER (*C. glomerata*) Tight clusters of upward-facing violet blooms in early summer on 24- to 36-inch-tall stems that need staking. Excellent cut flower. 'Superba' (deep purple flowers; is more heat-resistant). Zones 3–8.

❷ DALMATIAN BELLFLOWER (*C. portenschlagiana*) This groundcover grows 4 to 8 inches tall by 24 inches wide. Blue-violet flowers in late spring to early summer. Zones 3–8.

❸ SPOTTED BELLFLOWER (*C. punctata* 'Cherry Bells') Bright pink blossoms in early summer; 20 inches tall. The species has 12- to 24-inch-tall spires of tubular white blooms, marked inside with pink or purple from mid- to late summer. Aggressive spreader. Stems often need staking. 'Bowl of Cherries' (dark purple-red). 'Pantaloons' (light purple, hose-in-hose arrangement; 12 inches tall by 15 inches wide). Zones 5–9.

Big Betony
(*Stachys grandiflora*)

Flower spikes rise 8 to 10 inches above deer-resistant foliage clumps in late spring to early summer. Whorled around stems in groups of 10 to 20, the long-lasting blossoms open in pink and purple tones.

Best site

Plant in full sun to light shade in rich, moist, well-drained soil. Water frequently and mulch; aim for consistently moist, not soggy, soil. Zones 2–10.

Growing

Big betony grows 9 to 18 inches tall by 12 inches wide. Plants suffer in high heat and humidity; mitigate with part shade and consistent moisture. Big betony is short-lived in the South. Deadhead after blooming.

Design ideas

Plant in groups of three or more. Big betony's form and color beautifully suit a pondside setting, although the plant cannot tolerate continuously wet soil. Create a cottage look by combining it with roses, lady's mantle, and daisies. The blooms make wonderful cut flowers.

Blackberry Lily
(*Belamcanda chinensis*)

Fast-growing and fuss-free blackberry lily adds flair to the perennial garden with its swordlike foliage and crimson-freckled orange blooms. Plants bloom from midsummer to fall, each flower lasting one day. The seedpods are packed with shiny black berries.

Best site

Plant in full to part sun in well-drained, light soil. Cool, moist summers or wet winter soil challenge blackberry lily. Zones 4–10.

Growing

Plants grow 18 to 24 inches tall by 18 inches wide. Flower stems are 20 inches long; stake as needed. Blackberry lily is short-lived but self-sows. Divide plants every two to three years.

Blackberry lily is a type of iris and susceptible to iris borer and iris soft rot. Watch for leaf damage in spring; remove and destroy foliage showing symptoms. In fall, cut plants back; destroy the stems and leaves.

Design ideas

Good companions include ornamental grasses, blanket flower, and peach-leaf bellflower.

species:

❶ BETONY 'Hummelo' has lavender-rose blooms in midsummer on plants 18 to 20 inches tall and 18 inches wide. *S. monieri* bears rose-pink, spiky flowers on spikes above foliage. Zones 4–8.

varieties:

❶ 'FRECKLE FACE' 2-inch-wide blooms on 18- to 24-inch plants.
'HELLO YELLOW' Dwarf form with 1-inch pure yellow blooms atop 10-inch foliage.

Black-Eyed Susan

(Rudbeckia hirta)

Ignite a firestorm of color in the summer garden with hardy, reliable black-eyed susan. This sturdy perennial infuses the garden with long-lasting color, flowering from early summer to fall. Handsome foliage stands out beneath blooms.

YOU SHOULD KNOW

Scattering a few clumps of black-eyed susan throughout a perennial border will unify the planting and provide a steady shot of season-long color.

Best site

Plant black-eyed susan in soil with average fertility and moisture. Its sunny yellow blooms are a good clue that it grows best in full sun. Zones 3–10.

Growing

Plants grow 24 to 30 inches tall, and 24 to 36 inches wide. Water transplants regularly until plants are established. After that, drought tolerance reigns, and plants require little water or fertilizer. Black-eyed susan is relatively pest free, although during wet conditions it can develop fungal leaf spot disease. Thin the planting to promote good air circulation and reduce disease incidence. Deadheading regularly promotes rebloom and prevents excessive reseeding, as does cutting plants back in fall.

Divide plants every four to five years. Clumps can spread rapidly in fertile soil. Remove unwanted shoots from around the edge to keep the plant contained.

Design Ideas

Black-eyed susan features a coarse texture that shines with artful ease when matched with fine-textured and upright plants, such as ornamental grasses. It is a star in meadow and prairie plantings, where its golden daisies light up the summer landscape. Pair it with showy sedum for long-lasting interest from summer through winter. Blossoms of this classic wildlife garden plant lure butterflies and bees to the garden; seedheads are a favorite among birds. Gloriosa types, *R. hirta*, unfurl flowers in assorted hues, including orange, bronze, and bicolor blends.

species and varieties:

❶ 'INDIAN SUMMER' 34 to 48 inches tall and 12 inches wide; gold-yellow petals surround black centers.

❷ 'GOLDSTURM' (*R. fulgida*) 24 inches tall and wide. Long-blooming, traditional black-eyed daisies.

❸ 'PRAIRIE SUN' 30 inches tall and 12 to 18 inches wide; yellow daisies with green center.

❹ 'CHEROKEE SUNSET' 24 inches tall and 12 inches wide; double and semidouble 4-inch blooms in shades of yellow, orange, and bronze.

❺ 'TOTO' 10 inches tall and 12 inches wide; 4-inch gold flowers with brown center.

GIANT CONEFLOWER (*R. maxima*) 72 inches tall and 48 inches wide.

Blanket Flower
(*Gaillardia grandiflora*)

The cheerful daisylike blooms of blanket flower interject bright color into perennial gardens from early summer to fall. Flowers open in blends of red, yellow, orange, and gold, which weave ribbons of color in bouquets and enliven the tapestry of perennial beds.

Best site

Blanket flower performs best in full sun in sandy, well-drained soil high in organic matter, although plants tolerate poor, infertile soils. Zones 3–8.

Growing

Plants grow fast, reaching 12 to 30 inches tall and 24 inches wide. Heat and drought tolerant, blanket flower is a carefree bloomer except in soggy soil, where crown rot may develop. Stake tall varieties with grow-through supports to limit sprawl. Dwarf varieties, such as 'Goblin' and 'Baby Cole' form tight mounds that require no staking. Deadhead all types to prevent self-sowing, to promote continued bloom, and to keep the plant neat (it tends to look like a tangled mass). Self-sown seedlings of named cultivars do not come true to type; rogue out unwanted seedlings to maintain the desired variety. You can divide blanket flower every two or three years in spring to get more plants. Cut plants back in fall.

Design ideas

Blanket flower is a natural companion for yarrow, coreopsis, white gaura, globe thistle, and ornamental grasses. Combine it with other brightly colored perennials for a festive mixture. Its multicolor daisies attract butterflies, and it blooms nearly the entire growing season, making it a good choice for wildlife gardens. Grow blanket flower on steep slopes or in terraced gardens with a southern or western exposure. It will appreciate the good drainage and hot, dry conditions and reward you with long-lasting color.

YOU SHOULD KNOW
Horizontally spreading roots of blanket flower form an expanding clump, but they're not usually invasive because plants are short lived. Mulch in regions with cold winter weather to protect crowns.

species and varieties:

1 **'GOBLIN'** (also sold as 'Kobold') 12 inches tall. Deep red blooms edged with yellow.

2 **'BABY COLE'** 6 to 8 inches tall, 15 to 18 inches wide. 3-inch-wide, yellow-tipped red daisies with wine red center

3 **'ARIZONA SUN'** 10 inches tall and 12 inches wide. All-America Selections winner with uniform 3-inch-wide, red and gold blooms.

4 **COMMOTION 'TIZZY'** 18 to 24 inches tall and wide. Fluted russet or terra-cotta blooms.

5 **SLENDER BLANKET FLOWER** (*G. pinnatifida*) Yellow daisies with large red centers all summer; 18 inches tall and wide. Adapted to arid sites. Zones 7–9.

Bleeding Heart
(*Dicentra spectabilis*)

Old-fashioned bleeding heart fills a spring perennial garden with delicate, dangling heart-shape pink and white blooms. Other bleeding heart species—all featuring fernlike foliage, straight stems, and heart-shape flowers—keep the flower show going through summer.

YOU SHOULD KNOW

Full sun, dry soil, and high heat send old-fashioned bleeding heart into dormancy. Many gardeners in northern climes report success with repeat blooming into June by cutting back plants by one-half to one-third after flowering.

Best site

Plant in part to full shade in rich, moist, well-drained soil. Mix plenty of compost into planting beds; bleeding hearts like a humusy footing. Zones 2–8. Pacific (*D. formosa*) and fringed bleeding heart (*D. eximia*) can both stand a little more sun and are drought tolerant. Zones 3–10.

Growing

With old-fashioned bleeding heart, clumps can grow 24 to 36 inches tall and wide. There's no need for deadheading, division is rarely required, and plants are pest free.

Pacific and fringed bleeding hearts grow 9 to 12 inches tall and wide and bear flowers on stems that stretch 12 to 18 inches above foliage. Blossoms appear in late spring; plants rebloom sporadically throughout summer. When summer heat arrives, plants don't enter dormancy.

Deadhead to encourage rebloom or to prevent self-sowing of Pacific bleeding heart. If tattered foliage forms an eyesore, cut it back.

Design ideas

Summer dormancy in old-fashioned bleeding heart can leave a hole in your perennial garden. Tuck plants in the center or back of a planting bed, surrounding them with plants that disguise their absence. Good planting partners for old-fashioned bleeding heart include dwarf bearded iris, sweet woodruff, and variegated solomon's seal. Pacific and fringed bleeding hearts form a beautiful groundcover, spreading quickly by roots and seeds.

varieties:

❶ **OLD-FASHIONED BLEEDING HEART** Most varieties are pink with white central "drops." 'Alba' (white flowers and long-lasting blue-green leaves). 'Gold Heart' (pink blooms; chartreuse leaves scorch if they receive too much sun).

❷ **PACIFIC BLEEDING HEART** 'Adrian Bloom' (ruby red flowers, blue-green foliage). 'Aurora' (small white blooms, blue-green leaves). 'Luxuriant' (rosy pink flowers, blue-green foliage).

❸ **FRINGED BLEEDING HEART** 'Snowdrift' (white flowers). 'Stuart Boothman' (pink blooms; deeply cut, silvery blue-green foliage).

Boltonia
(Boltonia asteroides)
Drifts of 1-inch-wide daisies blanket sturdy branched boltonia stems from late summer to early fall. The plants resemble asters, opening flowers that attract butterflies and make excellent additions to autumn bouquets.

Best site
Plant in full sun to part shade in moist, well-drained soil of average fertility. Provide afternoon shade in hot climates. Zones 4–9.

Growing
Low-maintenance and mildew-resistant boltonia grows 12 to 24 inches tall; 5 feet tall when flowering. Stems need staking in windy sites, overly fertile soil, or part shade. Use grow-through supports. Cutting plants to 12 inches in late spring increases branching and flowers. Divide plants every three to four years to control size.

Design ideas
For late summer color, plant boltonia with goldenrod, joe-pye weed, 'Silver Feather' miscanthus grass, and pink muhly grass. Add to wildflower or wildlife gardens. Blooms make excellent cut flowers.

Bugbane
(Actaea simplex)
Good looks are part of bugbane's charm. Elegant, arching spires of white blooms hold court over coarsely lobed, eye-catching leaves in midsummer. Dark-leaf cultivars introduce strong season-long interest from colorful foliage.

Best site
Plant in part sun to full shade in well-drained, fertile soil. Provide afternoon shade in the South. Plants can survive full sun in the North if the soil is consistently moist. Zones 3–7.

Growing
The pest-free plant grows 24 to 36 inches tall and wide with 3- to 6-foot stems. In unidirectional light, stake plants. Grow-through supports work well. Spent blooms add interest; cut bugbane back in fall or early spring.

Design ideas
Mass bugbane at the back of a border. Planted in groups of three, bugbane forms spectacular drifts. Slow-growing bugbane pairs beautifully with shade lovers like hosta, rodgersia, monkshood, or heart-leaf brunnera.

varieties:

❶ **'SNOWBANK'** Small plant with 3- to 4-foot stems and white flowers.
'PINK BEAUTY' Pink blooms on 5-foot stems, silvery blue foliage.

species and varieties:

❶ **FRAGRANT BUGBANE** (*A. simplex*) Native; fragrant white blossoms, late summer.
'BRUNETTE' Pinkish white, fragrant flowers above dark, bronze-purple leaves. Zones 3–8.

Bugleweed
(*Ajuga reptans*)

A quick grower, bugleweed scrambles within planting beds to form a dense mat that crowds out weeds. Tightly packed violet, pink, or white flowers on spikes extend to 6 inches above low-growing leaves. They're magnets for bumblebees, hummingbirds, and butterflies.

YOU SHOULD KNOW

A fast-growing, aggressive spreader, bugleweed can easily overpower other perennials and nudge them out of planting beds. Contain bugleweed by planting it in areas bordered by a sidewalk or driveway.

Best site

Tuck plants into sandy, well-drained soil. Bugleweed tolerates clay and consistently moist, but not soggy, soil. Plant in part shade to full shade; some cultivars withstand more sun. In the northern end of its range, full sun is fine. Zones 3–11.

Growing

Leaves form a rosette 3 to 4 inches tall; flower spikes add another 4 to 6 inches. Plants spread 12 to 36 inches, depending on cultivar. Space plants 10 inches apart; keep the soil moist while roots establish. Primarily pest free, bugleweed is susceptible to crown rot in hot, humid climates.

This groundcover spreads by runners to form thick mats. Use caution when planting near a lawn or other perennials; it can quickly invade. Install edging to corral its wandering ways; a deep trench edge works well to hijack its invasion into unwanted areas.

Prune long shoots after flowering. To deadhead a large planting, set the lawnmower high and run over plants. Divide every two to three years in fall. Bugleweed spreads by runners that form small plants and root.

Design ideas

Bugleweed is ideal for areas too shady for grass. While it doesn't tolerate daily foot traffic, plants spring back from occasional treading. This groundcover spreads among stepping-stones and readily climbs hilly sites, slopes, and stone walls.

Use it to skirt spring-flowering shrubs or perennials, such as heart-leaf brunnera and yellow corydalis. Bugleweed pairs beautifully with caryopteris, coral bells, and hosta.

varieties:

❶ **'BLACK SCALLOP'** Dark purple to black leaves. Flower spikes 8 to 10 inches high. Foliage darkest in full sun. Powdery mildew resistant.

❷ **'BURGUNDY GLOW'** New growth unfurls burgundy red; leaves become white and dark pink with age. Spreads less aggressively than the species.

❸ **'CHOCOLATE CHIP'** Chocolate brown and green leaves are relatively small and narrow. Ideal planted between stepping-stones or in crevices in stone walls.

❹ **'GOLDEN GLOW'** Leaves splashed with yellow and mint green. Spreads less aggressively than the species. Protect from afternoon sun in southern regions.

Butterfly Weed
(*Asclepias tuberosa*)

With vivid orange flowers, butterfly weed adds sizzle to perennial plantings. It blooms in early to midsummer and fits perfectly into mixed borders and wildlife, meadow, and prairie gardens. Many butterflies sip its nectar; caterpillars of monarchs feed on its leaves.

Best site
Plant in full sun in light, lean, well-drained soil. Poor winter drainage can kill this perennial. Butterfly weed thrives in heat and won't perform as strongly in cool-summer climates. Zones 4–10.

Growing
Butterfly weed grows 24 to 36 inches tall and wide. Plants self-sow; deadhead before seeds form. Deadheading may produce a second, weaker bloom. Like all milkweeds, this perennial exudes milky sap that's not harmful.

Plants are slow-growing and long-lived. Butterfly weed forms a long taproot that makes it challenging to transplant. When digging to propagate, cut through the top of the root and obtain several eyes, along with a large piece of root, for each division.

If you allow plants to set seeds, harvest seedpods for dried flower arrangements. In spring, watch for volunteer seedlings. Allow them to grow six to eight weeks, then transplant. Keep seedlings well watered until roots establish.

Plants are generally pest free but do attract aphids. Apply insecticidal soap if pest levels become damaging.

Design ideas
Plant butterfly flower with fine-textured ornamental grasses that are shorter (blue oat grass) or taller (fountain or miscanthus grass). Low, mounded perennials such as coreopsis, catmint, and lavender cotton also complement butterfly weed. It blends nicely with other wildlife-friendly perennials, such as blanket flower, false indigo, coneflower, black-eyed susan, or prairie dropseed grass.

species and varieties:

1 **'GAY BUTTERFLIES'** Grown from seed, which yields a mix of flower colors—red, yellow, or orange. Stems 2 to 3 feet tall.

2 **'HIGH YELLOW'** Bright yellow blooms from midsummer to midfall. Grows 24 to 36 inches tall.

3 **SWAMP MILKWEED** (*A. incarnata*) Native wildflower that favors moist areas. Fragrant pink blooms atop 4- to 5-foot stems from summer through fall. Deadhead to ensure rebloom. 'Ice Ballet' (white flowers; 40 inches tall). 'Cinderellla' (rose pink blooms; 3 to 5 feet tall and 12 to 36 inches wide). Zones 3–9.

YOU SHOULD KNOW
Butterfly weed is a late riser in spring, emerging from soil long after spring bloomers are well into flowering. Surround this slow starter with early-season bloomers, such as spring bulbs.

Campion
(*Lychnis*)

Campion plants boast vibrant flowers that float atop colorful foliage. Blossoms open in early to midsummer, but offer a long flower show when you deadhead stems. A short-lived perennial, campion beautifully suits the carefree abandon of a cottage garden.

YOU SHOULD KNOW

Campion is a short-lived perennial, blooming little the first year, heavily the second, and deteriorating by the third. Plants self-sow, so by not deadheading all plants and letting some set seeds, you'll have a steady flower show from year to year.

Best site

Plant campion in full sun or light shade in moist, well-drained soil. Two types of campion are commonly planted: rose and Arkwright's. Rose campion combines silver woolly leaves with sizzling magenta blooms. Zones 4–10. Arkwright's campion tosses open electric orange-red flowers above bronzy foliage. Zones 6–10.

Growing

Rose campion forms a basal rosette of silver foliage that gives rise to 24- to 36-inches tall branched stems. Arkwright's campion grows 18 to 24 inches tall by 12 inches wide. Both continue to flower all summer with consistent deadheading. With large plantings, shear off flowers using hedge clippers. In late summer, allow a few stems to set seeds, so you have young plants to replace aging ones.

To dodge disease, keep rose campion foliage dry. With both campions, avoid overwatering and overfertilizing; both actions weaken the plant. Cut dead stems in late fall. Don't mulch over the crowns of plants.

Design ideas

Both plants hold their own in cottage gardens, where their self-sowing adds spontaneity to the design. Campions also fit well in naturalized or meadow plantings. In a cottage garden, good companions include lamb's-ears, lady's mantle, catmint, and prostrate rosemary. In a naturalized border, pair campion with joe-pye weed, coreopsis, or coneflower.

species and varieties:

❶ **ARKWRIGHT'S CAMPION** 'Vesuvius' (orange-red blooms, late spring to early summer; red-tinted leaves; 18 inches tall). 'Orange Gnome' (8 inches tall; dark purple-red leaves).

❷ **MALTESE CROSS** (*L. chalcedonica*) Striking four-petaled, scarlet blooms in dense clusters atop 18- to 24-inch-tall stems. Flowers briefly in early summer. 'Carnea' (pink blossoms on 4-foot-tall stems; flowers repeatedly from early summer if deadheaded). Zones 3–10.

❸ **ROSE CAMPION** 'Gardener's World' (24 inches tall; deep red-purple, double flowers all summer long; no self-sowing). 'Alba' (24 inches tall; white flowers). 'Oculata' (white blooms with cherry pink eye; 18 inches tall).

Cardinal Flower
(Lobelia cardinalis)

Dress the late summer to early fall garden in red flower spikes with the showy blooms of this native wildflower. Brilliant blooms beckon hummingbirds and butterflies, which extract nectar from the tubular, long-throated flowers.

Best site
Plant in full sun to part shade. Full sun works in cool climates; provide afternoon shade in the South. This bright bloomer prefers moist to continuously moist, fertile, acid, well-drained soil. In a sunny location, it needs more water. Zones 3–9.

Growing
Plants grow 20 inches tall by 12 inches wide, with 3- to 4-foot flower stems. Deadhead to extend bloom. In ideal conditions, plants will self-sow; allow a few flowers to set seeds to see what might happen. Cut back dead stems in fall or spring. Divide every two to three years in spring as needed.

Design ideas
Cardinal flower is breathtaking massed at edges of lakes, streams, ponds, or soggy spots. It pairs well with perennials that thrive in moist soil.

Caryopteris
(Caryopteris × clandonensis)

If you're hungry for blue, add caryopteris, or bluebeard, to your garden. This shrubby beauty flowers in late summer to early fall, opening fluffy, blue blossom clusters. The effect is light and airy, and the flowers have a frothy appearance.

Best site
Plant in full sun in dry, well-drained soil of average fertility. Zones 5–10.

Growing
Caryopteris grows 36 inches tall and wide. Technically, it's a deciduous shrub, though in Zones 5 and colder, only the roots are hardy; the stems die to the ground in winter. Cut dead stems in early spring when new growth appears. Thin dense shoots to increase air circulation.

Design ideas
Fine-textured, aromatic leaves create an airy backdrop for other perennials. The low mound blends artfully with ornamental grasses and late-season bloomers such as helenium and 'Autumn Joy' sedum, perennial sunflower, goldenrod, and joe-pye weed. Group several caryopteris plants together for a striking impact.

species and varieties:

❶ **CARDINAL FLOWER** Brilliant red blooms on 3-foot tall spikes. Needs moist shade. Zones 4–8.
BIG BLUE LOBELIA *(Lobelia siphilitica)* One inch long blue flowers. Needs moist shade. Zones 4–8.

varieties:

❶ **'BLUE MIST'** Powder blue blooms on plants 30 inches tall and wide.
'WORCESTER GOLD' Blue flowers and yellow to chartreuse leaves.

Catmint
(Nepeta racemosa)

It's tough to beat the billows of lavender-blue flower spikes that blanket catmint in early summer. The shrubby mounds of branching stems bear fragrant gray-green leaves. Tolerating heat, drought, wind, and foot traffic, catmint embodies low maintenance.

YOU SHOULD KNOW

If your garden's growing conditions don't favor lavender, try catmint as an alternative. Truly low maintenance and drought tolerant, this blue beauty flowers sporadically through summer with deadheading.

Best site

Plant this blue-tone bloomer in full sun in well-drained soil. Provide afternoon shade in hot climates. Zones 4–10.

Growing

Catmint grows 18 to 24 inches tall and wide. Plants tolerate foot traffic; although tolerant of many conditions, they do not like hot, humid weather. Help them survive summer's sultry weeks by deadheading. Shear plants back by one-third to one-half after the first flush of flowers. This keeps plants tidier in hot weather and promotes rebloom.

Stake floppy species using grow-through supports or branched twigs. Catmint transplants easily. Divide clumps in spring or fall every three to six years. Clean up plants in late fall or early spring, cutting stems to the ground.

Design ideas

Use catmint as an edging to soften paths or walls, or mass as a low-maintenance, drought-tolerant groundcover. Tuck several clumps along a bed edge to tie diverse plantings together with blue blossoms. A beautiful companion for coarse-texture bloomers, catmint shines when paired with bearded iris, cranesbill geranium, coneflower, blackberry lily, or lady's mantle. Skirt roses with catmint for a romantic planting.

Catmint makes a wonderful addition to a wildlife garden. Its flowers beckon butterflies, hummingbirds, and bees. If the blossoms are allowed to set seeds, goldfinches and other seed-eating fliers may come to feast.

species and varieties:

1. **'BLUE WONDER'** 6-inch flower spikes on 12- to 15-inch plant. More flowers and bigger leaves than the species.
2. **'DROPMORE'** Large flowers from early to midsummer on 12-to 18-inch-tall plant.
3. **'SIX HILLS GIANT'** 30 inches tall with large leaves and flowers. Violet blooms carried on 12-inch stems.
4. **'WALKER'S LOW'** Lavender-blue flowers on 18- to 24-inch plant. Stake stems to avoid flopping.
5. **'COOL CAT'** *(Nepeta subsessilis)* Blooms longer than other catmints. Can grow 12 to 40 inches tall.

Celandine Poppy
(Stylophorum diphyllum)

One of the spring garden's lovely native plants, celandine poppy unfurls gold blooms above deeply lobed gray-green foliage. The low-maintenance plant stands sturdily upright; flowers hover above leaves.

Best site
Plant celandine poppy in well-drained organic soil in part shade to full shade. It does not tolerate full sun or heat. Zones 4–9.

Growing
Celandine poppy grows 18 inches tall by 12 inches wide. It forms a clump that is fast growing and pest free. Celandine poppy self-sows profusely. Seedlings can overpower other plants; deadhead as needed. Plants don't rebloom. Division isn't necessary, nor is cutting back foliage in fall. Leaves decompose over winter.

Design ideas
Use celandine poppy to brighten shady areas. In a woodland setting, allow plants to self-sow and form naturalized drifts. Pair with yellow corydalis, small-leaf hostas, jacob's ladder, lungwort, and coral bells.

Centranthus
(Centranthus ruber)

Butterflies flock to the reddish pink blooms of centranthus. Arranged in dense clusters, the flowers start opening in late spring and continue until frost as long as you deadhead. Seedheads dangle in feathery clusters, prompting another common name, jupiter's beard.

Best site
Plant in full sun in well-drained alkaline to neutral soil. Water regularly the first year while roots are establishing. Plants don't tolerate the South's humidity. Zones 5–11.

Growing
Centranthus grows 24 inches tall and wide. Deadheading encourages rebloom and prevents self-sowing, which can be invasive. Cut back plants in early spring to encourage bushiness.

Divide clumps every two to three years. Centranthus is short lived, but allowing a few seedheads to mature improves the chances of its continued presence in the garden.

Design ideas
Plant centranthus with silvery lamb's-ears or artemisia. Dark-leaf perennials stage a striking backdrop for centranthus blooms.

species:

CHINESE CELADINE POPPY (*S. lasiocarpum*) Similar to celadine poppy but with larger, more deeply cut leaves, and red instead of yellow sap.

varieties:

❶ **'COCCINEUS'** Dark rosy red flowers.
'ALBUS' White blooms.

Chrysanthemum *(Chrysanthemum)*

Garden mums whisk colorful excitement into the perennial garden's fall flower mix with their madras shades—including orange, yellow, purple, green, and white. Their brightly colored blooms open from late summer to early fall, giving the garden a jewel-tone sendoff that's hard to beat. Mums earn their keep in beds or containers, blending beautifully with ornamental grasses. These bloomers attract butterflies and bees, serving up late season nectar in wildlife gardens.

Best site

Plant garden mums in full sun; they require part shade in the South. Provide average to fertile, well-drained soil. Mums need consistent moisture, but they won't tolerate soggy soil. Poor winter drainage will kill a mum. Zones 5–10.

Growing

Mounded in form, most mums grow 12 to 36 inches tall and wide. Plant mums four to six weeks before the last frost. Plants will withstand winter better the sooner they can be planted. If you're serious about garden mums, watch for plants in spring and add them to the garden at that time to allow maximum root development before frost.

Shorter days trigger flowering, which means you need to select the right plant for your region. If fall frost arrives early, plant types that flower early. Southern gardeners should choose mid to late bloomers. In mild climates, plant a mix of early, mid-season, and late mums to prolong the flower show.

With spring-planted and established mums, pinching promotes the greatest number of flowers and yields bushy, sturdy plants. Learn about pinching in the tip box Maximize Mums, on page 147. Pinching delays flowering a few weeks. If you desire big, loose, early-flowering plants, skip pinching and stake plants in late spring using grow-through supports to keep flower-laden stems from flopping.

Feed plants using a bloom booster fertilizer until you see flower buds. After blooming begins, deadhead faded blossoms to make some elbow room for developing buds. Divide plants every year or two in early spring, discarding the dead or weak sections, which usually appear toward the center of the clump.

In the late fall, when flowering is finished, cut plants back to 6 inches. After the ground freezes, mulch for winter protection using chopped leaves or straw. For the most effective winter protection, build a wire cage around plants and fill it with mulch.

Watch for aphids during spring and early summer, spider mites and Japanese beetles during summer, and mildew and rust in late summer and fall. Slugs and leaf spot disease can attack plants anytime.

Design ideas

Garden mums bring a traditional fall color palette to life with vivid orange, rich wine, saturated purple, or sparkling pink blooms. Mix and match mums with other strong fall performers to stage a stunning garden show. Monkshood, ornamental grasses, fall-blooming asters, Autumn Joy sedum, boltonia, and caryopteris shine when planted with garden chrysanthemums.

Names to watch for

Pacific chrysanthemum *(Chrysanthemum pacificum)* 12 to 15 inches tall and wide, silver-edged leaves are striking in the garden. Foliage is accented by gold balls of bloom appearing in fall in cold climates and early winter in warm zones.

Ox-eye daisy *(Chrysanthemum leucanthemum)* The classic wildflower daisy, with flowers on 12- to 24-inch stems from spring through summer.

YOU SHOULD KNOW
Some garden mums are short lived and meant to be signs of the season. These plants are designed to be nothing more than porch decor. For true perennial performance, ask garden center staff which mums are best adapted to your region.

varieties:

1 'DULUTH' Magenta petals with white zone near the center; yellow daisy center.

2 'SPARKLING CHERYL' Early-season bloomer with cheery yellow flowers atop sturdy stems. Blooms late summer to early fall.

3 'JAQUELINE' Double, rosy-lavender blooms from early to late fall. Plant is hardy and reliably overwinters. Zones 3–9.

4 'DEBONAIR' Pink-lavender flowers on strong stems, early to late fall.

5 'WARM IGLOO' Double bronze-orange blooms from early fall until frost.

Clematis *(Clematis)*

Some gardeners call clematis "queen of climbers." Beloved for its elegant blooms, this woody vine flowers from late spring to late summer in shades of blue, violet, red, white, pink, and bicolor blends. Seedheads form fuzzy balls of feathery threads. Clematis is a low-maintenance beauty, and although not truly a perennial, it fits easily into perennial gardens, weaving through plantings, adding a shrubby mound of color, or scaling a trellis.

Best site

Plant clematis in a spot that receives full sun to part shade. Give it, fertile, well-drained soil. Zones 3–9.

Growing

Count on two types of clematis to infuse your garden with color: shrubby or vining types. Vining types scramble from 4 to 12 feet, sometimes higher in milder climates, covering supports or wending through nearby shrubs or trees with the agility of a mountain goat.

When planting a clematis, dig a hole that's twice as deep as needed, and mix compost with the removed soil at a 1:1 ratio. Use this blend to backfill the planting hole and give roots a rich footing. If you garden in a region where winter brings snow, plant clematis early in the growing season to allow maximum root formation before frost. With vining types, bury 2 to 3 inches of stem, which will root into the soil. If clematis wilt attacks the vine, the buried stem will resprout and the plant will come back.

Clematis likes having its roots in shade and its leaves in sun. Mulch the root area of vines to shade and cool the soil, or plant the vines beside perennials or shrubs, which will help shade the roots. With established plants, heap compost around the base of the plants each fall. In early spring add slow-release fertilizer (compost works fine) around the plants.

These beautiful vines grow very slowly the first year; it may appear that growth is stalled, but roots are sinking into the soil. The second year, clematis vines creep along by inches. The third year, vines will leap out of the soil and begin to create a beautiful vine.

Prune vines to control growth, encourage flowering, and remove dead stems. With shrubby types, cut back to a pair of buds about 6 inches above the soil in early spring. With vining types, determine whether your clematis flowers on stems that formed last year, stems that will form during the current year, or a combination of both.

Trim vines that flower on last year's stems after they bloom. Typically, this group includes spring- and midseason-flowering varieties. Prune types that flower on the current year's growth in late winter or early spring. These are usually late bloomers. Cut young plants to 12 inches above the ground for the first three years, then to 24 inches above the soil for older plants. Clematis that bloom on new wood can quickly become overgrown and genuinely benefit from pruning.

For vines that flower on a combination of current and previous year's growth, prune vines in late winter or early spring. Pinch growing tips frequently to promote branching.

Clematis generally is pest-free, but it is susceptible to wilt disease. Affected plants seem healthy, then suddenly wilt. New growth may sprout from the base of a plant, especially if you buried the stem at planting time.

Design ideas

With shrubby clematis types, sprawling stems form a stunning groundcover that can transform a tree stump or slope into a waterfall of color. Staked, shrubby types create vertical interest. Consider growing a shrubby clematis through a tuteur-style support to form an eye-catching focal point. Or allow stems to weave gracefully through nearby shrubs or perennials.

Display vining types on a trellis, or let them scamper through a climbing rose, shrub, or small tree. Vines benefit from netting or wire fencing to help them cling to supports. Many gardeners intermingle two different clematis vines to ensure a steady show of bloom. If you do this, choose vines with similar pruning needs.

1

2

3

4

hybrid varieties:

① **'NELLY MOSER'** Large, flat, pink blooms 6 to 8 inches across with a single dark pink to lilac stripe. Flowers late spring to early summer. Plant in shade for longer-lasting blooms. Zones 4–9.

② **'COMTESSE DE BOUCHAUD'** Silvery rose blossoms 4 to 6 inches across all summer. Tolerates and flowers in part shade. Zones 4–9.

③ **'VILLE DE LYON'** Red flowers 4 to 6 inches across all summer. Zones 4–9.

④ **'MISS BATEMAN'** Heirloom clematis with blossoms to 6 inches wide. White petals initially have a pale green stripe fading to white. Contrasting chocolate red centers. Flowers late spring to early summer; second weaker bloom in late summer. Zones 5–9.

bushy clematis:

6 SOLITARY CLEMATIS (*C. integrifolia*) Bushy, sprawling mound 18 to 36 inches tall and wide. Without support, stems scramble along the ground. Large flush of nodding blue bells in late spring, continue to open sporadically through summer. Fuzzy seedheads persist into fall. 'Caerula' (porcelain blue blooms on 12- to 24-inch-tall plants). 'Rosea' (rosy-pink flowers on 24- to 36-inch-tall plants). 'Alba' (white, fragrant flowers on 24- to 36-inch-tall plants). Zones 4–9.

7 TUBE CLEMATIS (*C. heracleifolia*) Clusters of tiny blue fragrant blooms in late summer. Woody stems grow 24 to 36 inches tall and sprawl if not supported. Fuzzy seedheads persist through winter. Readily self-sows. Prune in midsummer to increase flower number and enhance clump formation. 'China Purple' (deep blue-violet bells in summer on 30- to 36-inch plants). 'Alblo', sold as Alan Bloom (large, vivid blue blooms; and stands up better than most tube clematis, except in shade, where it sprawls). Zones 5–9.

8 GROUND CLEMATIS (*C. recta*) Large clusters of fringed white flowers all summer long. Sprawls across the ground in a tangle. With stakes, stems soar to 4 feet tall and 36 inches wide. 'Purpurea' (small clusters of fragrant white blooms; leaves open purple, turning green as they mature). Zones 3–9.

9 DURAND CLEMATIS (*C. ×durandii*) 3- to 6-foot sprawling clump. Large blossoms of deep blue with yellow centers. Flowers open bell shape, then flatten to resemble other large-flower clematis. Zones 4–9.

vining clematis:

1 ALPINE CLEMATIS (*C. alpina*) Violet-blue bell-shape flowers. Zones 6–8.

2 SCARLET CLEMATIS (*C. texensis*) Nodding, small, pink, bell-shape blooms. Zones 4–8.

3 ANEMONE CLEMATIS (*C. montana*) Fast-growing vine with white blossoms. *C. montana rubra* has pink flowers. Zones 5–9.

4 JACKMAN CLEMATIS (*C.* 'Jackmanii') Large violet-purple blossoms in early summer and sporadically through summer. Zones 4–9.

5 VITICELLA CLEMATIS (*C. viticella*) Nodding flowers in hues of rose-purple, blue, and purple. Zones 5–7.

Columbine
(Aquilegia)

Beautiful and versatile, columbine decorates mid- to late spring with blossoms in blue, red, pink, white, and yellow. Leaves splash burgundy into the garden in fall. This North American native tolerates drought once established. Its flowers last long when tucked into bouquets.

Best site

Columbine thrives in part shade to full sun in rich, moist, well-drained soil. Plants prefer soils high in organic matter; mix compost into the planting hole. Zones 3–9.

Growing

These spring bloomers grow 12 inches tall and 12 to 18 inches wide. Flowers open atop stems 24 to 36 inches tall. Columbine has a short lifespan but happily self-sows. To ensure future crops of columbine, break off seedpods in late summer to early fall and sprinkle seeds in the garden. Conversely, if you have a large columbine patch, you can easily avoid excessive self-sowing by deadheading spent blooms. Trim plants to the ground after flowering to renew the planting.

Leaf miners frequently attack columbine. Remove any leaves containing tan leaf miner

trails and discard them in the trash; do not compost leaves with leaf miner damage. If the infestation is severe, cut plants to the ground in fall and remove any leaf litter around the plants, discarding it.

Design ideas

Partner columbine with other spring performers, such as moss phlox, meadow sage, or foam flower. The foliage looks nice paired with late bloomers, such as balloon flower, obedient plant, or coreopsis, or with the darker leaves of 'Chocolate Chip' or 'Black Scallop' ajuga. Columbine makes a nice cut flower in bouquets. The blooms attract hummingbirds, bees, and butterflies, giving columbine a natural place in a wildlife garden.

YOU SHOULD KNOW

If you're a hummingbird fan, tuck columbine into your garden. Their spring blooms help these zippy fliers refuel after long migratory treks.

varieties:

1. **CANADIAN COLUMBINE** (*A. canadensis*) Tall North American native growing 36 inches tall and 12 inches wide with ferny foliage. Droopy blooms with upright spurs are red outside, light yellow inside. 'Little Lanterns' (8 to 10 inches tall and wide). Zones 3–8.
2. **HYBRID COLUMBINE** Features large, upright blossoms in many different colors. McKana Hybrids (24 to 36 inches tall with flowers in blue, lavender, white, pink, red, and yellow). 'Nora Barlow' (double blooms in dark pink and white on plants 36 inches tall). 'Lime Frost' (variegated yellow and green splotched leaves on plants 14 to 18 inches tall). Zones 3–9.
3. **ROCKY MOUNTAIN COLUMBINE** (*A. caerulea*) Long-spurred blue and white blooms on 12- to 24-inch-tall plants. Zones 3–8.

Coneflower (*Echinacea purpurea*)

Tough-as-nails beauty reigns in coneflower. This drought-tolerant native of eastern North America features a rusty central cone that mimics a hedgehog in its spiny appearance. When flowers unfurl in mid- to late summer, petals fall away from the central cone, forming a purple-tinted petticoat. While the species is traditionally purple, breeding breakthroughs have added flowers in yellow, orange, cream, and burgundy.

Best site

Coneflower thrives in full sun in average, neutral to slightly alkaline, well-drained soil. Plants tolerate heat, humidity, drought, wind, and shade. Zones 3–10.

Growing

Fuss-free and fabulous coneflower grows 12 to 24 inches tall and 18 inches wide. Flower stems add another 12 inches to overall height. This low-maintenance plant is sturdy and rarely needs staking. When grown in rich soil, it has a tendency to become floppy and require staking. Use grow-through or linking supports (see page 151) to corral the entire clump.

Deadhead plants to prevent self-sowing and extend bloom time. With the straight species, if plants self-sow, seedlings will come true to the parent. With newer varieties and hybrids, however, seeds won't produce plants that mimic the parents.

Goldfinches and other birds like to feast on seeds. Allow a few stems to set seeds starting in fall to provide some winter forage. If you allow seedheads to remain for winter interest, cut back the stems in early spring. Otherwise, trim plants in late fall.

Divide clumps every four to five years, saving exterior portions of the clump and discarding any woody sections from the heart of the clump. Transplant the offsets that form around the base of the plant.

Deer-resistant coneflower is pest free, although crowded clumps can contract a viral condition known as stem dieback. If this condition manifests in your coneflower, there is no cure. Dig and discard the clump.

Design ideas

Coneflower is a great perennial for a wildlife garden—butterflies sip the blossom nectar; birds munch the seeds. Pair it with other critter-friendly plants, such as false indigo, ornamental grasses, showy sedum, or garden phlox, to outfit a wildlife bed-and-breakfast.

Coneflower shines when planted with balloon flower, white guara, globe thistle, and Russian sage. It's a natural plant to include in sunny borders, cottage gardens, and streetside plantings. Combine it with gayfeather, caryopteris, 'Autumn Joy' sedum, and blue fescue for a drought-tolerant planting with season-long good looks. Coneflower makes a wonderful addition to garden bouquets; flowers last long in the vase.

Names to watch for

MEADOWBRITE SERIES Semidroopy to flat daisies with slender petals. Height varies from 18 to 30 inches, making this group a clear choice for container plantings.

Mango Meadowbrite Yellow daisies on 30-inch stems. **Orange Meadowbrite** Orange-petaled daisies on 24- to 36-inch-tall stems.

Pixie Meadowbrite Pink blooms on dwarf 18-inch plants. Zones 5–9.

BIG SKY SERIES Semidroopy petals on blossoms with a fragrance like roses. Most are 18 to 24 inches tall.

'Harvest Moon' Orangish yellow petals surround a golden orange central cone. **'After Midnight'** Magenta-purple petals with a black cone; 12-inch stems.

'Summer Sky' Petals cherry red at the base fading to peach at the tips.

'Sunrise' Glowing buttery yellow blooms.

'Sunset' Bright orange daisies with dark orange centers on 30-inch stems. Zones 5–9.

YOU SHOULD KNOW
Coneflowers beckon butterflies and bees during the flowering season, and as seeds ripen, birds like goldfinches flock to feast from the spiny, seed-laden cones.

varieties and species:

❶ **'MAGNUS'** Bright rose-pink blooms with a sienna-tone cone open on 24- to 36-inch stems. Petals stand out rather than droop. Zones 2–9.

❷ **'RAZZMATAZZ'** Fully double with purple-pink petals forming a fringe surrounding a puffy, pom-pom center. Stems are 36 inches tall. Flowers develop normally at first, with traditional cones forming, then petals begin to emerge from the central cone, until the pom-pom is fully formed. Zones 5–10.

❸ **'FRAGRANT ANGEL'** Double, white, fragrant coneflower. Petals held out horizontally from cone. Zones 4–10.

❹ **TENNESSEE CONEFLOWER** (*E. tennesseensis*) Pink, flat-top flowers. Zones 5–9.

Coral Bells (*Heuchera*)

Celebrate variety when you add coral bells to your perennial garden. Colorful foliage unfolds in shades of purple, pink, silver, amber, chartreuse, and various combinations of these—and other—hues. Leaf form includes lobed, ruffled, rounded, and frilled. Dainty bell-shape blooms appear as loose spikes in late spring to early summer. Flowers are typically red, pink, or white and attract hummingbirds.

Best site

Plant in full sun to part shade. In cool climates, full sun is fine; plants need part shade in hot regions. Some hybrids with pale foliage hybrids need more shade for the leaves to develop the strongest hue. Give coral bells moist, well-drained soil rich in organic matter. Mix compost into the planting hole to increase the organic matter content. Zones 3–10.

Growing

This low-maintenance perennial grows 6 to 10 inches tall and wide; flower stems add another 12 to 24 inches to height. Deadhead flowers, removing the entire spike, to allow foliage to take center stage. Remove any dead leaves in spring; use clippers to avoid dislodging the plant.

Coral bells is susceptible to frost heave. Prevent this by mulching plants after the ground freezes. Laying evergreen boughs over plants also helps insulate the soil. Divide plants every few years to stimulate flowering.

Design ideas

Coral bells is one of the perennial garden's most versatile players. Ideal for mixing with other perennials in cottage and woodland gardens, it also forms an attractive edging along beds and paths. Grow it at the front of a perennial border as edging, or use one of the boldly tinted hybrids as a focal points. Amber-tinted coral bells blend especially well with other perennial foliage.

Mass coral bells as a groundcover under trees. In this use, you'll need to apply 1 to 2 inches of compost every fall to give roots a boost of easily accessible nourishment.

Next to large-leaf hosta, coral bells foliage takes on a fine textural appearance. With astilbe, the leaves appear to have a chunkier texture. In a sunny border, pair coral bells with 'May Night' meadow sage or coreopsis.

Names to watch for
PURPLE FOLIAGE

'Obsidian' Deep black-purple leaves tolerate heat and humidity. 10 inches tall and 16 inches wide. Zones 5–7.
'Berry Smoothie' Rose-pink foliage on plants 18 inches tall and 20 inches wide. Zones 4–9.
'Chocolate Ruffle' Leaves chocolate color on top and reddish purple underneath. 10 inches tall and 12 inches wide. Zones 3–9.

AMBER FOLIAGE

'Amber Waves' Ruffled amber-gold foliage shows strongest color on new growth. Use as a neutral color with other perennials, blends with every shade. 8 inches tall and 17 inches wide.
'Southern Comfort' Leaves emerge peachy-orange, mature to amber, turn coral-orange in fall. Tolerates heat and humidity. 14 inches tall and 24 inches wide. Zones 4–8.

CHARTREUSE FOLIAGE

Dolce Key Lime Pie Bright chartreuse leaves with prominent veins and mottling. Color darkens in cool weather. Clump grows to 16 inches wide. Zones 4–8.

YOU SHOULD KNOW
Some gardeners grow coral bells solely for the foliage and actually dislike the blooms, cutting stalks as soon as they appear. Coral bells blossom spikes make long-lasting cut flowers, adding an airy touch to bouquets.

varieties:

❶ 'PARIS' Silvery leaves with dark green veins. Strong flower show on plants 9 inches tall and 15 inches wide. Zones 4–8.

❷ 'PEWTER VEIL' Metallic silver foliage with purple-gray veins on plants 12 inches tall and 12 to 18 inches wide. Zones 4–9.

Coreopsis (*Coreopsis*)

Low-maintenance, long-blooming coreopsis fills a garden with color all summer long. Yellow daisies with notched petals open in early to midsummer and continue until frost. Blossoms rise above large species but hover like butterflies over short kinds.

YOU SHOULD KNOW
Nothing stops coreopsis, except rich, wet soil. In this setting, even short-stemmed types can grow lanky and flop. Stake stems with grow-through supports.

Best site
Plant coreopsis in full sun in moist, well-drained soil. This workhorse perennial tolerates heat and drought but won't flourish in soil that stays moist through winter. Zones 4–10.

Growing
Plants grow 6 to 36 inches high and 12 to 36 inches wide. Deadhead to encourage flower formation by shearing the whole plant back after blossoms fade; use grass shears or scissors. In late fall or early spring, cut plants to the ground. Divide plants every three years in spring. In shaded locations, powdery mildew often attacks coreopsis leaves.

Design ideas
Coreopsis is a natural fit in wildflower or prairie gardens, along with perennials like coneflower, gayfeather, and blanket flower. It stages a low-maintenance, season-long performance in a sunny border and also thrives in container gardens. The yellow blossoms look lovely with blue bloomers, such as globe thistle, lavender, and Russian sage. Add coreopsis to a wildlife garden, since its blossoms beckon hummingbirds and butterflies.

Names to watch for
TICKSEED COREOPSIS (*C. grandiflora*)

'Early Sunrise' Yellow flowers on 24-inch stems that rise above over 12-inch foliage. Long season of bloom if deadheaded regularly.
'Baby Sun' Fine-texture leaves with 2-inch daisies on 20-inch stems.
'Rising Sun' Yellow flowers on 24-inch stems that hover over 12-inch foliage.

THREADLEAF COREOPSIS (*C. verticillata*)

'Moonbeam' small, pale yellow daisies on 8 to 10-inch-tall plant with fine, threadlike leaves. Fast growing with a long season of bloom. Zones 4–10.

'Crème Brulee' Butter yellow daisies on sturdier stems than 'Moonbeam'; Grows 12 inches tall and 36 inches wide. Good powdery mildew resistance.
'Zagreb' Bright yellow daisies on plant up to 24 inches tall.

species and varieties:

① LANCELEAF COREOPSIS (*C. lanceolata*) Yellow 2-inch-wide daisies on 24-inch-tall plant. 'Sterntaler' (gold daisies with burgundy-brown eye). Zones 3–8.
② PINK COREOPSIS (*C. rosea*) Fine, threadlike leaves with tiny, pink daisies. Zones 7–9. 'Sweet Dreams' (white daisies with raspberry centers. Zones 6–8).
③ 'AUTUMN BLUSH' Gold daisies with mahogany red centers on 36-inch stems. Zones 5–9.

Crocosmia
(Crocosmia)

Summer sizzles when you add exotic crocosmia to the garden. Brilliant yellow, orange, or fiery red blossoms open in mid- to late summer atop long stems that soar from a clump of sword-shape leaves. Flowers form 2-inch-wide trumpets displayed side by side along a horizontal stem.

Best site
Plant in full sun to light shade in rich, moist, well-drained soil. Water frequently and mulch. Zones 5–11.

Growing
This bold bloomer tolerates heat and humidity, making it an excellent choice for Southern gardens. Wet soil, poor drainage, or droughty conditions lead up to a poor performance. Winter loss is normally caused by poor drainage.

Design ideas
Crocosmia infuses a sense of tropical beauty into plantings. Use it as a midsize perennial tucked in the middle of the border or plant in clumps for a strong presence. Ornamental grasses make wonderful planting companions, as do perennials with orange, yellow, or white blossoms.

varieties:

1 **'LUCIFER'** Fiery red flowers on 36- to 42-inch tall stems.
'EMBERGLOW' Orange-red blooms with a hint of blue.

Culver's Root
(Veronicastrum virginicum)

Give your garden a native touch with culver's root, a tall, clump-forming perennial. Bluish white spires about 5 inches long reach above leaves from early summer to fall. Tiny blossoms opening from the bottom of the spike upward. The flowers attract butterflies and bees.

Best site
Plant culver's root in part shade to full sun, giving it moist soil high in organic matter. This native of eastern North America tolerates heat and humidity. Zones 4–8.

Growing
This high-rise perennial grows 4 to 6 feet tall and 2 to 4 feet wide. Deadheading prolongs blooming. Cut the entire plant back in late fall or early spring. If your plant tends to topple, insert grow-through supports early in the growing season.

Design ideas
Culver's root belongs at the back of the border, where its strong architectural presence handily anchors a planting bed. Use it as a vertical accent. Pair it with mounding bloomers, such as hardy hibiscus, or ornamental grasses, like miscanthus grass.

varieties:

1 **'ALBUM'** White flower spires tipped with green. Flowers open midsummer to midfall.
'ERICA' Red buds contrast with pale pink flowers. Blooms midsummer to early fall.

Daylily *(Hemerocallis)*

A perennial favorite, daylilies are true garden heroes, with showy blossoms backed by easy-growing dispositions. These hardy and robust plants cope with nearly every growing condition. The flowers, which live for one day and open from late spring to frost, come in nearly every color imaginable; the only missing hues in the palette are pure white and blue. With more than 30,000 daylily varieties, you can find the flower of your dreams.

Best site

Daylilies thrive in full sun to part shade in moist, humus-rich, well-drained soil—but they'll grow in nearly any condition. Plants adapt to drought, heat, shade, wind, salt spray, flooding, and foot traffic, but many of these conditions diminish the flower show. You'll be rewarded with the most flowers when you give daylilies soil that's rich in organic matter. Zones 3 to 11.

Growing

Size varies among different daylily cultivars, but typically plants grow 18 to 30 inches tall and 18 inches wide. Flower stems skyrocket above the arching fountain of foliage. You'll see increased blossom numbers when plants receive adequate water until bloom time. Flowers last one day, and plants look best when faded blooms are snapped from flowering stems. Use caution when deadheading; don't accidentally snap developing flower buds. When all buds on a flowering stem have opened, cut the entire stem as far back in the clump of foliage as possible.

Plant or divide at any point in the growing season. Early spring is the least stressful on plants, but you can also divide after flowering. If you divide later in the season, cut back foliage on divisions by two-thirds before replanting to reduce stress on developing roots. Daylilies typically need dividing every three to five years, or whenever you start seeing flower numbers diminish. For the maximum number of blooms, divide plants every three years.

Pests include slugs, snails, woodchucks, deer, and rabbits. Daylily rust and leaf streak can also infect plants. To limit diseases, give daylilies optimum growing conditions or plant disease-resistant cultivars.

Design ideas

Daylilies fit nearly any garden use. These rugged plants survive competition from tree roots, sparkle in heat-baked parking strips, and flourish in containers. Mass daylilies for a flowering, low-maintenance groundcover or plant a few choice specimens in a mixed border for a steady parade of color. For a summerlong daylily show, choose cultivars with different flowering windows.

once-blooming varieties:

❶ **'PEACH SUMMER DANCE'** Peach-apricot flowers early in the season on plants 24 to 36 inches tall and wide.

❷ **'HYPERION'** Fragrant, large, lemon yellow flowers through peak summer on plants 36 inches tall.

❸ **'RUBY SPIDER'** Deep red, spider-type flowers with gold throats. Early season bloomer to 36 inches tall.

YOU SHOULD KNOW
In cold climates, frost heave can lead to crown rot during the first year of growth. Mulch newly planted daylilies for their first two winters to help plants establish.

reblooming varieties:

1 'STELLA DE ORO' Gold flowers all summer on 12-inch plants.

2 'EARLY BIRD CARDINAL' Bright red, 4-inch blooms with contrasting gold throats start blooming early in the season. 21-inch stems.

3 'LAVENDER VISTA' Large lavender blooms with yellow and green throats on 24-inch stems.

4 'BITSY' Lemon yellow flowers from spring to fall on plants 17 to 28 inches tall. Zones 4–9.

5 'LADY ELIZABETH' 5-inch, ruffled, near-white blossoms with a rich green throat. 18 to 28 inches tall and wide.

Delphinium
(*Delphinium*)

Delphiniums grace a garden with a stately air, thanks to their lofty stems that soar above the shiny foliage. Blossoms come in hues of blue, pink, white, or purple in early to midsummer. These plants thrive in cool-summer areas but can make a striking show in other regions.

YOU SHOULD KNOW

With tall types, staking is key to beautiful delphiniums. Single stakes provide sturdy stem support; branches effectively support the lower portion of flower stems.

Best site

Plant delphiniums in full sun to light shade. Give plants rich, moist, well-drained soil high in organic matter. Avoid sites where winds whip through the garden. Zones 3–10.

Growing

Delphinium foliage grows 12 to 36 inches tall and 36 inches wide. Flower stems reach 18 inches to 7 feet. These elegant bloomers are heavy feeders. Satisfy their appetites by heaping compost around plants in early spring. Chemical fertilizers high in nitrogen produce foliage at the expense of flowers.

Stake blossom stems as they start to soar. Use single stakes, tying stems every 12 inches, or insert grow-through or branches to support the lower portion of flower stems. This type of staking exposes tall stems to wind damage; be prepared to stake individual flower stems if high winds are forecast.

Cut flower stems back inside the mound of foliage to hide spent stems. After frost zaps foliage, cut stems back to 1 or 2 inches above the soil. Delphinium are usually short-lived perennials, lasting three to five years. In the South, plant delphiniums in the fall, treating them as cool-season annuals.

Leaf spot disease, crown rot, and powdery mildew can affect plants. Pests include slugs, snails, and stem borers.

Design ideas

Delphinium infuses any design with English-garden charm. Position tall types toward the back of the border, pairing them with other towering plants, such as joy-pye weed.

species and varieties:

❶ **BELLADONNA GROUP** Multiple flower stalks. Perform better in warm climes. 1 to 2 feet tall with 3- to 4-foot flower stems. 'Bellamosum' (bright, deep blue flowers).

❷ **CENTURION STRAIN** Double blooms in blue, rose, and white on 4- to 6-foot stems. Zones 3–7.

❸ **CHINESE DELPHINIUM** (*D. grandiflorum*) Flowers in loose spikes. 'Blue Butterfly' (deep blue flowers with a hint of purple; 14 inches tall). Zones 3–9.

❹ **PACIFIC GIANT GROUP** 'Round Table' comes in blue and purple shades, white, or bicolors on 5- to 6-foot-tall stems.

❺ **PACIFIC GIANT GROUP** 'Magic Fountains' (dark-eyed blue, pink, and white blooms on 30- to 36-inch-tall plants). 'Summer Skies' (sky-blue flowers on 5- to 6-foot stems in early summer).

Evening Primrose
(Oenothera)

These are fast-growing North American natives. Some, like Ozark sundrops, open their flowers in the evening. Others, such as evening primrose, open flowers during the day. Blossoms of both types last only a few days, but flower buds are continually forming.

Best site
Plant evening primrose in full sun in well-drained soil. Zones 4–9.

Growing
Evening primrose spreads quickly by seeds or spreading roots. Deadheading extends blooming and prevents self-sowing.

After flowering, cut back upright growers by one-third to promote fresh growth. You can also cut plants to the ground. Divide plants every four or five years in spring or early fall, discarding the central portion of the clump.

Design ideas
Evening primrose is a vigorous spreader, which works well in wildflower gardens, meadows, or wildlife gardens. Good companion plants include 'Karl Foerster' feather reed grass and catmint.

False Indigo
(Baptisia australis)

An easy-care, long-lived perennial, false indigo brings understated beauty to the garden. In late spring to early summer blue flower spires steal the show, but afterwards it's the blue-green foliage and its subtle, steady note of color. Blossoms fade to form eye-catching seedpods.

Best site
Give false indigo full to part sun and lean, well-drained to dry soil. Zones 3–10.

Growing
False indigo is slow to awaken in spring; mark the planting to avoid disturbing the crown. Stems often flop after flowering. Cut spring growth back by one-third to encourage strong stems. To let seedpods ripen, insert grow-through supports over clumps in early spring. False indigo doesn't transplant well. Cut the plant back to the ground in late fall and early spring.

Design ideas
Use this drought-tolerant, deer-resistant beauty in wildlife gardens. Plant with prairie favorites, such as blanket flower, gayfeather, coneflower, or black-eyed susan.

YOU SHOULD KNOW
Dried seedpods of false indigo make a clattering noise when shaken and were often used by pioneer children as rattles. Use them in dried flower arrangements; the foliage makes a stunning addition to fresh bouquets.

species:

1 SUNDROPS (*O. fruticosa*) Upright spreader with large yellow blooms atop sturdy stems in summer. Native to eastern North America. Thrives in moist, well-drained soil. Zones 4–9.

species and varieties:

1 FALSE INDIGO The species grows 4 to 5 feet tall, and bears pale to deep blue spires of blooms. **'CAROLINA MOONLIGHT'** Pale yellow flowers on 40- to 50-inch stems. Zones 4–9.

False Sunflower
(*Heliopsis helianthoides*)

Give your perennial garden a touch of sunflower cheer with one of its cousins, false sunflower. This fast-growing beauty opens yellow daisies from early to late summer. The 3-inch-wide blooms attract butterflies and make a wonderful addition to seasonal bouquets.

Best site

Plant in full sun and well-drained soil high in organic matter. Provide afternoon shade in the hottest regions. False sunflower tolerates part shade, drought, and a variety of soil types including heavy clay. Poorly drained soil, however, yields a lackluster performance and a long, slow death. Zones 3–9.

Growing

False sunflower grows 3 to 6 feet tall and 2 to 4 feet wide. Deadheading prolongs blooming and prevents self-sowing. With dwarf and variegated types, seedlings don't come true to parents and are typically inferior plants. Floppy stems signal a need for sunnier growing conditions, better drainage, or more water and fertilizer. If growing well and in tight quarters, plants may require support to maintain a tidy, upright, vase shape.

Use grow-through or linking supports as shown on page 151.

Design ideas

Include false sunflower in planting beds for its long bloom time. Nectar-laden blooms suit a wildlife or meadow garden, luring butterflies, bees, and hummingbirds. Flowers last long in a vase. Use false sunflower as a backdrop in the garden, or skirt it with short bloomers such as meadow sage, catmint, or blanket flower to form an eye-pleasing combination. Pair it with crocosmia for a texturally striking foliage display. It works well in prairie gardens, combined with native grasses and Russian sage.

varieties:

 'SUMMER SUN' Soft yellow, double flowers on 3- to 5-foot stems. Plants are taller in northern areas; shorter in the South. Heat tolerant. Good choice for Southern gardens.

❷ **'LORAINE SUNSHINE'** White leaves with green veins. Yellow daisies on 30-inch stems.

❸ **'TUSCAN SUN'** Yellow, 2-inch blooms with an orange-gold center. Dwarf plant 12 to 24 inches tall and 9 to 15 inches wide.

Ferns

Woodland gardens and shady borders come to life when ferns are added to the mix. These graceful, native plants introduce unique textures in a package that's deer resistant. A foliage plant, ferns blend well with many other perennials and add unique visual interest to shade garden plantings.

Best site

Give ferns part to full shade and rich, well-drained soil. Plants need protection from afternoon sun in all climates to prevent drying and leaf scorch. Zones 3–10.

Growing

Ferns can grow from 12 inches to 6 feet tall, depending on the species. These foliage standouts prefer a humusy, acid soil; mix ample compost into the planting holes and mulch annually with composted oak leaves. Ferns aren't demanding in their care. Keep the soil moist with mulch, provide shade, and your plants will flourish.

Divide ferns in spring or fall. Keep divisions well watered until plants are established. Ferns are generally pest free.

Design ideas

In a woodland setting, ferns introduce an elegant element with arching, artistic-looking fronds. These foliage favorites combine effortlessly with other shade-loving perennials, such as hosta, solomon's seal, astilbe, and heart-leaf brunnera. Combine different types of ferns to craft a textural masterpiece.

You can also count on ferns to form a low-maintenance groundcover that suppresses weeds. Use ferns in this way beneath trees with high canopies that create light shade, on a slope, or in a woodland garden.

Names to watch for

CHRISTMAS FERNS (*Polystichum*)
Upright, evergreen ferns offer medium to bold texture with lustrous green fronds. These ferns thrive in moist, well-drained soil in light to full shade. Continually moist soil is key to healthy plants. Clip brown leaves in early spring before new growth emerges.

Western sword fern (*P. munitum*) Glossy deep green fronds 3 to 4 feet tall and wide. Medium texture. Plants thrive in coastal settings. Zones 5–10.

Tassel fern (*P. polyblepharum*) Dark glossy evergreen fronds 18 to 24 inches tall and 10 inches wide. Grows well in containers. Zones 6–10.

HAY-SCENTED FERN (*Dennstaedtia punctilobula*) Fronds smell like hay when bruised or crushed. This upright native fern has arching, yellow-green lacy fronds that form a beautiful woodland groundcover. Plants grow 36 inches tall and wide. Hay-scented fern tolerates a range of growing conditions, but thrives in part to deep shade and rich, moist, well-drained, slightly acid soil. Established plants tolerate dry shade. Zone 3–8.

SENSITIVE FERN (*Onoclea sensibilis*)

Light green, wide fronds introduce a coarse texture and grow up to 24 inches tall. This wide-spreading fern prefers moist shade and forms an excellent groundcover for moist shade or beside shaded ponds. Also known as bead fern. Zones 3–8.

YOU SHOULD KNOW
Ferns can be slow to awaken in spring, lingering long in winter slumber. If you have a specimen fern in a planting bed, consider marking its location to avoid mulching over its crown in early spring.

LADY FERNS (*Athyrium*)
Forms vary greatly, from upright to spreading. Fronds are deciduous. Plants grow best in part to full shade in soil with a neutral pH.

Japanese painted fern (*A. niponicum* 'Pictum') Silver fronds brushed with red and blue tints unfurl atop burgundy stems. Reaches 12 to 18 inches tall and to 24 inches wide. Grows in dark corners, but fronds color best when receiving at least a few hours of morning sunshine. Thrives in containers or planting beds. Zones 4–9.

MAIDENHAIR FERNS (*Adiantum*)
Airy, delicate-looking ferns have a hardy disposition that thrives in full shade to part sun. Prefer neutral to alkaline soil enriched with organic matter. Slender stalks unfurl broad leaflets at the tip of the stem, creating an umbrella-like appearance. Plants are striking when grouped in a woodland or shady border.

Northern maidenhair fern (*A. pedatum*) Upright blackish purple stems topped with arching branchlets arranged like fingers on a hand. Tough but dainty fern is deciduous and grows 24 inches tall and wide. Prefers dappled shade. New growth on 'Miss Sharples' (light yellow-green new growth; leaflets larger than species). 'Japonicum' (pinkish bronze new growth). Zones 5–8.

Southern maidenhair fern (*A. capillus-veneris*) Bright green fronds on blackish stems 18 to 24 inches tall. Native to the southern half of the United States. Thrives in heat and humidity; requires consistently moist soil. Part to full shade. Zones 7–10.

OSMUNDAS (*Osmunda*) One of the largest ferns for home gardens. Plants require very moist soil to survive and grow in light to full shade.

Cinnamon fern (*O. cinnamomea*) Deciduous fern that grows wild in moist to wet soils in sun or shade. Sterile light green fronds can reach 5 feet tall in a 24-inch-wide clump. The center of the plant bears erect, 36-inch-tall reddish brown spore-bearing fronds. Grow at the edge of ponds or in woodlands. Zones 4–9.

Interrupted fern (*O. claytoniana*) Forms clumps 36 inches tall and 6 feet wide. Upright fronds bow at the tips; leaflets bearing spore cases form at the center of fronds, producing an interrupted appearance. Zones 3–6.

Royal fern (*O. regalis*) Leathery light green, deciduous foliage turns gold in fall. Thrives in part shade. Clumps grow 2 to 6 feet tall in wet, boggy, or lakeside soils. Zones 4–9.

OSTRICH FERN (*Matteuccia struthiopteris*) Forms a vase-shape clump 36 inches tall and wide. In ideal growing conditions, fronds can stretch to 6 feet. A classic fern look that spreads rapidly by thick, braided rhizomes. Do not plant this fern in combination with other tidy, clump-forming perennials. It will overpower them. Give ostrich fern a shady spot to roam, and it will form a luxurious groundcover with a jungle effect. Average to moist soil is ideal. Tolerates sun as long as the soil never dries. When soil dries in shady locations, fronds burn; they're that sensitive to dry soil. Zones 3–8.

WOOD FERNS (*Dryopteris*) Tough and adaptable, medium-size ferns offer strong form and texture in the shade garden. Some species are evergreen; others are deciduous. These woodland ferns prefer neutral to acid, well-drained, fertile soil high in organic matter. Dividing clumps every three years or so maintains the symmetrical form. Undivided clumps become large and unattractive.

Male wood fern (*D. filix-mas*) Fronds form a clump 36 inches tall and wide. Can be evergreen in protected locations. Zones 3–8.
Autumn fern (*D. erythrosora*) Coppery new growth matures to green; ruddy fall color. Evergreen fern grows to 18 inches tall and wide.

Goldie's fern (*D. goldiana*) Light green fronds in clump feet tall and 24 inches wide. Zones 6–8.
Marginal shield fern (*D. marginalis*) Evergreen fronds grow 18 inches tall and 24 inches wide. Zones 3–8.

Foam Flower
(*Tiarella*)

Foam flower forms a wonderful groundcover in woodland settings or shady borders in midspring. White or pink blooms open on spikes held above the short foliage. Lobed leaves offer long lasting interest in summer and display degrees of autumn color.

Best site

Plant foam flower in part to full shade in moist, well-drained, humus-rich soil. Foam flower doesn't tolerate drought. Zones 3–9.

Growing

Space plants 12 to 15 inches apart. There's no need to cut growth back in fall. Divide plants every three to four years to curtail their spread. Between dividing sessions, pull runners to keep foam flower in check.

Design ideas

Foam flower thrives in moist woodland settings and shady borders. This diminutive groundcover grows nicely with other shade-loving perennials, such as ferns and yellow corydalis. It's especially lovely planted with bleeding heart, lenten rose, and barrenwort.

Foamy Bells
(×*Heucherella*)

Foamy bells results from a cross between coral bells and foam flower. Flower spikes carry bell-shape blooms in white, pink, or cream. Leafy mounds shift in color through the season, displaying marbled greens to burgundy, bronze, chartreuse, purple, and yellow.

Best site

Plant in full sun to part shade in rich, moist, well-drained soil, preferably high in organic matter. Plants can adapt to full shade, but yellow- and pale-tone varieties may burn. Zones 4–10.

Growing

Pest- and disease-resisant foamy bells grows 5 to 9 inches tall and wide, 15 to 23 inches in bloom. Plants require consistently moist soil; mulch to conserve soil moisture. Add compost in early spring to maintain high organic matter.

Design ideas

Use foamy bells to edge a border or path. Mass it beneath shrubs; match leaf color to a flowering shrub's blooms. It's excellent in containers. Companions include hosta, cranesbill geranium, and black mondo grass.

species and varieties:

① **ALLEGHENY FOAM FLOWER** (*T. cordifolia*) Midspring white or pink blooms above green leaves.
② **'BLACK SNOWFLAKE'** Leaves have dark purple veins and nearly black new growth. Zones 4–9.

varieties:

① **'RUNNING TAPESTRY'** Leaves change hues from blue, to green with rich burgundy veins. **'GOLDEN ZEBRA'** Bright yellow leaves with maroon centers on deeply cut leaves. Zones 6–10.

Gayfeather
(*Liatris*)

Introduce vertical interest to a sunny planting with gayfeather. A prairie native, it sends up tall purple flower spikes that open in early to midsummer. Grassy leaves whorl around stems. Foliage and flowers combine to create a bottlebrush effect—a striking plant form.

YOU SHOULD KNOW

Blossom spikes open from the top down, creating color that lingers in the garden over several weeks. The flowers are a favorite of butterflies and bees.

Best site

Plant gayfeather in full sun in fertile, well-drained soil. Established plants are drought, heat, and wind tolerant. Zones 3–10.

Growing

Sturdy stems form a clump roughly 12 inches tall and wide. Flower spikes soar 2 to 5 feet. Tall plants may require staking, especially when grown in average to dry soil. Use single stakes or insert grow-through supports in early spring. Deadhead after flowering to extend blooming and prevent self-sowing. Remove spent stems at the base. In late fall or early spring, cut plants back to the ground.

Divide gayfeather every three to five years in spring to maintain plant health. Plants grow from tuberous roots and transplant easily. Slugs

and snails occasionally trouble gayfeather, but for the most part, these plants are pest free.

Design ideas

Include gayfeather in wildlife or prairie gardens, where its drought-tolerant nature and nectar-laden blooms will easily earn the plant its keep. Count on this upright beauty to add vertical interest to planting beds, containers, and cut flower arrangements.

In combinations, gayfeather shines when partnered with larger, coarser leaves and mounded plant forms. Plant it with tree mallow, bearded iris, geranium, or hardy hibiscus. Gayfeather also shines when partnered with ornamental grasses or perennials bearing daisy-like blooms, such as false sunflower, coneflower, or black-eyed susan.

species varieties:

❶ KANSAS GAYFEATHER (*L. pycnostachya*) Mauve-purple flower spikes to 20 inches on plants that grow 5 feet tall. Stems require staking. Moist, well-drained soil. Zones 3–9.

❷ SPIKE GAYFEATHER (*L. spicata*) Plants grow 3 to 4 feet tall and 24 inches wide. Flower stems comprise 6 to 15 inches of overall height. Mauve-purple blooms in early to midsummer. 'Alba' (white flowers on 40-inch plants). 'Floristan Violet' (violet blooms on strong stems; excellent choice for cut flowers). 'Floristan White' (white blooms; strong stems). 'Kobold' (rosy-purple spikes on 24-inch plant). Zones 3–10.

Geranium
(*Geranium*)

Perennial geraniums introduce carefree color in plants that form spreading clumps or round mounds. Five-petaled flowers in shades of blue and pink accent lobed foliage. Blossom time varies. Some geranium species have foliage that displays autumn hues—red, gold, or orange.

Best site

Geraniums grow in full sun to full shade. In a full sun setting, plants need good watering. In heavy shade, flower numbers may diminish. Ideal conditions are a half day of full sun. Plants need part shade in the South and West. Give geraniums moist, moderately fertile, well-drained soil. Zones 3–9.

Growing

Plant size varies based on species, but geraniums grow from 4 inches to 4 feet tall and to 36 inches wide. Deadheading isn't necessary for rebloom. After the first flush of flowers, shear plants near the base to promote new, tidy growth and prevent self-sowing. Trim frost-damaged foliage in late fall or early spring. Geraniums are easy to transplant. Divide plants every five to six years to renew vigor.

Design ideas

Geraniums prove versatile in the perennial garden. Vary border position based on plant size. Give short types a front-of-the-border position; tall types can nestle mid-border. Once established, geraniums form a dense flowering groundcover, even beneath trees. These hardy bloomers are also perfect for creating soft mounds around the base of leggy shrubs. Team geraniums with ornamental grasses, asters, and 'Autumn Joy' sedum for a pretty fall planting.

Names to watch for

BIGROOT GERANIUM (*G. macrorrhizum*)
In spring magenta blossoms open in spring on 18-inch-tall stems that form a dense, weed-smothering groundcover. Ideally sited in full sun and well-drained, moist soil; also grows in dry shade. Leaves develop red and yellow fall color. Don't shear after flowering; foliage looks good all season. Zones 5–8.
'Bevan's Variety' Deep magenta flowers all summer long on plants 12 inches tall and 18 inches wide.

BLOODY CRANESBILL

(*G. sanguineum*) Free-flowering plant tolerates heat and cold better than other geranium species. Brilliant magenta blooms from spring into summer on spreading plants 18 inches tall and 36 inches wide.

'Alba' White blooms on plants 6 to 12 inches tall. Light-color flowers show up nicely in part shade. Zones 4–8.

Striped bloody cranesbill
(*G. sanguineum striatum*) Pale pink flowers striped with magenta in late spring to early summer. Sporadic rebloom through summer. Foliage turns red in autumn. Zones 4–10.

YOU SHOULD KNOW

Geraniums combine several admirable qualities to earn a place in any garden: drought tolerance, deer and rabbit resistance, and summerlong color. With dozens of species, the hardest part of growing geraniums is figuring out which ones to grow.

HYBRID GERANIUMS

'Brookside' Blue flowers with white eyes appear on plants 24 inches tall and 36 inches wide. Foliage turns red in fall. Zones 4–7.

'Rozanne' Violet-blue blooms 2½ inches across from early summer to fall on plant 20 inches tall and 24 inches wide. Marbled dark green leaves turn mahogany in fall. Zones 5–8.

'Johnson's Blue' Best known of the blue geraniums, reknowned for clear blue, 2-inch-wide flowers. Cut back after flowering. Plant grows 12 to 24 inches high and wide. Zones 5–8.

'Summer Skies' bears violet-blue blooms above 2-foot-tall and wide mounds of gray-green foliage.

'Wisley Blue' produces blue blooms on 24-inch-tall plants.

MEADOW CRANESBILL

Meadow cranesbill (*G. pratense*) Late spring purple flowers on plant 36 inches tall and 24 inches wide. Cut to the ground after flowering. Zones 5–7.

'Midnight Reiter' Dark purple leaves throughout the growing season. Violet flowers in spring. Zones 5–8.

'Splish-Splash' White blossoms streaked, daubed, and splashed with blue to lavender. Mounding plant 30 inches tall and 24 inches wide. Cut back after first bloom to induce more flowers. Zones 4–8.

Globe Thistle
(*Echinops bannaticus*)

Globe thistle fills midsummer with spiny, deep blue, globe flowers. The 2-inch-diameter blooms last a month; use for fresh or dried cut flowers. Leaves unfurl gray-green above and downy white beneath. Plants resist browsing critters, but the blooms lure bees and butterflies.

Best site

Plant in full sun in well-drained soil. Easy-to-grow globe thistle thrives in many soils—fertile, poor, or sandy—but it demands good winter drainage. Zones 4–9.

Growing

Plants grow 36 inches tall and 24 inches wide. Fertile soil yields floppy stems. This thistle isn't invasive, but deadheading prevents self-sowing and keeps plants looking good. Stems may rebloom if pruned to basal leaves after flowering. Divide plants every four years in early spring.

Design ideas

Use globe thistle in sunny borders, cottage gardens, roadside beds, or seaside plantings. The blooms blend nicely with pink muhly grass or gayfeather.

species and varieties:

❶ 'ARCTIC GLOW' (*E. sphaerocephalus*) Red stems bear 2-inch white globes. Zones 5–8.

'STAR FROST' Pearly white blooms on stems 36 inches tall and 18 inches wide.

Goatsbeard
(*Aruncus dioicus*)

Goatsbeard brightens shady nooks with open plumes of white flowers in early summer. Ferny, deep green leaves unfurl a coarse texture to create plants with strong architectural interest. Goatsbeard's large stature provides a striking backdrop in any shaded setting.

Best site

Plant in part shade in moist, well-drained soil. In cool-summer climates, full sun is fine; in warm regions, provide afternoon shade. Plants don't thrive in heat and humidity. Zones 3–9.

Growing

Goatsbeard grows 24 to 36 inches tall (4 to 6 feet in flower) and 4 feet wide. Deadhead to keep seedheads from forming. In hot conditions, leaf spot and rust diseases can develop. Dry soil causes leaf scorch. Plants are difficult to move. Thick roots often require a chainsaw to divide.

Design ideas

This tall perennial is a natural choice for a shady stream or pondside planting. Use it to accent a moist woodland garden. It partners well with hosta, ferns, astilbe, or rodgersia.

varieties:

① **'KNEIFFII'** 36 inches tall in bloom; flower stalks 18 inches long. Lacy leaves.

Goldenrod
(*Solidago*)

This perennial is well known for its golden plumes in late summer to fall. A North American native, goldenrod is a favorite of bees, butterflies, and other beneficial insects. Adaptable, deer resistant, and drought tolerant, goldenrod is a cinch to grow.

Best site

Plant in full sun to light shade. Goldenrod adapts to sandy well-drained soil. Zones 3–9.

Growing

Plants grow 12 to 36 inches tall and wide. As flowers form, stems bow, creating a fountain effect. Reduce flowering height by cutting plants back by one-third to one-half in late June. Clumps in fertile soil may need staking. Clean up plants in fall. Goldenrod spreads aggressively; dig and yank far-ranging stems in early spring.

Design ideas

Plant goldenrod in the front or middle of a late-season border. Combine it with fall bloomers, such as Russian sage, aster, garden mum, and ornamental grasses. Include goldenrod in butterfly, meadow, or wildflower gardens.

varieties:

① **'FIREWORKS'** (*S. rugosa*) A selection of rough-stemmed goldenrod. Grows 3 to 4 feet tall and wide with 18-inch-long flower plumes. Rust resistant.

Grasses

Ornamental grasses give a garden year-round interest with motion and gentle rustling. Grasses also stage a seasonal show with textural foliage that forms a fountain in shades of blue, chartreuse, red, gold, green, or variegated patterns. Leaves fade to lovely brown, pink, or dusk shades in winter. Seedheads soar above the foliage in summer, adding eye-catching interest through winter.

Best site

Plant most ornamental grasses in full sun to part shade in fertile, well-drained soil. Some species, such as golden hakone grass, grow in deep shade and prefer acid soil. Others, like switch grass, thrive in sandier soil. Good winter drainage is important for all grasses. Zones 3–9, depending on species.

Growing

Ornamental grasses grow in varying sizes depending on species, from a petite 6 inches tall and 10 inches wide, to an imposing 8 feet tall and 4 feet wide. Grasses either form tidy clumps that increase in size over time or spread by underground stems. If situated in ideal growing conditions, spreaders can quickly overrun a garden. When planting a spreader, confine it in some kind of containment system that runs at least 12 inches underground.

If you plant a grass that readily self-seeds, cut off seedheads before seeds begin to disperse. When self-seeding isn't an issue, allow seedheads to remain in place through winter to contribute structure to the garden. In either case, leave the foliage in place for a winter show.

Remove dead foliage in spring before new growth emerges, cutting to within a few inches of the soil. With large clumps, an easy way to remove foliage is to gather it together with a string and use electric hedge clippers to slice the stems. The string also helps to bundle the cut stems.

Divide ornamental grasses as needed to renovate the clump. Grasses are pest free.

Design ideas

Use short ornamental grasses to edge a border, fill containers, or create a drift of color beside midrange perennials. Count on tall species to command attention as a focal point, create a hedge, or shield an unpleasant view. Incorporate grasses into planting schemes to take advantage of foliage color and variegation. Because ornamental grasses provide such strong winter interest, consider siting one where it's visible from indoors during the garden's off-season.

Names to watch for

BLUE FESCUE (*Festuca glauca*) Fine-textured blue foliage forms a rounded tuft 6 to 10 inches tall and wide. Foliage colors best in full sun; plants survive in light shade. Tan seedheads form in midsummer; many gardeners remove these as they form. Blue leaves are semi-evergreen; cold temperatures brown foliage. Clip and remove damaged leaves in spring. Clump dies out in the center over time. Divide every few years to renovate the clump. Zones 4–10.

'Blue Glow' 8 to 10 inches tall with icy blue foliage.

'Blue Sea' 6 inches tall with grayish blue tufts.

'Elijah Blue' grows 8 to 10 inches tall with blue leaves.

BLUE OAT GRASS (*Helictotrichon sempervirens*) Silvery blue evergreen foliage forms a clump 24 inches tall and wide. Plant in dry soil with excellent drainage. Cut foliage back in late spring. Divide every three years. Fungal diseases like rust plague plants in humid climates. Not a good choice for the Deep South. Mulch over plants in Zone 4 in winter. Zones 4–10.

'Sapphire' grows 30 inches tall; is rust-resistant.

FEATHER REED GRASS

(*Calamagrostis acutiflora*) Light green foliage in spring; flowers in early summer shift from pink to light purple, ripening to golden, wheatlike sheaves by midsummer. Seedheads remain strongly upright through winter. Full sun to part shade and moist, well-drained soil rich in organic matter. Tolerates wet clay and salt spray. Divide in spring after new growth begins but before flowering. Zones 4–10.

feather reed grass varieties:

❶ **'KARL FOERSTER'** Forms a stiff, 5-foot-tall and 24-inch-wide column in bloom.

❷ **'OVERDAM'** Variegated with a green midrib surrounded by white; it grows 36 inches tall.

FOUNTAIN GRASS (*Pennisetum alopecuroides*) Graceful arching green stems fade to gold in fall and almond in winter. Upright foxtail seedheads open green, mature to silvery pink or white, and turn tan by winter. Strong upright seedhead stems remain through winter. Clumps 36 inches tall and 24 inches wide; 4 feet in flower. Plant in full sun in well-drained, moist, fertile soil. Can self-sow in warm climes to point of invasiveness. Zones 5–10.

 'Hameln' More compact at 24 inches tall and wide. Creamy white blooms in midsummer. Arching stems create a compact mound.

'Little Bunny' Only 8 to 12 inches tall.

'Little Honey' Variegated version of 'Little Bunny' with a similar size and plant form.

 'Moudry' Dark brown to black flower plumes in late fall on plants 24 to 36 inches tall. The plumes are excellent in fresh-cut or dried flower arrangements.

GOLDEN HAKONE GRASS (*Hakonechloa macra* 'Aureola') Vivid yellow leaves with green stripes brighten shady nooks with elegant cascades of foliage 18 inches tall and wide. Resembles bamboo; pairs nicely with hosta. Part sun to full shade in rich, well-drained, slightly acid soil rich in organic matter. Remove faded foliage in spring before new leaves grow. Zones 4–9.

'Albostriata' Dark green leaves with white stripes on the margins.

'All Gold' Yellow leaves; 8 inches tall.

'Beni-kaze' Develops red fall color; is green in summer; it grows 24 to 36 inches tall.

PINK MUHLY GRASS (*Muhlenbergia capillaris*) Light pinkish plumes in late summer fade to gold in fall; flowers draw butterflies. Mound is 12 inches tall (36 inches in bloom), 3 to 4 feet wide. Fine-textured grass makes great edging. Tough native plant; tolerates heat, salt spray, drought, poor, wet, and sandy soil. Zones 6–10.

'White Cloud' White blooms 4 feet tall.

'Regal Mist' Dusky pink in late fall; 36 inches tall and wide. Does well in Southwest.

PRAIRIE DROPSEED (*Sporobolus heterolepis*) Native warm-season clumping grass. Foliage resembles a fountain of green hair, fades to orange, bronze, and tan. Flowers appear late summer. Grows slowly; buy the largest plants you can. Plant in well-drained soil of dry to average moisture. Tolerates drought and heat. Doesn't self-sow freely. Seeds attract birds. Zones 3–9.

PURPLE MOOR GRASS (*Molinia caerulea*) Elegant green leaves form a dense tuft 18 inches tall and wide; use as groundcover. Plant in full sun and acid to neutral, moist soil. Needs part shade in southern climates. Divide when plants outgrow their boundaries. Clumps are deciduous and lose leaves in fall. Zones 4–9.

'Variegata' White-striped green leaves.

TALL PURPLE MOOR GRASS (*M. arundinacea*) Low, 24- to 36-inch fountain of foliage. Flowers stalks rise 7 to 8 feet. Use as gauzy screen. **'Skyracer'** Erect flower stems and yellow-orange fall color. Zones 5–10.

SWITCH GRASS (*Panicum virgatum*) Fine-textured foliage in a narrow upright clump 5 feet tall and 24 inches wide. Leaves have fall color before turning tan for winter. Gauzy, open blooms. Plant in moist, well-drained soil in full sun. Tolerates drought and salt spray once established. May self-sow in ideal conditions. Check with local extension service to see if self-sowing is an issue in your region. Forms a nice living screen. Zones 3–9.

'Cloud Nine' Slender icy blue leaves and clouds of rust-color blooms; 6 feet tall.

'Dallas Blue' Develops drooping, pale blue leaves; huge rosy purple seedheads ripen to tan; 5 feet tall.

'Heavy Metal' Powder blue leaves turn yellow in fall; 3 to 4 feet tall.

'Rotsrahlbusch' Excellent red fall color; 3 to 4 feet tall.

'Shenandoah' Purple-tinged green leaves turn deep wine red in autumn; 36-inch clump.

MISCANTHUS GRASS

(*Miscanthus sinensis*) Many cultivars with leaves of varying colors, forming clumps 3 to 7 feet tall and wide. Late summer or early fall, showy pink, tan, silver, or bronze flower plumes rise above leaves; seedheads persist into winter. Leaves quiver and rustle in wind. Plant in moist, well-drained, fertile soil in full sun to light shade. Established plants tolerate salt spray and drought. Early flowering cultivars can be invasive. Divide clumps that have grown too large or that are dying in the center. Large clumps may require a saw for dividing. Zones 4–10.

miscanthus grass varieties:

1. **'MORNING LIGHT'** Green leaves with white edges; clumps 4 to 6 feet tall and 2½ to 4 feet wide; white plumes at maturity persist well through winter.
2. **'SILVER FEATHER'** Silver flowers from September through winter. Dense, 6- to 9-foot-tall form; use for hedges and screens.
3. **'STRICTUS'** Porcupine grass. 6- to 8-foot-tall columnar foliage clump; 3 to 4 feet wide. Leaves green with horizontal yellow bands.
4. **'VARIEGATUS'** Green blades, gold edges. 5- to 6-foot stems; 6- to 8-foot plumes; 20 inches wide.
5. **MAIDEN GRASS** Green, gracefully arching leaves; clumps grow to 7 feet tall by 8 feet wide. Deer resistant. Use individually as a specimen or several in a row as a hedge.

Hardy Begonia
(*Begonia grandis*)

Hardy begonia brings late summer to life with a spreading mound decorated with dangling sprays of pink blooms. Heart-shape leaves enhance the color show, with red-flushed undersides topped with olive green. Red leaf stems and veins give the plant season-long good looks.

Best site

Plant in moist, fertile, well-drained soil high in organic matter. Wet soil causes root and crown rot. Zones 6–10.

Growing

Hardy begonia grows 18 to 24 inches tall and 18 inches wide. Plants appear in late spring. Deadhead to extend flowering. Tiny bulbs form along the stem, dropping to the earth in fall and sprouting in spring. Cut plants down in fall. Mulch crowns thickly before winter.

Design ideas

Use hardy begonia as a groundcover in part shade or woodlands. It suits confined areas, such as a bed edged by a sidewalk or driveway. Planting companions include Japanese painted fern, hosta, and heart-leaf brunnera.

species and varieties:

❶ HARDY BEGONIA
'HERON'S PIROUETTE' Pink and lavender flowers hang on much longer stems.

Hardy Hibiscus
(*Hibiscus moscheutos*)

Give your garden a taste of the tropics with the mid- to late summer blooms of hardy hibiscus. Exotic-looking flowers open in shades of pink, red, and white on towering plants. New cultivars offer smaller stature with luxuriously large 10-inch flowers.

Best site

Plant in full sun in moist soil that is high in organic matter. Hardy hibiscus tolerates part shade. Avoid windy locations. Zones 5–10.

Growing

Plants grow 3 to 6 feet tall and 3 to 4 feet wide. It's a marshland native, so water during dry spells. Plants are slow to emerge in spring. High temperatures promote flower formation.

Cut plants to 6 inches in late fall. Mulch crowns for winter. Japanese beetles and caterpillars may infest plants.

Design ideas

Use hardy hibiscus to create a focal point, or grow several together as a seasonal hedge. Planting partners include ostrich fern, culver's root, joe-pye weed, and Siberian iris.

Names to watch for

DISCO BELLE SERIES Short plants, 24 to 36 inches tall with 9-inch-wide pink, rose, red, white, or bicolor blooms. Deadhead after bloom to prevent self-seeding.

'Lady Baltimore' 7-inch-wide, ruffled, dark-eyed, pink flowers on 4- to 6-foot plant.

'Lord Baltimore' 10-inch-wide bright red blooms on 4-foot plant.

CORDIALS SERIES Large flowers, maple leaf–shape foliage, 4-foot-tall plants. 'Brandy Punch' flowers in pink with red shades.

Heart-Leaf Bergenia
(Bergenia cordifolia)

The cabbage-style leaves of heart-leaf bergenia introduce bold texture. An architectual beauty forming an impenetrable groundcover in part shade, this plant is deer resistant, low maintenance, and slow spreading. Pink, cupped flowers appear on thick, red stalks in spring.

Best site

Plant in part shade and moist soil high in organic matter. Provide afternoon shade in southern regions. Excessive heat disrupts flower bud formation. Zones 4–10.

Growing

Plants grow 12 inches tall and wide to 18 inches tall in bloom. Winter winds shred leaves; protect plants with mulch or burlap screens. Heavy snow flattens leaves, which perk up after snow melts. In early spring, remove winter-damaged growth. Clip flower stalks after blossoms fade. Divide if plants become crowded. Slugs feast on leaves.

Design ideas

Use as edging or part of a rock garden planting. Thick, leathery leaves are evergreen in mild climates, semi-evergreen in harsher zones.

varieties:

❶ **'BRESSINGHAM WHITE'** Flowers open pink and change to white.
'RUBY ELF' 6 inches tall; red-purple flowers; ruby red winter color.

Heart-Leaf Brunnera
(Brunnera macrophylla)

This perennial decorates the spring garden with tiny blue flowers held above a low mound of large, heart-shape leaves. Hairy stems and leaves resist slug attacks. A native of Siberia, heart-leaf brunnera forms a low-maintenance groundcover.

Best site

Plant in part shade in moist soil high in organic matter. Plants can grow in full sun or in regions with cool summer climates as long as roots are in consistently moist soil. Leaves scorch in hot regions. Zones 3–10.

Growing

Plants grow 12 inches tall (18 inches in bloom) and 24 inches wide. Wear gloves to protect against prickly stems. Deadhead by cutting flowering stems at the base. Allow seeds to ripen if you're using the plant as a groundcover. Seedlings of variegated cultivars won't resemble and are likely to outgrow parents.

Design ideas

Plant heart-leaf brunnera along paths as edging, or use it to create a flowering groundcover.

varieties:

❶ **'JACK FROST'** Silver leaves with green edges are 3 to 5 inches wide. Heat tolerant.
'SILVER WINGS' Gray-green leaves with large silvery splotches between veins.

Helenium
(*Helenium autumnale*)

A North American native, helenium thrives in moist meadows. Flowers in wonderful autumn hues and blends of red, gold, bronze, orange, and russet open for 8 to 10 weeks or more starting in midsummer. Petals of this daisylike flower flare out from a large center.

YOU SHOULD KNOW

Tall varieties typically need staking; insert supports in early spring. Another option is to cut plants back by one-third in late spring or early summer to reduce final height and produce compact, branched plants.

Best site

Plant in moist to wet soil in full sun. The soil should not be allowed to dry out. Add organic matter to dry soil to make it more moisture retentive. Zones 3–10.

Growing

Plants grow 3 to 5 feet tall and 2 to 5 feet wide, although height can vary based on moisture availability. Deadhead after flowering to promote rebloom. Fertilize plants lightly in spring, when stems are emerging from soil, and again after flowering.

Whenever clumps become crowded, divide in early spring, when new growth is about 2 inches tall. Lift the clump free, and pry off the outer portions for the strongest divisions. Discard any woody central portions of the root ball. Powdery mildew and leaf spot diseases often afflict plants that lack sufficient air circulation. If disease attacks foliage, cut down plants after flowering and discard leaves.

Design ideas

Helenium holds its own in the middle to the back of the border. Use it to punch up the late summer garden's color quotient. Flower centers look wonderful covered with a light snow; allow seedheads to remain for winter interest.

Butterflies flock to this rugged native, making it a logical choice for wildlife gardens. Pair helenium with other moisture-loving meadow flowers, like joe-pye weed, bee balm, or hardy hibiscus. It also looks stunning with miscanthus grass and tall asters.

varieties:

1. **'BUTTER PAT'** Gold flowers with yellow centers on 4-foot-tall plant.
2. **'INDIAN SUMMER'** Coppery red blooms with a yellow center.
3. **'MARDI GRAS'** Nondrooping orange-red flowers marked with yellow and a dark center.
4. **'CHELSEY'** Nondrooping crimson flowers marked with yellow and a dark brown center.
5. **'DOUBLE TROUBLE'** Nondrooping, double, yellow daisies with a yellow center.

Hollyhock (*Alcea rosea*)

Old-fashioned charm abounds in hollyhock's soaring flower spires and round leaves. Hollyhock is a staple in cottage gardens. In early to midsummer, flowers of bright pink, red, maroon, purple, yellow, or white open from the bottom of the spike upward, attracting butterflies, hummingbirds, and bees.

Best site

Plant in full sun in rich, well-drained, moist soil. Adding compost around plants annually helps build soil that's high in organic matter and able to hold moisture. Zones 3–10.

Growing

Consider wind when deciding where to put hollyhocks. Locate these towering plants away from windy aspects of the garden. Stake tall varieties, inserting stakes in early spring. It's worth the time to stake individual flower stems. Many gardeners deadhead after flowering to keep plants tidy. You can also allow seeds to ripen and self-sow. If plants begin to look ratty during late summer, cut tall flowering stems back to fresh foliage.

Leaf miners, Japanese beetles, and hollyhock rust are the main problems. Select rust-resistant types. Help prevent rust outbreaks by cutting plants down in fall, removing foliage and stems, and destroying them. Hand pick beetles, and remove leaves with telltale leaf miner trails.

Design ideas

A classic cottage garden perennial, hollyhock gives any planting the feeling of old fashioned, country garden charm. A clump of these towering plants can easily serve as a focal point. Hollyhock also can be pressed into service as a flowering screen to hide a building, fence, or unsightly view.

Dwarf cultivars thrive in containers or along the front of borders. Consider making hollyhock part of a wildlife garden, since the flowers beckon hummingbirds and butterflies. Good companions include meadow sage, ladybells, ornamental grasses, and Shasta daisy.

YOU SHOULD KNOW
It's easy to start hollyhocks from seed you save or to allow plants to toss seeds in the garden. Volunteer seedlings often bloom in different colors than the parent plants.

varieties:

❶ **'CHATER'S DOUBLE' HYBRIDS** Double blooms in shades of pink, red, maroon, white, yellow, violet, and salmon.

❷ **'CREME DE CASSIS'** Large, heavily veined, white-rimmed, dark raspberry flowers on 5- to 6-foot-tall stems. Double, semidouble, and single flowers can appear on the same stalk.

❸ **'OLD BARNYARD' MIX** Rust resistant. Bright pastels, deep jewel colors, and bicolors, including brick reds, oranges, yellows, and rosy reds. Stems 5 to 6 feet tall.

❹ **FIG-LEAF HOLLYHOCK** (*A. ficoides*) Yellow flowers open along stems with irregularly lobed leaves resembling a fig. Plants grow 5 to 7 feet tall and are rust free and cold tolerant.

❺ **'NIGRA'** Deep maroon single flowers on 5- to 6-foot spikes.

Hosta (*Hosta*)

Most gardeners prize hosta for the wonderful array of leaf colors and sizes. The foliage flaunts hues of gold, white, blue, or green, along with variegated patterns. Leaf surfaces can be wavy, smooth, shiny, puckered, or quilted. In summer, white to lavender flowers open on stalks that extend above leafy mounds. The blossoms attract bees and butterflies and also make excellent cut flowers in garden bouquets.

Best site

Plant in moist, well-drained soil in part shade. Hostas like to sink their roots into soil that's rich in organic matter. In hot regions, give plants full shade and plentiful moisture. Morning sun is ideal in cool climes. Yellow-leaf cultivars perform better in sun than blue-leaf types. Hostas don't tolerate drought. Zones 3–9.

Growing

Plant size varies from diminutive miniatures (2 inches tall and 4 to 6 inches wide) to gigantic specimens (nearly 4 feet tall and 6 feet wide). Before planting, improve the soil with compost or well-rotted manure to create a fertile, well-drained bed. If planting in spring, fertilize with a continuous-release product or use soluble fertilizer starting three weeks after tucking hostas into beds. Stop fertilizing six to eight weeks before the average first fall frost.

Deadhead after flowering. Some gardeners remove flowers before they open. With blue-leaf cultivars, deadheading causes rebloom. Cut back plants after foliage dies in fall. Divide crowded clumps in spring or fall.

Rabbits, deer, slugs, and snails like to feast on hosta. Thick, quilted leaves are more slug resistant. Look for slug resistance when purchasing hostas. Hailstorms can also significantly damage hosta leaves. Clip damaged leaves to tidy the plant, and scratch a slow-release fertilizer into the soil around plants or add a layer of compost over the roots to encourage new leaf formation.

Design ideas

Versatile and beautiful, hosta can fill a chorus line role in a perennial border or stand in the spotlight as a focal point. Small to medium hostas create a lovely edging along paths. Mix several hostas together to fill a woodland garden with subtle beauty, or mass hostas to create a groundcover. Hostas look pretty gathered at the base of evergreens. The flowers show staying power in fresh-from-the-garden bouquets.

Finding the right hosta can be difficult. Focus on leaf color to make selection easier.

Planting companions include mat-forming perennials (bugleweed, bunchberry, and barrenwort), plants with a strong vertical form (bugbane and goatsbeard), or perennials with fine-textured foliage (ferns, astilbe, and yellow corydalis). Other planting partners include bleeding heart, lungwort, solomon's seal, and heart-leaf brunnera.

Thousands of hosta species are available. Don't miss the hosta specialist nurseries listed in the Resources (pages 278–279); they carry unusual types that might be hard to find at local garden centers. This listing represents a mere sampling of the variety available.

Names to watch for
VARIEGATED WHITE-LEAF VARIETIES

 'Christmas Candy' Creamy white leaves edged with a slender green streak. 16 inches tall and 20 inches wide.

 'Fire and Ice' Bright white leaves unfurl with green edges. 8 to 10 inches tall and 12 to 15 inches wide.

'Golden Meadows' Variegated green, white, and chartreuse foliage. Full sun bleaches the chartreuse color to white. 36 inches tall and 36 to 48 inches wide.

YOU SHOULD KNOW
Hostas bring bold texture to perennial combinations with broad leaves that are oblong or pointed. Their round form makes it easy to incorporate symmetry into plantings.

blue-leaf varieties:

① **'HALCYON'** Spear-shape foliage. 10 to 18 inches tall and 3 to 4 feet wide.

② **'BLUE MAMMOTH'** Puckered light blue leaves are slug resistant. 4 feet tall and 6 feet wide. Use as focal point or screen.

③ **'CAMELOT'** Powder blue foliage. 14 inches tall and 40 inches wide plants.

④ **'HADSPEN BLUE'** Thick gray-blue, heart-shape leaves are slug resistant. 18 inches tall and 4 feet wide.

⑤ **BLUE HOSTA** (*H. ventricosa*) Heavily textured, large, dark blue-green leaves. Fast grower to 18 inches tall.

'Patriot' Cupped, slight wavy leaves with dark green centers surrounded by white margins. 18 inches tall and 30 inches wide.
'Orphan Annie' Miniature hosta 2 inches tall and 4 to 6 inches wide. White leaf margins encircle green centers.

YELLOW-LEAF VARIETIES

'August Moon' Leaves vary from gold to chartreuse, depending on amount of sun received. Leaves are brighter in sunny sites. 18 inches tall and 4 feet wide.

Fragrant hosta (*H. plantaginea*) Rather plain looking, growing 24 inches tall and 4 feet wide. Sweetly fragrant white flowers on 5-foot stems appear in August. Individual blossoms at least 6 inches long open in late afternoon. This is the southern-most naturally occurring hosta. Tolerates heat and humidity but rises early in spring and is often the victim of late frosts. Plants generate new foliage all season, replacing damaged leaves. 'Aphrodite' has double, pure white blooms.

'Sun Power' Oval-pointed chartreuse leaves occur on plants 24 inches tall and 36 inches wide.

'Sum and Substance' Sun-tolerant, huge, round, puckered chartreuse leaves can reach 20 inches across. Plants grow 24 inches tall and 3 to 6 feet wide.
'Zounds' Gold, cupped, heavily puckered leaves create mounds 30 inches tall and 4 feet wide.

GREEN-LEAF VARIETIES

'Elegans' (*H. sieboldiana* 'Elegans') Large, heart-shape, blue-green leaves with heavily corrugated texture. Plants grow 2 to 3 feet tall and 3 to 5 feet wide.
'Krossa Regal' Oval leaves open on vase-shape plants 30 inches tall and 48 inches wide.

variegated yellow varieties:

❶ 'FRANCES WILLIAMS' Corrugated, rounded blue-green leaves with gold edges. 32 to 36 inches tall and a little wider.

❷ 'GOLDEN TIARA' Small, gold-edge heart-shape leaves. Dense clump 8 to 12 inches tall and wide. This is a heavy bloomer with purple flowers. Use to edge beds and paths.

❸ 'GOLD STANDARD' Golden-green foliage is highlighted with gold variegation, especially along leaf edges. 10 to 18 inches tall and 3 to 4 feet wide.

❹ 'GUACAMOLE' Leaves have bright gold centers surrounded by green edges. White to light purple, intensely fragrant blooms in late summer. 18 to 42 inches tall and 42 to 48 inches wide.

❺ 'RHINO HIDE' Narrow gold centers surrounded by blue-toned margins. Thick, cupped, puckered leaves are slug resistant. 22 inches tall and 30 inches wide.

Hyssop (*Agastache*)

Give your perennial garden an infusion of fragrance with hyssop. These sturdy plants possess gray-green, fragrant foliage; leaves release an anise scent when brushed, rubbed, or crushed. A long bloomer, hyssop opens spiky blooms from midsummer to fall. Hybrids offer the most boldly tinted blossoms.

Best site

Plant in well-drained soil in full sun. Rich or wet soils and abundant fertilizer produce floppy plants with compromised winter hardiness. Plants tolerate drought, heat, and humidity once established. Zones 4–10.

Growing

Plants grow 2 to 4 feet tall and 24 to 36 inches wide, depending on species. Pinch plants in early spring, removing the center pair of leaves to produce full plants with more flowers. Deadheading can prevent self-sowing and trigger rebloom. Threadleaf giant hyssop and hybrids need winter protection in coldest areas of Zone 5. Plants are pest free.

Design ideas

Hyssop blends beautifully into the center of the border, where its knobby knees (bare lower stems) can be easily camouflaged by short perennials, such as Carpathian or Dalmatian bellflower, pincushion flower, or catmint. Add hyssop to a wildlife garden, since its nectar-rich blooms lure butterflies, bees, and hummingbirds. Flowers last long in bouquets; use dried leaves and blossoms in potpourri.

Names to watch for

ANISE HYSSOP (*A. foeniculum*) Sturdy, upright plants 18 to 30 inches tall and wide. Short, dense flower spikes packed with edible, licorice-flavor blossoms. Dry leaves to brew herbal tea. Plants self-sow easily. Deadhead after flowering or plant in an area that can be overrun with seedlings. Goldfinches feed on seeds. Powdery mildew develops in hot, dry weather. Zones 5–10.

YOU SHOULD KNOW
The delicate beauty of hyssop blooms belies a tough-as-nails constitution. These perennials offer deer- and rabbit-resistance on plants that withstand drought and sizzling summer heat.

VARIETIES SIMILAR TO ANISE HYSSOP
'Black Adder' Dark violet-blue blooms on plants 12 to 36 inches tall. Grows well in part shade.

'Blue Fortune' Dense, bright purple-blue blooms. 3 to 4 feet tall and 24 inches wide.
'Tutti Frutti' Pink-lavender flowers, 4 to 6 feet tall and 24 inches wide. Sweetly fruit-scented foliage.

THREADLEAF GIANT HYSSOP (*A. rupestris*)
Native to mountain ranges in the Southwest. Sometimes called sunset hyssop; blossoms offer

a mix of red, purple, and orange. Flowers last eight weeks or more and rebloom after deadheading. 24 to 36 inches tall. Excellent drainage required.

'Apricot Sunrise' Light orange flowers.

'Ava' Long spikes of dark raspberry blooms in midsummer. Plant has a loose, airy appearance. 4 to 5 feet tall.
'Summer Love' Large, bubble-gum pink flowers (pictured, top).
'Desert Sunset' Multicolor blooms in lavender, pink, and orange.

TEXAS HYSSOP (*A. cana*) Dense spikes of raspberry blooms. 12 to 36 inches tall. Tolerates full sun and dry soil. Zones 5–9.

Iris (*Iris*)

Irises fill the spring to early summer garden. The flowers consist of three upper petals (called standards) and three lower petals that dangle (called falls). The petals boast a rainbow of hues: purple, blue, white, pink, burgundy, yellow, and bicolor blends. All irises make excellent additions to garden bouquets. Two types of irises exist: ones that grow from bulbs and ones that grow from rhizomes.

Best site
Plant in moist, moderately fertile, well-drained soil in full sun. Some species thrive in wet or boggy soil. Zones 3–10.

Growing
Irises are easy to grow and reliable. Perennial rhizomatous irises fall into three categories: bearded, beardless, and crested. All flower in late spring and early summer. Plant rhizomes shallow right at the soil surface. Iris borer can attack plants.

Design ideas
Irises introduce an upright, often coarse texture to the garden. Good companions include catmint, coreopsis, aster, creeping phlox, ornamental grasses, coral bells, cranesbill geranium, and lady's mantle.

Names to watch for
BEARDED IRISES

This group of irises sports fuzzy hairs, or beards, in the center of the falls. Every color unfurls with the exception of true red. The group includes German iris (*I. germanica*) and sweet iris, also known as sweet flag (*I. pallida*).

German iris Flowers from 1 to 8 inches; some are fragrant. Add bonemeal to soil at planting. Remove stalks after buds have faded. Divide every three to four years. 8 to 36 inches tall and 12 to 24 inches wide.

Sweet flag Two to three fragrant bluish purple flowers per stem. Less susceptible to iris borer than other irises. 24 to 30 inches tall and 12 inches wide.

CRESTED IRISES
Crested irises have a crest or ridge down the center of each fall.

Dwarf crested iris (*I. cristata*) Native to the Southeast. Fragrant, yellow-crested, lilac-blue blooms on 2- to 3-inch stems. Use as a groundcover for dry shade; pair with barrenwort. Leaves 4 to 6 inches tall. Zones 3–8.

Roof iris (*I. tectorum*) Also a crested iris. Blue or white flowers atop sword-shape leaves. 12 to 18 inches tall and 36 inches wide. Zones 5–8.

bearded varieties:
① **'PROUD TRADITION'** German iris. Pale blue standards, deep blue falls, blue beard. Huge flowers.
② **'MAKING EYES'** German iris. Dwarf; purple falls and white standards with a yellowish white beard.
③ **'AUREA VARIEGATA'** Sweet flag. Wide, yellow stripe on each leaf.
④ **ARGENTEA VARIEGATA** Sweet flag. Wide, white stripe on each 12-inch leaf; lilac blooms.

YOU SHOULD KNOW
For the most part, irises bridge the seasons of spring and summer, adding color during the transition. All irises suit a cottage or informal garden style, and the strongly upright foliage of some species fits a formal setting.

BEARDLESS IRISES

These irises lack fuzzy falls and a crest. Flowering in spring and early summer, they include Siberian iris (*I. sibirica*), Japanese iris (*I. ensata*), Louisiana iris (*I. fulva*), and yellow flag (*I. pseudacorus*).

beardless varieties:

1 SIBERIAN IRIS Thrives in moist, fertile, well-drained soils; adapts to other soils. Grassy foliage 24 to 36 inches tall and 24 inches wide. 'Caesar's Brother' (above) is one of the most popular varieties. White, blue, or lavender varieties are also available. Zones 3–9.

2 JAPANESE IRIS Horizontal flowers in blue, purple, pink, or white. Plant in full sun to part shade in rich, moist to boggy, acid soil. Sword-shape leaves 5 feet tall and spreads 36 inches wide. 'Dark Lightning' is pictured.

3 LOUISIANA IRIS Purple, blue, copper, yellow, pink, or white blooms; attract hummingbirds and butterflies. Heat-tolerant; thrives in the South. Plants are 18 to 60 inches tall and spread fast in boggy soil. Zones 4–11.

4 YELLOW FLAG IRIS Light yellow flowers with slender petals. Moist to wet soil. Plants need part shade in hot summers. Leaves 3 to 5 feet long.

Jacob's Ladder
(*Polemonium caeruleum*)

Jacob's ladder graces the garden with fine-textured beauty. Small leaves arranged like the rungs of a ladder climb along short, arching stems. Collectively the stems form a dense mound of foliage that comes to life with blue-violet or white flowers in mid- to late spring.

Best site
Plant in full sun to part shade in moist, well-drained soil high in organic matter. Good drainage is vital to success. Plants tolerate shade and alkaline soils, but decline in extreme heat, drought, and high humidity. Zones 3–8.

Growing
Plants grow 8 to 12 inches high (24 inches in bloom) and 18 to 24 inches wide. They sometime need staking. Clip flower stems after blooming to prevent self-sowing; variegated forms are less aggressive seeders. Deadheading often promotes rebloom.

Design ideas
In woodland gardens, this perennial's self-sowing creates naturalized plantings. Variegated forms pair nicely with heart-leaf bergenia.

varieties:

❶ 'PURPLE RAIN' (*P. yezoense*) Clustered blue flowers rise above a 24-inch mound of ferny, purplish foliage.

Jerusalem Sage
(*Phlomis russeliana*)

A Mediterranean native, fast-growing Jerusalem sage is drought tolerant and low maintenance. It sends up tall spikes with tiers of hooded yellow blooms from late spring to early summer. The gray-green foliage is rabbit and deer resistant.

Best site
Plant in full sun in light, well-drained soil. Plants are heat tolerant and require little water. Zones 4–11.

Growing
Plants typically grow 24 to 36 inches tall and wide, but can reach 5 feet tall. Sturdy stems don't need staking. Deadheading prolongs the bloom. In the coldest climates, mulch plants in late fall to protect crowns. Stems add interest to winter scenery. Clip old foliage in early spring. Divide clumps every two to three years in early spring.

Design ideas
Use this architecturally interesting perennial in low-water-use landscapes and wildlife gardens, where the yellow blooms beckon bees. This beauty partners well with lavender cotton, yarrow, coneflower, purple moor grass, and aster. The blossoms make long-lasting cut flowers—fresh or dried.

Names to watch for
SHRUBBY JERUSALEM SAGE (*P. fruticosa*)

Bright yellow blooms from June to August. Plants grow 4 feet high and 36 inches wide. Beautiful with catmint, balloon flower, or blue oat grass. Zones 6–11.

SAGE-LEAF MULLEIN (*P. tuberosa*)

Mauve-pink, hooded flowers on crimson stems all summer long. Less demanding of perfect drainage. Plants grow 4 feet high and 36 inches wide. Zones 5–11.

'Amazone' Lavender-pink flowers on reddish stems late spring to early summer; 5 feet tall and 4 feet wide. Zones 5–11.

Joe-Pye Weed
(Eupatorium maculatum)

For back-of-the-border beauty, it's hard to beat joe-pye weed. Mauve blooms open atop stately burgundy stems in late summer. Foliage forms a good-looking mass prior to flowering. Blossoms beckon butterflies and bees; plant with great rudbeckia to lure goldfinches too.

Best site
Plant in moist, well-drained, fertile soil, in full sun to part shade. Zones 3–9.

Growing
Plants grow 4 to 6 feet tall and 4 feet wide in an upright clump. Sturdy stems don't usually require staking. Pinch plants once or twice prior to July 4 to increase branching and flower number—and reduce final height.

Flowers form flat clusters 10 to 12 inches across. Deadhead before windborne seeds ripen to prevent self-sowing. Powdery mildew can attack plants. Thin the stems to improve air circulation. Divide plants in spring.

Design ideas
Use joe-pye weed in the back of the border. Pair it with tall ornamental grasses.

varieties:

❶ **'GATEWAY'** More compact than the species; 5 feet tall.

Lady's Mantle
(Alchemilla mollis)

Luxurious, velvety foliage clothes lady's mantle with elegance and charm. Clusters of tiny chartreuse blooms dangle above and among foliage from late spring to midsummer. Flowers make great additions to fresh or dried bouquets. This plant is pest and disease free.

Best site
Plant in moist, well-drained soils in part shade. Full sun is fine in cool climates. Zones 4–9.

Growing
Lady's mantle grows 18 to 24 inches tall and wide. Space plants 12 to 18 inches apart. For groundcover use, allow plants to self-sow. To tend a single clump, deadhead the plant. Cut last year's dead foliage in early spring, before new growth appears. Divide in spring. Renew plants in summer by cutting back leaves.

Design ideas
Use lady's mantle to soften path edges or form a lovely groundcover in a lightly shaded spot along a wall or under a tree. Team it with coral bells, Japanese painted fern, heart-leaf brunnera, and other cottage garden plants.

varieties:

❶ **'THRILLER'** More erect with large leaves. 18 inches tall.
ALPINE LADY'S MANTLE (*A. alpina*) White-edged green leaves on plants 5 to 6 inches tall.

Ladybells
(*Adenophora confusa*)

Large, purple-blue bells dangle along flowering stems from late spring to midsummer. Bees happily buzz inside hanging blossoms, which make excellent cut flowers. Plants self-sow to form a dense groundcover along the edge of a woodland setting.

Best site
Plant in full sun or part shade in well-drained, evenly moist soil. Zones 3–10.

Growing
Ladybells grows 36 to 40 inches tall, 12 inches wide, and is pest free. It doesn't transplant well; put it where you're sure you want it. Plant in early spring, keeping it moist and shaded until the roots establish.

Plants self-sow freely to the point of invasiveness. Deadhead by cutting down stems; use shears to deadhead large clumps. Plants often rebloom after deadheading.

Design ideas
Allow ladybells to naturalize beneath tall shade trees, or position it in the center of a sunny border or flowerbed.

varieties:

❶ **PURPLE LADYBELLS** (*A. pereskiifolia*) Blue flowers on plants 18 to 24 inches high. More heat tolerant than bellflower; plant in place of it in the South.

Lamb's-Ears
(*Stachys byzantina*)

Give your garden a velvet touch with the silvery foliage of lamb's-ears. The leaves form an impenetrable groundcover that suppresses weeds and glows a luminous white at dusk. Many gardeners prize the felty foliage, clipping flower stems as they form.

Best site
Plant in dry, sandy to loamy, very well-drained soil in full sun. Zones 3–10.

Growing
Plants grow 8 inches tall and 24 inches wide. Flower stems add another 10 inches to plants. If you allow flowers to form, deadhead after bloom. In wet conditions, leaves may rot. Check plants in midseason and remove any damaged leaves. Divide plants every four to five years to renew the clump and keep spread in check.

Design ideas
Drought tolerant lamb's-ears thrives atop stone walls and in sunny borders. Use it as edging along planting beds. Plant with lavender, 'Crème Brulee' coreopsis, Jerusalem sage, globe thistle, or big betony.

varieties:

❶ **'BIG EARS'** sold as 'Helene Von Stein'. Heat tolerant with few or no flowers. 8 to 10 inches tall with leaves twice as big.

Lavender *(Lavandula)*

This woody, evergreen shrub fits easily into perennial gardens, with its clumps of gray-green leaves and spiky purple blooms. Flowers and foliage yield a sweet, distinctly clean perfume. Plants suit sunny borders, Mediterranean-style gardens, and rock gardens. The blossoms attract butterflies and bees.

Best site

Plant lavender in full sun in well-drained, somewhat fertile, somewhat alkaline soil. Excellent drainage is key to survival. To grow lavender in a planting bed with acidic soil, amend the soil around the lavender with lime at planting. You can also line the planting hole with limestone gravel and use the gravel as a mulch. In future years, slip a piece of blackboard chalk into soil near the root zone. Zones 5–10.

Growing

Lavender forms clumps up to 24 inches tall and 36 inches wide; plants can be up to 36 inches tall in bloom. Plants tolerate heat, drought, and wind, but won't survive high humidity, wet soil, or poor drainage. Root rot attacks plants grown in wet conditions. Shear faded flowers after blooming to shape plants and promote reblooming.

Prune lavender in spring after stems leaf out, treating the plant like a shrub. Place first cuts to remove dead or damaged stems, then clip leggy stems. Finally, prune to shape as desired. To help plants survive winter, mulch crowns with loose, airy mulch. If lavender is borderline hardy in your region, help it to overwinter successfully by placing straw around the plant crown and then adding evergreen boughs.

Lavender plants are woody and aren't propagated through division but by stem cuttings. Surround your lavender plantings with gravel areas, allow plants to set seed, and you'll likely discover lavender seedlings popping up in the gravel the following season. Transplant these for new lavender plantings.

Design ideas

These fragrant plants are beloved favorites in herb gardens and also thrive in rock gardens, where drainage is typically sharp. Use lavender to create a lovely short hedge or mass planting. The fragrant beauty is often pressed into service as a path edging. Flowers attract many bees; consider this as you choose to use lavender for edging walkways. On hot summer afternoons, the scent of lavender saturates a planting. Use lavender to surround a seating area or bench to provide a perfumed retreat.

Lavender also performs well in sunny borders and herbal knot gardens; situate it in the middle of a bed for the best effect. Good companions include germander, penstemon, pink muhly grass, and black-eyed susan.

Names to watch for

'GROSSO' (*L. × intermedia*, also called lavandin). The most intensely fragrant lavender, grown for its essential oil. Flowers opens dark violet on long spikes. Grows to 24 inches tall. Zones 6–10.

grosso lavender varieties:

1 'PROVENCE' Mauve blooms make excellent cut flowers. 36 inches tall and 24 inches wide. Plants rebloom with deadheading.

YOU SHOULD KNOW
To dry lavender cut flowers when spikes are partly open. Gather stems into bundles 1 inch in diameter and hang them upside down in a dark, dry place with good air circulation. Store dried blooms in an airtight container.

ENGLISH LAVENDER (*Lavandula angustifolia*) Traditional star-petal blooms arranged along a spike. Blossoms in varying shades of purple, pink, and white and rise on slender stems that soar above foliage. Zones 5–10.

english lavender varieties:

1 **'BLUE CUSHION'** Blue flowers above silvery, 16-inch-tall leaves.

2 **'HIDCOTE'** Deep purple blooms on compact silver plant; 24 inches tall. Good in cold climates.

3 **'LODDEN PINK'** Light pink flowers on 18-inch-tall plants.

4 **'MUNSTEAD'** Blue-purple blooms on 18-inch-tall plant. Good in cold climates.

5 **'NANA ALBA'** White flowers on 12-inch-tall plant.

SPANISH LAVENDER (*L. stoechas*) Wands of dark purple bracts topped with lilac-purple rabbit-ear petals shaped like rabbit ears above silver foliage. Zones 7–10.

spanish lavender varieties:

6 **'WILLOW VALE'** Lavender-purple blooms on upright plant to 36 inches tall and 24 inches wide.

7 **'OTTO QUAST'** Royal purple blooms from late winter to early summer.

8 **'KEW RED'** Magenta-pink flowers on plant that can reach 4 feet tall.

'LEMON LEIGH' Chartreuse flowers on 24-inch-tall plant with silvery foliage.

Lavender cotton
(*Santolina chamaecyparissus*)

Lavender cotton forms a fuss-free, low maintenance mound of silvery, fragrant foliage. The leaves are edged with tiny teeth to create a wonderful, fine texture. Yellow button blooms on stem tips appear in summer. This woody shrub is deer and rabbit resistant.

Best site
Plant in full sun in average garden soil. Good drainage is a must. Zones 6–10.

Growing
Plants grow 12 inches tall (18 inches in flower) and 24 to 36 inches wide. Lavender cotton tolerates salt spray and dislikes high humidity. Keep plants dense and compact by cutting to 6 to 8 inches in early spring before growth starts. Shear as needed to maintain shape. Trim plants post-bloom; the striking good looks will return.

Design ideas
Use lavender cotton to edge rock gardens or planting beds. Sheared plants make a low hedge suitable for knot or herb gardens. Mass plantings form a groundcover. Plant with heart-leaf bergenia, Japanese fountain grass, or yucca.

varieties:
① 'NANA' Strongly scented foliage on 10-inch plant.

Lenten Rose
(*Helleborus orientalis*)

Lenten rose is an evergreen, deer-resistant groundcover with 2½-inch-wide flowers that last for months. Blossoms, opening in late winter or early spring, are single or double and cupped or nodding. Colors include green, white, yellow, pink, purple, red, and blends of these hues.

Best site
Plant in part to full shade in rich, humusy, well-drained soil. Avoid wind or wet and poorly drained soil. Zones 4–10.

Growing
Lenten rose grows 18 to 24 inches tall and 24 to 30 inches wide. Plants tolerate alkaline or dry soil and thrive in full sun in cool climates. Plants self-sow, seedlings often in new bloom colors.

Apply winter mulch in Zones 4–5. Clip dead leaves in late winter. Fertilize in spring as new growth appears. If needed, divide plants in spring, but they may not flower the next year.

Design ideas
Add Lenten rose to woodland or shade gardens, or grow it as a groundcover under trees.

species:
BEAR'S FOOT HELLEBORE (*Helleborus foetidus*) Yellow-green flowers late winter to early spring.
CHRISTMAS ROSE (*Helleborus niger*) White flowers tinged with green, often in December.

Lily (*Lilium*)

Exotic and showy, lilies fill the summer garden with color that returns reliably year after year. Clumps increase in size over time, building the flower show. Blossoms open from summer to fall, depending on the type of lily. Flowers trumpet or dangle atop sturdy stems that often don't require staking. Leaves whorl around stems in shiny deep green, forming a striking fringe below flowers.

Best site

Plant lilies in full sun to light shade in well-drained, organic soil. Plants adapt to most growing conditions except dry heat. Lilies will flower in as few as four hours of sun (ideal in hot climates) but generally prefer six hours of sun daily. Zones 3–11.

Growing

There are many lily species and varieties. Size ranges from 18 inches to 8 feet tall. All need cool roots. Shade them either with surrounding plantings or a 2-inch mulch layer. Water and fertilize regularly while the plants are growing.

Purchase lilies as potted plants or bare bulbs. With potted lilies, plant bulbs at the same depth they are in the pot. Space large lilies 12 inches apart. Lilies won't bloom again the first year after planting. When planting bulbs, dig the hole deep enough that bulbs will have 2 inches of soil over them. Eight inches deep is usually adequate; plant Asiatic lilies 10 inches deep. Because roots form along the underground stem, a deeper planting ensures well-anchored stems. For tall types, insert stakes at planting time, being careful to avoid spearing bulbs.

Design ideas

Plant a variety of lilies to ensure a succession of bloom from these pretty bulb bloomers. Arrange bulbs in drifts, not straight lines, for a more natural appearance. Locate lilies in a sunny border according to their height: short types in front, towering ones in back. Lilies blend well with many perennials, such as Japanese anemone, lady's mantle, bellflower, clematis, and meadow sage.

Names to watch for

ASIATIC HYBRIDS Flower in early summer on stems 2 to 5 feet tall. Blooms in shades of orange, yellow, red, pink, lavender, or white measure 4 to 6 inches across. Some petals have freckles in darker shades. Compact growth.

MARTAGON HYBRIDS 2- to 4-inch flowers in early summer on plants 3 to 6 feet tall. Colors include white, lavender, yellow, orange, and mahogany. Flowers hang down and petals curve back.

CANDIDUM HYBRIDS Heavily fragrant 4- to 5-inch flowers in early summer on plants 3 to 4 feet tall.

AMERICAN HYBRIDS Hybrids of North American native lilies. 4- to 6-inch flowers in late spring and early summer on plants 4 to 8 feet tall.

LONGIFLORUM HYBRIDS Include the familiar white, fragrant Easter lily and its hybrids. Stems are 36 inches tall; summer blooms. Zones 6–11; with protection, may survive in Zone 5.

TRUMPET HYBRIDS Summer-flowering lilies with 6- to 10-inch-long blooms on 4- to 6-foot stems. Group includes Aurelian and Olympic hybrids, which have trumpet-shape flowers. Other hybrids in the group have star-shape, pendent, or flat, open blossoms.

ORIENTAL HYBRIDS Richly fragrant hybrids that flower in late summer, opening 12-inch-wide blooms. Various hybrids range from 24 inches to 8 feet tall. Bowl-shape blossoms have petals that curve back. Colors include white, pink, deep red, and bicolors.

SPECIES LILIES Includes lilies native to North America, Europe, and Asia.

Gold-banded lily (*L. auratum*) Bears up to 35 fragrant flowers per stem.

Martagon lily (*L. martagon*) Hardy species; opens dozens of dangling blossoms with recurved petals.

Regal lily (*L. regale*) Fragrant, trumpet-shape flowers.

YOU SHOULD KNOW
Fall is the best time for planting lilies, except for Madonna and candidum lilies, which should be set out in late summer to early fall. Most bulbs hit the market in spring; if you buy them then, plant them at that time.

species and varieties:

1 **'PURPLE RAIN'** Asiatic hybrid. White blooms brushed with a deep burgundy-purple blotch at the base of each petal. 32 inches tall. Zones 3–9.

2 **MARTAGON** (*Lilium martagon*) Clusters of red-purple or pink blooms have petals that peel back. Plant in moist, well-drained soil; provide part shade in hottest regions. To 6 feet tall. Zones 3–7.

3 **MADONNA LILY** Candidum hybrid. White, trumpet-shaped, richly fragrant blooms from late spring to midsummer. Zones 3–7.

4 **TURK'S CAP LILY** American hybrid. Flowers in clusters atop 3- to 8-foot stems; orange petals with black freckles reflex strongly. Open midsummer to early fall and attract hummingbirds and butterflies. Prefers rich, moist soil. Zones 3–8.

5 **LONGIFLORUM HYBRID** Produced by crossing traditional Easter lilies with Asiatic hybrids. Flowers unfurl in a variety of hues and have a light fragrance. Zones 3–10.

6 **'BLACK BEAUTY'** Oriental hybrid. Dark crimson, fragrant blooms edged in white on stems 4 to 6 feet tall. Protect from hot afternoon sun; provide support to protect stems during summer storms. Zones 4–10.

7 **'TOUCHING'** Orienpet hybrid. (Orienpet lilies result from crossing Oriental and trumpet lilies.) Fragrant, pale, ivory-yellow blooms with rosy brush strokes on petals and light raspberry freckles. 24 to 36 inches tall. Zones 4–8.

8 **GOLD-BANDED LILY** (*L. auratum*) Bears up to 35 heavily fragrant flowers per stem. Zones 5–9; with mulch, will survive in colder climates.

Liriope *(Liriope muscari)*

Low maintenance and drought tolerant once established, liriope is a Southern favorite, used heavily for edging and as a groundcover to hide the soil beneath shrubs and small trees. Purple blooms open on spikes in late summer to fall. The flowers fade to black berries.

Best site
Plant in full sun to full shade in moist, well-drained soil. Give afternoon shade in the South. Acid soil yields best growth. Zones 5–11.

Growing
Liriope grows 8 to 12 inches tall and 18 inches wide. Use slow-release fertilizer at planting. Until plants establish, water regularly and deeply—when the soil feels dry 3 inches down. Deadhead faded flowers. In a mass planting, refresh liriope in spring by mowing plants on the highest mower setting. Divide in spring or fall.

Design ideas
Use as a groundcover under shrubs and trees, or a grassy covering for hard-to-mow slopes. Liriope works well in containers. Good companion plants in a border include cranesbill geranium, heart-leaf brunnera, and meadow sage.

species and varieties:

❶ **'VARIEGATA'** Lavender flowers on 10-inch plants; white-edged green leaves.
CREEPING LIRIOPE *(L. spicata)* Finer leaves. Grows in full sun or full shade.

Lungwort *(Pulmonaria)*

Brighten the shade garden with the one-two punch of lungwort. Also known as Bethlehem sage, blossoms open in early spring. Buds burst to reveal pink blooms that fade to blue, giving plants a two-tone flower show. When blossoms fade, leaves with silver or white splotches steal the spotlight.

Best site
Plant in part to full shade in moist soil enriched with organic matter. Lungwort tolerates drought or heat—just not at the same time. Zones 3–8.

Growing
Plants grow 12 inches tall and 12 to 24 inches wide. They self-sow, often producing seedlings with different leaf markings. Allow them to self-sow and select your own cultivars, or deadhead to prevent self-sowing. Plants rarely require division. Foliage decomposes over winter. If powdery mildew attacks, cut stems to the ground and water to encourage new growth.

Design ideas
Lungwort's coarse foliage anchors tall shade-loving plants, such as solomon's seal, blue lobelia, astilbe, and ferns. Mass as a groundcover, or use as edging along beds or paths.

varieties:

❶ **'MRS. MOON'** Large, silver-spotted leaves.
'EXCALIBUR' Almost completely silver leaves; 10 inches tall and 20 inches wide. Mildew resistant.

Lupine *(Lupinus)*

Lupines fill the spring to early summer garden with spectacular flower spikes in bright shades: purple, red, white, pink, blue, and other hues. Plants form mounds of coarse-textured foliage with eight-finger leaves featuring green silky threads. The entire effect is striking, unusual, and beautiful.

Best site

Plant in full sun to part shade in consistently moist, well-drained, acid soil. Hybrids prefer light, sandy soil, cool summers, and mild winters. Zones 4–8.

Growing

Plants grow 36 inches tall and 24 inches wide. Space plants 18 to 24 inches apart. Mulch in summer and in winter for protection.

Deadheading may promote rebloom. Plants self-sow easily. Hybrid lupine seedlings aren't true to parents but offer interesting color combinations. Deep taproots resent transplanting. There's no need to divide.

Design ideas

Lupines look stunning massed in planting beds or combined with mounded perennials such as lady's mantle, cranesbill geranium, and catmint.

varieties:

❶ **'THE CHATELAINE'** Pink and white bicolor flowers. Zones 5–8.
GALLERY HYBRIDS Dwarf series growing to 18 inches tall.

Meadow Rue *(Thalictrum)*

When airy clusters of dainty flowers open in shades of lavender in mid- to late summer, the plants tower to 6 feet. The gray-green foliage offers a delicate, divided texture. Meadow rue is deer resistant and a favorite among butterflies and bees.

Best site

Plant in part shade in deep, consistently moist soil with abundant organic matter. Full sun is fine in northern gardens, but plants require more water. Meadow rue doesn't tolerate humidity, heat, or drought. Zones 4–9.

Growing

Meadow rue grows 36 inches tall and wide, to 6 feet in bloom. Usually doesn't need staking. If stems bow in summer storms, rig a support with stakes and string. The seeds are decorative but can self-sow. Remove seedheads before winter.

Divide every five years to renew vigor. Meadow rue doesn't move easily. Keep the soil moist around transplants until wilting stops.

Design ideas

Before flowering, meadow rue foliage adds fine texture to the garden.

species and varieties:

❶ **COLUMBINE MEADOW RUE** (*T. aquilegifolium*) Pink flowers in late spring to early summer. Leaves resemble columbine's.
'LAVENDER MIST' Graceful, tall, pink flowers.

Mondo Grass
(*Ophiopogon japonicus*)

Mondo grass isn't a true grass—it just looks like one. Slender, shiny, dark evergreen leaves form tidy clumps that spread slowly to form a groundcover. Little lilac flowers open in late spring to early summer. The blooms aren't highly visible and fade to blue pea-size berries.

Best site
Plant in full sun to part shade in moist, fertile, well-drained soil with abundant organic matter. Zones 6–10.

Growing
Mondo grass grows 6 to 12 inches tall and 12 inches wide. In full sun, plants require more water. Mow or cut plants back in early spring before new growth appears. Divide overcrowded clumps in spring. In parts of Florida and Texas, mondo grass can be invasive. Contact your local extension office to double-check that it is non-invasive in your area.

Design ideas
Use mondo grass to edge paths and planting beds. Under high shade trees, it makes a wonderful groundcover.

species and varieties:

❶ **BLACK MONDO GRASS** (*O. planiscapus* 'Niger') Violet-black leaves. Zones 5–10.

Monkshood (*Aconitum*)

For late season color, include monkshood in your garden. Hooded blooms in shades of purple, white, or blue and resembling the cowl of a monk's robe open in late summer to early fall. Tall, upright flower stems start to form in midsummer, slowly rising above the foliage.

Best site
Plant in full sun or part shade in well-drained soil. Full sun is okay in cool summers or with consistently moist soil. Provide afternoon shade in hot climes. Zones 3–8.

Growing
Monkshood grows 24 inches tall (3 to 5 feet in bloom) and 12 inches wide. In full shade, monkshood grows slightly taller and flowers later. Stems in shade often need staking. Insert grow-through supports over plants in spring.

Cut plants down after frost. Mulch in Zones 3–4 to aid winter survival. Poor winter drainage kills plants. Divide every five years in spring.

Design ideas
Pair monkshood with ornamental grasses, asters, and joe-pye weed.

species:

❶ **AZURE MONKSHOOD** (*A. carmichelii*) Deep purple blooms on plants 2 to 4 feet tall. **COMMON MONKSHOOD** (*A. napellus*) Purple-blue flowers in late summer.

Mountain Bluet
(Centaurea montana)

Mounds of divided gray-green foliage provide a petticoat for mountain bluet's blue-violet blooms. Flowers rise above leaves on 18-inch stems in midspring to early summer, unfurling 2-inch-wide daisies with wispy petals. Blossoms attract butterflies and bees.

Best site

Plant in full sun to part shade in well-drained soil. Plants tolerate drought, wind, heat, and high pH. Soggy winter soil will kill plants. Zones 3–10.

Growing

Mountain bluet grows 12 to 18 inches tall and 12 inches wide. Cut plants after flowering to encourage new growth and prevent self-sowing. Plants often rebloom in midsummer when deadheaded. Foliage decomposes over winter.

Divide clumps every two to three years. Plants spread by self-sowing and underground stems. Take care when moving plants; any root sections remaining will sprout. This plant can be invasive.

Design ideas

Use mountain bluet to fill in around late spring risers, such as balloon flower and butterfly weed.

varieties:

❶ 'AMETHYST IN SNOW' Purple-centered white daisies.

'GOLD BULLION' Violet-centered blue blooms above chartreuse foliage.

Mullein (Verbascum)

Offering ephemeral beauty in the garden, mulleins are short-lived, low maintenance plants. Spikes dressed with yellow, pink, or white blooms soar above the leaves in early to midsummer. They make a nice addition to bouquets. Deer resistant foliage forms a broad rosette with a coarse texture.

Best site

Plant in full sun in sandy, alkaline soils. Mullein tolerates other soil types, heat, wind, and drought. Plants don't tolerate poor drainage, wet soil, or high humidity. Zones 5–10.

Growing

Mullein grows 18 to 24 inches tall (to 4 feet in flower) and 2 feet wide. Fertilize lightly. The tall stems don't need staking. Deadhead as seedpods start to swell at the base of the flowering stems. Clip bloom stalks at the base to tidy. Remove remaining flower stems in fall after seeds have ripened. Allow the foliage to remain.

Design ideas

Mullein adds a strong vertical accent to beds. Mass plants in the middle of a flower border. Self-sown seedlings create serendipitous charm.

varieties:

❶ 'SUMMER SORBET' Hot raspberry pink blossoms on 24-inch stems.

OLYMPIC MULLEIN (V. olympicum) Yellow flowers on branched, 6- to 7-foot stems.

New Zealand Flax
(*Phormium tenax*)

Grow this broadleaf grassy ornamental for its striking foliage in dark green, yellow-green, red, rust, or variegations. Drought tolerant New Zealand flax introduces drama to any setting, in planting beds or containers.

Best site
Plant in full sun. Provide a sheltered spot and deep, fertile, moist soil. For the healthiest foliage, give colorful cultivars afternoon shade in desert regions. Many cultivars are slightly less cold hardy than the straight species. Zones 8–11.

Growing
New Zealand flax grows 5 to 7 feet tall and 4 to 8 feet wide. Water plants regularly to keep the soil moist. Divide plants in spring.

Design ideas
Color coordinate New Zealand flax with shrub or perennial blooms or foliage. This strappy grower suits waterside plantings, xeriscapes, and rock gardens. Gardeners in northern climates typically grow it in a container, moving it indoors near a bright window for winter.

varieties:

❶ **'MAORI CHIEF'** Bronze leaves streaked with pink and red; 6 feet tall and 10 feet wide. Zones 9–11.
'YELLOW WAVE' Bright yellow leaves edged in green; 3 to 4 feet tall. Zones 9–11.

Obedient Plant
(*Physostegia virginiana*)

Dress the late summer garden in obedient plant's shades of pink, purple, or white. Blossoms open along densely packed spikes and attract hummingbirds, butterflies, and bees. Gently push individual blooms on the spike to one side or the other and they'll stay put.

Best site
Plant in full sun in fertile, acid soil. Obedient plant tolerates most soils and light conditions. Zones 4–9.

Growing
Obedient plant grows 2 to 4 feet tall and 36 inches wide. Plants in partial shade have fewer flowers. Insert grow-through supports early in spring. Pinch early in the season to reduce flowering height. Deadhead to prolong flowering. In moist, fertile soils, plants are invasive. Variegated forms are less invasive. Divide plants every two to three years to limit spreading. Cut plants back in late fall or early spring.

Design ideas
Pair the plant with butterfly weed or balloon flower. The blooms make excellent cut flowers.

varieties:

❶ **'VIVID'** Deep pink dwarf; 18-inch stems. Fast spreading; can become invasive.
'VARIEGATA' Pink blossoms on 24-inch stems. Cream-edged green leaves.

Oriental Poppy
(*Papaver orientale*)

Stunning crepe-paper petals unfurl atop fuzzy stems on Oriental poppy. This perennial blooms in red, white, pink, and orange in late spring to early summer. The upward-facing, cupped blooms often have dark centers. The sturdy flower stems don't need staking.

Best site
Plant in full sun in moist, deep soil rich in organic matter. Zones 3–10.

Growing
Plants grow 12 to 18 inches tall and 24 inches wide. Flower stems soar 24 to 36 inches. Poppies demand good drainage year-round and protection from strong winds. Plants thrive in cool climates and don't tolerate heat, humidity, or wet soil.

Deadhead or allow seedheads to develop for dried arrangements. After flowering, leaves die and disappear. New growth emerges in late summer to fall. Don't clip or touch this growth; it will disappear next summer after bloom.

Plants rarely need division and are difficult to transplant. You'll have best success with seedlings that appear in early fall. Move these,

keeping them well watered to prevent wilting. Allow poppies to self-sow by letting weather disperse seeds. You can also scatter seeds yourself before winter but after frost.

To sow seeds successfully in areas with warm summers (Zones 7–10), gather ripe seedpods in summer. Place seeds or pods in a paper bag and stash them in the refrigerator until fall. Check them often, tossing any that become moldy. The seeds are tiny. Mix them with sand to make sowing easier. In fall, scatter the seeds.

Design ideas
Poppies are stunning in large drifts. Surround them with late-blooming perennials such as Japanese anemone, aster, and false sunflower.

Poppies make wonderful cut flowers. When cutting, dip the cut stem ends into boiling water or sear them with a lighted match.

YOU SHOULD KNOW
In regions with warm winters, poppies won't reliably flower. That's because in order to bloom, poppies need a period of dormancy—during a warm summer season—followed by a cool winter period.

varieties:

1. **'BEAUTY OF LIVERMERE'** Red orange blooms with a dark eye and black splotches at the base of petals.
2. **'PATTY'S PLUM'** Pinkish purple petals with a black raspberry eye.
3. **'ROYAL WEDDING'** White petals with a deep black eye.
4. **'KING KONG'** Large flowers with red orange, ruffled petals and a black base.
5. **'HELEN ELIZABETH'** Salmon pink, clear blooms on 24-inch stems.

Ornamental Allium
(*Allium*)

These pretty, edible onion cousins grow from bulbs, unfurling grassy leaves with a light onion scent. Straight, leafless stems are topped with spherical or flat blossoms, which are actually clusters of individual flowers that attract butterflies and bees.

Best site
Plant in full sun to part shade in well-drained soil. Alliums like consistent soil moisture; avoid planting in wet, waterlogged soil. Zones 3–10.

Growing
Plants grow from a diminutive 7 inches tall to a towering 5 feet, depending on species. Alliums are fast growing and low maintenance. If you find potted alliums in spring, add them to the garden. Otherwise, plant bulbs in the fall and roughly 5 inches deep. The leaves of many species ripen after flowering. Don't cut ripening foliage; allow it to yellow and die naturally.

Alliums multiply to form increasing clumps, spreading by self-sowing or by forming small bulbs alongside large bulbs. Crowded clumps typically signal the need for division by diminished flower number. Divide clumps in spring by digging them up and separating the bulbs.

Design ideas
The leaves of many species die back after flowering, but flower stalks and dried flowerheads remain. Surround alliums with other perennials that will hide ripening foliage and add interest to the garden. Small allium species make colorful edgings along planting beds or paths or lovely accents in rock gardens. Plant large species in the middle of the border among other perennials or position them as focal points.

Names to watch for
BLUE GLOBE ONION (*A. caeruleum*, pictured at top). Densely packed, bright sky blue, 1-inch-wide flowers in early summer. Plant grows 12 to 24 inches tall. Zones 5–7.

GARLIC CHIVES (*A. tuberosum*) Showy white flowers in late summer on plants 9 inches tall and 6 inches wide. Curtail invasiveness by deadheading before seeds ripen. Attracts bees and butterflies.

GERMAN GARLIC (*A. senescens* 'Glaucum') Lilac to mauve blooms on 12-inch-tall plants in late summer. Foliage swirls around a central point, forming a clump that grows 6 inches wide. Good choice for edging or rock gardens.

GIANT ALLIUM (*A. giganteum*) Purple balls of blooms 5 to 6 inches across on 3- to 5-foot stems in early to midsummer.

GOLDEN GARLIC (*A. moly*) Yellow flowers 1-inch wide on 10- to 12-inch stems in late spring. Use in rock gardens, containers, or borders.

NODDING ONION (*A. cernuum*) Loose clusters of bright pink lily-of-the-valley-shape blooms on 24-inch stems. North American native.

PERSIAN ONION (*A. aflatunense*) Purple flowers 2 to 3 inches across last for several weeks in early spring. Grows 24 to 36 inches tall. Foliage dies back as flowers start to form.

STAR OF PERSIA ALLIUM (*A. christophii*) Large flowers measure 8 to 10 inches across. Strappy, broad leaves often die back before blooms are fully open. 24 inches tall and 8 to 10 inches wide.

Penstemon (*Penstemon*)

For a strong flower show, it's tough to beat penstemon. It sends up spikes covered with tubular blooms in shades including orange, yellow, red, purple, and white. Rabbit- and deer-resistant plants blossom from late spring through summer and attract hummingbirds.

Best site

Plant in full sun to light shade in well-drained soil. Penstemon tolerates wind, heat, and humidity; wet soil in any season will kill it. Zones 2–10.

Growing

Penstemon grows 24 to 30 inches tall and 12 to 24 inches wide. A North American native, penstemon originates from the Desert Southwest or the East. Desert species tolerate droughty, hot conditions. Eastern species prefer moist, fertile, rich soil that isn't wet over winter. If desert species are grown in moist, fertile soil, plants flower less, become floppy, and die.

Natural amounts of rainfall provide adequate water for penstemon. Water deeply, as needed, during drought. Deadhead to promote rebloom. Plants in part shade can be floppy; stake as necessary. Penstemon self-sows. Allow a few seedlings to develop to replace aging, short-lived plants. Seedlings often have different flower colors and heartier constitutions than their parents. Seedheads have an unpleasant odor.

Add a thin layer of compost around plants in early spring. In fall fertilize with a low-nitrogen, high-phosphorus product. Cut plants back in late fall or early spring. Divide in spring or fall every four years to maintain vigor.

Design ideas

Penstemon generally looks best in the garden when planted in drifts. Tuck short species in rock gardens or along the edge of a planting bed. Tall types blend effortlessly in wildflower plantings or the back of the border.

Penstemon makes a wonderful cut flower. Blooms attract hummingbirds, making this low maintenance beauty a natural choice for a wildlife garden. Companion plants include ornamental grasses, geraniums, artemisias, pinks, and catmint.

Scarlet-flowered penstemons look striking with lady's mantle or 'May Knight' salvia. Plant pineleaf penstemon in large drifts in a wildflower garden.

Names to watch for

COMMON BEARD TONGUE (*P. barbatus*)
Western native (pictured above). Open, 30-inch spikes with large red, pink, purple, blue, or white blooms in early summer. Zones 4–9.

FIRECRACKER PENSTEMON (*P. eatonii*)
Native to Southwest and cold desert areas. Long, tubular, scarlet blooms with white stamens in spring; 24 to 36 inches tall and 12 inches wide. Zones 4–10.

PINELEAF PENSTEMON (*P. pinifolius*)
 Southwest native. Scarlet blooms on 18-inch stems from summer to fall. Evergreen, needlelike leaves. Thrives in average to lean garden soil. Needs a little more water than other penstemons. Good choice for first-time penstemon growers. Zones 4–10.

ROCKY MOUNTAIN PENSTEMON (*P. strictus*)
Native to Rocky Mountains and Southwest. Purple flowers provide month-long bloom on 24- to 36-inch stems in late spring to summer. Tolerates typical garden conditions. Good choice for first-time penstemon growers. Zones 4–9.

SMOOTH WHITE PENSTEMON (*P. digitalis*)
 White blooms in midsummer. 24 to 36 inches tall and 18 inches wide. Thrives in heat and humidity. Zones 4–10. 'Husker Red' has red-tinted blooms, stems, and leaves.

YOU SHOULD KNOW

Plant penstemon high, leaving the top edge of the root ball above surrounding soil. Keep the crown above soil and unmulched. If you want mulch, choose a material that won't hold moisture against the plant, such as gravel.

Peony (*Paeonia*)

Peonies are beloved for their luxurious blooms overflowing with petals and fragrance. Flowers in shades of pink, red, white, or cream open in late spring to early summer. The blossoms can be single, double, or semi-double. New cultivars add bicolors, yellow, and coral to the flower palette. Long lived, peonies last for generations.

Best site

Plant in full sun and moist, well-drained soil. Peonies tolerate a wide range of growing conditions. Zones 2–9.

Growing

Peonies grow 24 to 36 inches tall and wide. Plant in fall, when root growth is greatest. Space them 36 inches apart, placing the pink buds (called eyes) just 1 inch underground. If roots are planted deeper, plants won't flower. With potted peonies, plant so that the roots are at the same level they were in the pot. Newly planted peonies can take up to three years to flower.

When shoots appear in early spring, add compost around the plants or gently scratch a slow-release fertilizer into the soil. Stems get top heavy under the weight of blooms; insert grow-through, grid, or linked supports (see page 151) early in the season. Ants crawl on buds as they're opening. Folklore states that ants are necessary for flowers to open, but the insects are merely attracted to nectar that escapes buds as they swell.

Deadhead after flowering. In late fall, cut stems to the ground. Divide plants every 8 to 10 years to renew the planting and soil. Botrytis blight affects peonies, causing dark spots on leaves or purple-brown streaks on stems. Flower buds affected by botrytis often turn dry and shrivel. To reduce the occurrence of botrytis, remove and discard petals as they drop from flowers; deadhead flowers and dispose of them; clean up and dispose of foliage and stems in fall.

Peonies fail to flower for several reasons, including being planted too deep or being newly transplanted. Plants need at least four to six hours of sunlight daily. Too much nitrogen encourages lush foliage at the expense of flowers. Removing leaves in late summer can diminish flower number the following spring, as can an extremely droughty summer. Flower buds can appear but fail to open when a late freeze occurs, fungus attacks the buds (they'll turn brown and mushy; just clip them), or plants are undernourished.

Design ideas

Peonies are a staple on Midwest family farms, where plants are lined out in a staggered double row to form a low, wide hedge. These bloomers are strong performers when tucked into perennial borders. They add floral color early in the season and a wonderfull dark-leaf backdrop for other plants later in the summer. Peonies also make a great partner for spring-flowering bulbs, with peony foliage covering ripening bulb leaves. Extend the flowering season by planting several types that bloom at different times.

Peonies make excellent cut flowers for bouquets; to avoid carrying ants inside, shake the blooms before taking them indoors. Clip leaves all summer to add greenery to bouquets.

Names to watch for

'Cheddar Charm' Overlapping white outer petals surround a large gold center. Fragrant, midseason blooms.

'Scarlet O'Hara' Single red flowers with gold stamens. Good for the South.

TREE PEONY (*Paeonia suffruticosa*) is actually a shrub with woody stems that don't die back to the ground over winter like herbaceous peonies. Plants grow slowly, reaching 3 to 5 feet tall over several decades. Site tree peonies in rich, moist, well drained soil in part shade. You'll get more flowers from plants placed in sunny sites, but blooms last longer in shade. Blossom colors include purple, maroon, green, and yellow—shades not available in herbaceous peonies. Tree peony flowers are larger and open a few weeks earlier than herbaceous peonies. Zones 4–6.

YOU SHOULD KNOW
Peony roots require chilling to 40°F (or colder), which is why many peonies don't flower well in warm climes. These cultivars bloom reliably in warm zones: 'Festiva Maxima', 'Sea Shell', and 'Sarah Bernhardt'.

varieties:

1 'SARAH BERNHARDT' Fragrant, soft pink, double blooms. Late season. Good for the South. Zones 2–8.

2 'BARTZELLA' Fragrant, bright yellow, double flowers. Zones 4–8.

3 'RED CHARM' Bright scarlet flower with ruffled central ball surrounded by flat petals. Zones 3–9.

4 'FESTIVA MAXIMA' Large, white, double blooms flecked with red. Fragrant. Good for the South. Zones 3–8.

5 'PRINCESS CHIFFON' Tree peony with 7- to 8-inch semidouble, ruffled, clear pink blooms. Strong fragrance. Zones 4–8.

Perennial Sunflower
(*Helianthus*)

Perennial sunflower warms the late season garden with its large, 2- to 3-inch-wide yellow daisies with bronze centers. The single or double blooms attract butterflies and have staying power in the vase. This is a reliable, low-maintenance perennial.

Best site
Plant in moist, well-drained soil in full sun. Provide afternoon shade in the South. Plants tolerate clay and a wide pH range. Zones 3–10.

Growing
Plants grow 4 to 6 feet tall and 3 to 4 feet wide. Control height by pinching several times from early spring to midsummer. Deadhead to extend flowering. To prevent stem flopping, insert stakes in spring. Divide in spring every few years to prevent disease and improve air circulation.

Design ideas
This beauty creates a deep green backdrop for other perennials. Pair it with taller ornamental grasses, Russian sage, or monkshood. Skirt with shorter, mounding perennials, such as lady's mantle, coreopsis, catmint, or meadow sage.

varieties:

❶ 'LEMON QUEEN' Single light yellow daisies on a plant 5 feet tall.

Phlox (*Phlox*)

Lavish flower shows make phlox a garden favorite, with species that bloom in nearly every season. Garden phlox and other tall varieties blossom in mid- to late summer; moss, creeping, and woodland phlox flower in early to midspring. Masses of pink, magenta, white, or lavender-blue blooms cover plants.

Best site
Plant phlox in moist, well-drained, fertile soil. Phlox tolerates wind and a range of soil pH but can't withstand drought, heat, or humidity. Plant woodland phlox in full to part shade; garden and moss phlox need full sun. Zones 2–9, depending on species.

Growing
Phlox height varies by species and ranges from 6 inches to 5 feet tall. Plants need deep watering, regular fertilizing, and organic matter in the soil. Stake garden phlox, inserting grow-through supports early in the season. If stems are weak and floppy, thin clumps by removing stems and increase water and fertilizer next spring.

Deadhead garden phlox to encourage rebloom and prevent self-sowing (seedlings don't come true to parents). Shear moss phlox after flowering. Allow woodland phlox to self-seed and create a carpet of color. Divide phlox every three to four years. Thin moss phlox whenever plantings are crowded.

Cut garden phlox to the ground in late fall; remove the clippings. Mulch shallow-rooted moss phlox for winter.

Design ideas
All types of phlox belong in cottage gardens. Woodland phlox suits a shady setting, and garden phlox blends into a meadow planting with ease. Good companions for garden phlox include daylily, Shasta daisy, fountain grass, centranthus, and speedwell. Moss phlox partners well with spring bulbs and shrubs.

Names to watch for

CREEPING PHLOX (*P. stolonifera*) Evergreen, shade-loving groundcover to 6 inches tall. Blue, pink, white, or purple flowers in spring. This is the most fragrant phlox. Zones 3–9.

MOSS PHLOX (*P. subulata*) Evergreen, sun-loving groundcover 3 to 6 inches tall. Blue, pink, white, or purple blooms in early to midspring. Moss-looking foliage is slightly prickly. Zones 2–9.

WOODLAND PHLOX (*P. divaricata*) Evergreen, shade groundcover to 12 inches tall. Purple, pink, or white, slightly fragrant flowers in late spring. Zones 4–9.
'Plum Perfect' Dark-eyed, pale purple flowers; best mildew resistance.

CAROLINA PHLOX (*P. caroliniana*) Native that blooms earlier than garden phlox, filling the early summer garden with fragrant pink to magenta blooms atop 3- to 4-foot stems. Zones 3–9.
'Magnificence' Mildew-resistant phlox with clear pink blooms. Zones 4–9.

MEADOW PHLOX (*P. maculata*) also known as wild sweet william. Lilac, lavender-rose, or white blooms in early to midsummer. Stems grow 12 to 36 inches tall. Zones 4–8.
'Natascha' Bicolored flowers white petals striped pink. Zones 3–8.

GARDEN PHLOX (*P. paniculata*) Summer showstopper of the phlox family. Large flowerheads open mid- to late summer on plants 12 inches to 5 feet tall. Fragrant blooms perfume summer evenings and attract butterflies, hummingbirds, and sphinx moths. Zones 4–8.
'Goldmine' Deep magenta blooms and gold-bordered, green leaves; mildew-resistant. 30 inches tall.

YOU SHOULD KNOW
Tall garden phlox is prone to powdery mildew. Beat this disease by planting mildew-resistant varieties and thinning clumps to five or six stems to increase air circulation.

garden phlox varieties:

1. **'DAVID'** White flowers, sturdy stems, mildew resistant. 4 to 5 feet tall.
2. **'SHORTWOOD'** Bright pink blossoms with deep pink eyes, mildew resistant. 4 to 5 feet tall.
3. **'KATHERINE'** Lavender flowers with white eyes, mildew resistant. 3 to 4 feet tall.
4. **VOLCANO SERIES** Available in several colors, including pink, white, red, purple, and bicolors. Sturdy, mildew resistant purple bicolor blooms; mildew resistant. 24 to 30 inches tall. Zones 4–10.

Pincushion flower
(*Scabiosa caucasica*)

Wiry-stemmed flowers dance above mounds of ferny foliage from summer to fall. This long-flowering beauty opens tufted blue blooms that attract butterflies. Delicate stamens rise above flower centers like pins stuck in a pincushion. Blossom stems grow to 30 inches long, giving the plant an airy appearance.

Best site

Plant in full sun in fertile, well-drained soil that's slightly alkaline. Cool, humid climates are best. High heat, humidity, poor drainage, and wet winter soil harms plant. Zones 5–10.

Growing

The plant grows 18 to 30 inches tall and wide. If your soil is acidic, treat the area near the roots with ground limestone annually in early spring.

Plants take light frosts in stride. They self-sow readily, but seedlings won't look the same as parents. Divide plants every three to four years.

Design ideas

Combine pincushion flower with substantial perennials, such as artemisia, coral bells, and garden mums. It makes a superb cut flower.

Pinks *(Dianthus)*

Kick off the garden season with the spicy fragrance of pinks, sometimes called carnations or dianthus. These dainty bloomers open clove-scented flowers in pink, white, red, rose, or bicolor blends from late spring to early summer, depending on species. The foliage creates an eye-catching evergreen mat of grassy blue-green.

Best site

Plant in full sun in well drained, fertile, slightly alkaline soil. Provide afternoon shade in the South. Pinks don't tolerate wet soil, pH below 6, or heat and high humidity. Zones 3–10.

Growing

Pinks grow from 4 to 12 inches tall and 12 inches wide. Deadhead to extend bloom; cut plants back after flowering to keep foliage compact. Divide every two to three years to renew vigor.

Pinks are susceptible to leaf diseases. Avoid overhead watering or water early in the day so foliage dries before dusk. Apply a low-nitrogen fertilizer in spring.

Design ideas

Place pinks at the front of a border, in rock gardens, or atop a stone wall.

species and varieties:

1 **'BUTTERFLY BLUE'** (*S. columbaria*) Plants are 18 to 24 inches in bloom (lavender-blue blooms on 12- to 18-inch stems). Zones 3–10.

varieties:

1 **CHEDDAR PINKS** (*D. gratianopolitanus*) Tolerates heat and humidity. Flowers open in pink and rose shades in early to midsummer; deadheading brings blooms all summer.

Primrose (*Primula*)

The spring garden comes to life with frilly pink, snow white, magenta, pale purple, or bicolor blooms when you add primrose to the roster. Flowers open in early to late spring, rising in clusters above ground-hugging foliage. Blossoms feature rich hues; the foliage has a corrugated or pebbly texture.

Best site

Plant Japanese primrose in light shade in acid soil that's high in organic matter. Plants can withstand a little sun as long as the soil doesn't dry out. Zones 5–9.

Siebold primrose prefers cool and moist, acid soil that's high in organic matter. Zones 3–8.

English primrose takes part shade or full sun if the soil is constantly moist. Zones 4–8.

Plant cowslip in light to full shade in consistently moist, fertile soil that's slightly alkaline. Zones 4–9.

Growing

Japanese primrose grows 18 to 24 inches tall and 15 to 18 inches wide. Mulch plants to keep roots cool; water during dry spells. Plants often go dormant in the heat of summer, reappearing in fall. Divide plants every three years. Handpick or trap slugs and snails, or use bait.

Siebold primrose grows 4 to 8 inches tall and 8 inches wide. Plants go dormant in the heat of summer, returning the following spring. Plants prefer morning sun and afternoon shade. Protect crowns in winter with a thick mulch or consistent snow covering. Every three years divide plants in early spring or after flowering.

English primrose grows 6 to 9 inches tall and 9 inches wide. Mulch plants to keep roots cool during the growing season. In regions with mild winters, plant in fall for winter flowers.

Cowslip grows 6 to 12 inches tall and wide. Plants self-sow freely, making a wonderful groundcover in a woodland setting. Deadhead to prevent self-sowing.

Design ideas

Japanese primrose looks lovely massed in a woodland setting. Plant Siebold primrose beneath azaleas and rhododendrons, on the north side of a garden shed or home, or in a lightly shaded, moist woodland setting. Mass English primrose in a woodland setting, or plant it near evergreen shrubs for a stunning spring show. Cowslip adds fragrant color to dappled shade gardens in areas with moist soil. It's a good choice for streamside plantings or the edge of moist thickets. Good companions for all primroses include Japanese painted fern, woodland phlox, Lenten rose, hosta, and astilbe.

Names to watch for

JAPANESE PRIMROSE (*P. japonica*) High-rise flower stems accent low-growing leaves.
'Miller's Crimson' Red-purple blooms on 24-inch stems.
'Redfield Strain' Mix of shades, from red to white to pink and hues in between.

SIEBOLD PRIMROSE (*P. sieboldii*) opens 1-inch-wide blooms at the tips of erect 12-inch-tall stems that rise from thick rosettes of fuzzy, bright green leaves.
'Snowflakes' White flowers with fringed petals.
'Lacy Snowflake' White, 1½-inch diameter blossoms open from creamy yellow buds.
'Pink Snowflake' Pink flowers with fringed edges on 12-inch stems.

ENGLISH PRIMROSE (*P. vulgaris*) The species of choice for Southern gardens.
'Blue Sapphire' Double, deep blue blooms.
'Marie Crousse' Lavender-purple flowers on 6-inch plants.
'Prinic' Double, yellow blossoms all summer.

YOU SHOULD KNOW

Some people contract dermatitis from handling primroses. Wear long sleeves, pants, and gloves when working among primroses until you know what your reaction level is.

species and varieties:

1 JAPANESE PRIMROSE (*P. japonica*) Eye-catching blooms with blossoms whorled around a flower stalk that stands above foliage.

2 SIEBOLD PRIMROSE (*P. sieboldii*) Easy to grow and rewards with beautiful blooms that are single or double, fringed, flat, starry, or slightly cupped. Clumps grow steadily larger over time.

3 ENGLISH PRIMROSE (*P. vulgaris*) Flowers in a rainbow of bright hues, including purple, white, pink, red, orange, and bicolors. Plants thrive in full to part shade and are deer resistant.

4 COWSLIP (*P. veris*) Clusters of nodding, fragrant yellow blossoms in spring atop 10-inch stems. Leaves are evergreen to semi-evergreen. Success hinges on providing plants consistently moist, fertile soil.

5 VIALL'S PRIMROSE (*P. viallii*) Flowers feature a spike encircled with small, individual lavender blooms that open from the bottom of the spike up. Flowers stems are 12 to 24 inches. Zones 5–8.

6 CANDELABRA PRIMROSE (*P. beesiana*) Rose, mauve, magenta blooms in late spring to early summer; arranged in whorls around upright stems 18 to 26 inches tall. Zones 4–9.

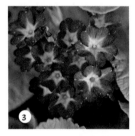

Queen-of-the-Prairie
(*Filipendula rubra*)

This North American native with its towering flowers makes a powerful presence in the garden. Fluffy, 6-inch-long and -wide, fragrant plumes of cherry pink rise to 6 feet above leaves in early to midsummer. The plants are deer and rabbit resistant.

Best site
Plant in full sun to part shade in moist, fertile, well-drained to boggy soil. Zones 3–8.

Growing
Plants grow 12 to 24 inches tall and 18 to 24 inches wide; in flower, height soars to 3 to 6 feet. Cultivars are shorter. Queen-of-the-prairie forms dense colonies in moist to soggy soil in full to part sun. Plants flower and stand tall better in full sun, rarely needing staking. Plants in shade or dry soil tend to be floppy. Add a layer of compost and organic mulch in spring, followed by a thin layer of mulch in fall. Consider cutting the foliage to the ground when it starts to brown in early fall. Attractive seedheads make deadheading unnecessary. Cut back plants in early spring. If powdery mildew attacks, cut down foliage to encourage new leaves to form.

Design ideas
Use queen-of-the-prairie in woodland settings, moist meadows, wildflower gardens, or to fill in boggy sites. Plant it in the back of the border, where its green foliage can provide a backdrop for other perennials. Queen-of-the-prairie looks lovely in a pondside planting, especially when grouped with astilbe, sensitive fern, and royal fern. Round out the combination with a dainty primula to toss in some spring color.

Names to watch for

DROPWORT (*F. vulgaris*) White blooms open from pink buds. Plumes are less dense than queen-of-the-prairie's. Plants grow 12 to 18 inches tall and 18 to 24 inches wide. Grows in part shade and tolerates hot sites if given moisture. Tolerates dry soil in cool climates. Does well in high humidity, wind, and alkaline soil. Cut back in early spring; deadhead to prolong bloom and limit self-sowing. Divide every five to six years. Zones 3–9.
'Multiplex' (also sold as **'Flore Plena'** and **'Plena'**) Double white blooms on 10- to 15-inch-tall stems).

QUEEN-OF-THE-MEADOW (*F. ulmaria*) More compact than queen-of-the-prairie, growing 3 to 4 feet tall and 36 inches wide. White blossoms in early summer. Zones 3–9.
'Aurea' Foliage unfurls bright gold; matures to yellow-green.
'Variegata' Dark green leaves with yellow splotches or stripes. Best color on both cultivars is with part shade. Leaves scorch in full sun in hot climes.

YOU SHOULD KNOW
The plumelike blooms of queen-of-the-prairie attract bees and butterflies. Flowers also attract compliments when cut to use in fresh bouquets. Gather dry blooms and seedheads for dried arrangements.

varieties:

① **'KAHOME'** Dwarf, 12 inches tall and 10 inches wide. Rosy-pink flowers mid- to late summer. Zones 3–8.
② **'VENUSTA'** (*F. rubra*) Deep pink blooms on 4-foot-stems. 'Venusta Alba' (white flowers).

Rodgersia (*Rodgersia*)

Massive and impressive, rodgersia issues a command performance in moist soil, unfurling huge, dark green leaves up to 36 inches across. Fuzzy plumes of tiny pink, red, or white flowers soar above the foliage in spring or mid- to late summer, depending on the species.

Best site
Plant in part sun to full shade in continuously moist to soggy soil high in organic matter. Rodgersia tolerates heavy clay, but not full sun or heat unless plants are kept wet. Zones 5–8.

Growing
Rodgersia grows 24 inches tall (3 to 4 feet in bloom) and 3 to 4 feet wide. Space plants 3 feet apart. Mulch to keep roots cool and moist. Deadhead to tidy plants. When top growth dies in fall, cut plants back. Rodgersia rarely needs division and is hard to move. When moving, keep soil moist around transplants so they don't wilt.

Design ideas
Use this dramatic perennial as a focal point in a planting bed, with partners such as hosta, bugbane, and royal fern.

species:

❶ BRONZELEAF RODGERSIA (*R. podophylla*) Bronze-green, five-leaflet foliage; turns red in fall. Yellow-white blooms in midsummer.

Rose Turtlehead (*Chelone obliqua*)

For the shade garden or a moist spot, count on rose turtlehead to contribute beauty in late summer and fall. Small, deep rose-purple blooms, clustered along upright stems, attract butterflies and bees, making the plant a great addition to a wildlife garden.

Best site
Plant in dense shade in moist, neutral to acid soil. Turtlehead tolerates heavy clay and alkaline soils, along with full sun, provided soil is constantly moist. Zones 4–10.

Growing
Rose turtlehead grows 24 to 36 inches tall and 12 inches wide. Plants spread by shallow rhizomes, forming wide, dense colonies. Layer plants with 1 to 2 inches of compost in fall to renew their vigor.

Design ideas
Rose turtlehead has glossy foliage and a strong vertical form. Pair it with hosta, astilbe, or sensitive fern in a moist, shady spot. In a sunnier spot, companions include meadow rue, daylily, queen-of-the-prairie, and ornamental grasses.

species:

❶ PINK TURTLEHEAD (*C. lyonii*) Forms pale rose flowers. 'Hot Lips' (shorter variety with hot pink blooms).

Russian sage
(Perovskia atriplicifolia)

Russian sage adds beauty to gardens while making few demands. Long-lasting lavender blooms sparkle amid lacy, gray-green leaves from mid- to late summer. Tiny blossoms covering 12 or more inches of stem tips makes for a stunning show. Foliage smells like sage when bruised.

Best site
Plants prefer light, alkaline, somewhat dry soils, but will grow in average, well drained soil. Russian sage tolerates drought, heat, humidity, and wind, but does not take shade or poor drainage. Zones 4–10.

Growing
Russian sage grows 4 feet tall and wide. Plants don't normally need staking, unless growing in fertile or moist soil. In these conditions, insert grow-through supports or tree branches early in the season. Supports will disappear nicely as stems grow.

Prune plants in spring, treating them like a woody shrub. Remove any dead or damaged wood, and place cuts to shape the plant. Shorten stems by cutting to a bud facing the direction you want growth to head. For better flowering and more upright stems, cut plants to the base.

Mulch plants in Zones 3 and 4 for winter protection. In climes where stems die to the ground and only roots survive, cut plants back in early spring.

Design ideas
Soft, finely divided foliage combines well with ornamental grasses, perennial sunflower, coneflower, and caryopteris. Other good companions are lamb's-ears, white garden phlox, and coral bells.

Plant hyssop, penstemon, and coreopsis with Russian sage to stage a drought-tolerant, deer-resistant combination. Surround plants with dark mulch for a striking scene, or plant in front of dark evergreens or highbush cranberry for a pretty late season show.

YOU SHOULD KNOW
Russian sage spreads by natural layering. Whenever a stem touches the ground, it roots and produces a new plant. Dig and share these starts with friends or use them in your own garden.

varieties:

1. **'BLUE SPIRE'** Hybrid with deep violet-blue blooms on plants 24 to 36 inches tall. Stems more upright than the species.
2. **'LITTLE SPIRE'** Flowers appear earlier in summer on 24-inch stems. Plants rebloom in fall in mild climates.
3. **'LONGIN'** Finely dissected, coarse foliage.
   'FILLIGRAN' Finer texture and dissected leaves.

Salvia, Sage (*Salvia*)

Salvia plants open showy flowers in blue, purple, red, white, and pink. Blossoms appear from late spring to fall, depending on species, and are a favorite of bees, butterflies, and hummingbirds. As a group, salvias offer deer and rabbit resistance. Plants vary from small perennials to large woody shrubs and are covered with dark green or grey-green and smooth or pebbled leaves.

Best site

Plant in full sun and average, well-drained soil. Zones 4–10.

Growing

Plant autumn sage in full sun in lean to average, well-drained soil. It thrives in heat, drought, and alkaline soil. Plants become leggy in shade or rich soil and don't tolerate wet soil. Cut back to 4 inches in late winter and late summer.

Site blue anise sage in full sun and well-drained soil. Plants in shade produce few flowers and lanky stems that need support. Cut back by one-third in early spring to reduce final height. Water and deadhead regularly during summer. Cut plants to the ground in late fall.

Give common sage full sun and slightly acid to neutral, well-drained soil. Water during drought. Avoid shade and wet soil. Prune as needed to control height and shape.

Plant perennial salvia in moist soil that's well drained in every season. Wet winter soil can kill plants. Deadheading extends blooming. Divide in early spring every three years.

Design ideas

Use autumn sage in a border to create a backdrop for other small perennials or as a focal point shrub. A natural fit in a butterfly or hummingbird garden, plant it with lavender, penstemon, or Russian sage. In cold regions, autumn sage is often grown as a container annual.

Blue anise sage thrives in planting beds or containers. Good companions include pink- or yellow-flower perennials, such as threadleaf coreopsis, goldenrod, coneflower, or butterfly weed. This is an excellent plant for fall color; use it as an annual in northern zones, exposing it in full sun. Pair it with ornamental grasses and pink-flowering asters. Common sage makes a charming edging and blends well with catmint or lavender. Plants also grow well in potted herb gardens. If the soil is too rich, leaf flavor will diminish.

Perennial salvia looks fantastic massed in a border or planted beneath roses. Underplant it with pinks or violets for a pretty spring scene, or pair it with lady's mantle or 'Bowles' Golden' sedge.

Names to watch for

AUTUMN SAGE (*S. greggii*) Blossoms open in red, white, or violet from midsummer to fall. In mild climates, plants flower from February to November. The bright blooms are a magnet for hummingbirds. It becomes a dense shrub 36 inches tall and wide; extremely heat and drought tolerant. Leaves are gray-green, contrasting nicely with blooms. Zones 7–10.
'Furman's Red' Bright red flowers, hardy to Zone 6.
'Purple Pastel' Light purple blooms.

BLUE ANISE SAGE (*S. guaranitica*) Intense blue flowers start opening in midsummer and continue until frost. Becomes a woody shrub 36 inches tall and wide, topped with flower stems that soar 12 to 24 inches above leaves. Zones 7–10.

COMMON SAGE (*S. officinalis*) Most commonly grown as a culinary herb. Plants grow 2 to 2½ feet tall and wide; larger in mild zones. Zones 4–10.
 'Tricolor' Leaves with irregular cream margins, some tinged with red. It can be used as an herb too. Hardy to Zone 6.

YOU SHOULD KNOW
Perennial salvia stages a long flowering season if you faithfully deadhead plants. The first bloom is the strongest, followed by looser spikes. Established plants tolerate heat, drought, and humidity.

PERENNIAL SALVIA (*S. nemerosa*) Purple-blue flowers rise on upright stems above dark green foliage. Plant grows 12 to 18 inches tall and wide; bloom spikes soar 12 to 24 inches. This is one of the longest-blooming cold-hardy salvias. Flowers open in late spring to early summer; plants rebloom with deadheading. Zones 4–10.

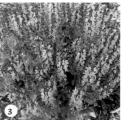

perennial salvia varieties:

1 **'MAY NIGHT'** (also sold as 'Mainacht') Dark blue-violet spires. Grows 18 to 24 inches tall.

2 **'EAST FRIESLAND'** (also sold as 'Ostfriesland') Deep purple spikes on 18- to 36-inch plants.

3 **'SENSATION ROSE'** Light pink flowers on compact 12-inch stems.

Sea holly (*Eryngium*)

Prickly sea holly is a head-turning perennial. Steely blue to deep purple thistlelike flowers open over a long period in July and August. The blooms are beautiful in fresh flower arrangements or in dried bouquets. The plants are drought tolerant and deer resistant.

Best site
Plant in full sun in well drained soil. Cool nights yield the best color. Sea holly adapts to sandy soil and salty conditions. Zones 2–10.

Growing
Sea holly grows 24 to 36 inches tall and 18 to 24 inches wide. Plants need staking when grown in rich soil. A deep taproot makes them difficult to move. Sea holly is disease and insect resistant.

Plants spread by seeds; deadhead to prevent self-sowing. To eliminate seeds, grow the sterile cultivar 'Sapphire Blue'.

Design ideas
Place sea holly against a dark evergreen to make its blue color pop. In a border, combine it with yarrow, artemisia, coneflower, and ornamental grasses.

varieties:

❶ AMETHYST SEA HOLLY 24 inches tall and wide. Most cold hardy species.

Sedges (*Carex*)

Well-known water garden plants, sedges also perform in the perennial garden. The foliage sports stripes and colors including blue-green, gold, and white. Sedges resemble ornamental grasses, forming clumps or low-arching mounds of narrow leaves. In mild climates, the foliage is evergreen, adding interest to the winter garden.

Best site
Plant in full shade to part shade in hot climates; full sun to full shade in cool regions. Sedges need moist, well-drained soil. Zones 5–10.

Growing
Plants are 6 to 24 inches tall and wide, depending on species. Avoid overwatering. In regions with cold winters, cover plants in late fall with a loose mulch, like straw or pine boughs. Cut damaged foliage after removing mulch in early spring. Divide plants in early spring.

Design ideas
Use sedges as edgings or accent plants. Massed, sedges form a dense groundcover. Plants thrive in rock gardens or water gardens. In Southern gardens, foliage provides multiseason interest. Good companion plants include foamflower, astilbe, ferns, foamy bells, hosta, and coral bells.

Names to watch for
GOLDEN-TUFTED SEDGE (*C. elata* 'Aurea') Yellow-edged bright green leaves grow 24 inches tall and wide. Zones 5–10.

JAPANESE GRASS SEDGE (*C. morrowii*) 'Goldband' Broad, white leaf edge. 12 inches tall, 24 inches wide.
'Ice Dance' Thin, white leaf edge; 12 inches tall.

WEEPING BROWN SEDGE (*C. flagellifera*) Linear reddish bronze evergreen leaves resemble tufts of hair. Arching, 18-inch clump. Use as edging and in containers. Zones 6–9.
'Bronzita' 12-inch tall and wide.
'Toffee Twist' Bronzy clump 18 to 24 inches tall and wide. Zones 7–11.

YOU SHOULD KNOW
When transplanting sedge, keep plants well watered until roots form. Once sedges are established, they typically need watering only during the driest parts of the growing season, in peak summer.

species and varieties:

1 **'BOWLES' GOLDEN'** Slender, gold-green leaves with thin green margins; 24- to 36-inch mounds. Zones 6–9.

2 **'ISLAND BROCADE'** (*C. ciliatomarginata*) Green leaves edged in yellow. 6 to 10 inches tall. Use as groundcover under trees, as edging, or in containers. Zones 6–9.

3 **JAPANESE GRASS SEDGE** (*C. morrowii*) Green leaves ½ inch wide. Zones 5–9.

4 **'THE BEATLES'** (*C. caryophyllea*) Mophead of blue-green, fine-textured foliage on clump 6 inches tall and 24 inches wide. Zones 5–9.

5 **WEEPING BROWN SEDGE** (*C. flagellifera*) Forms an arching mound of bronze foliage. 12 to 18 inches tall. Zones 5–9.

Shasta Daisy
(*Leucanthemum*)

Give your garden vintage charm by planting a drift of classic white daisies with yellow centers. These early summer bloomers feature single or double flowers that rise from a low mound of dark green foliage. Blossoms make great additions to bouquets. Plants are easy-care, low-maintenance beauties.

Best site
Plant in full sun in well drained, alkaline soil. Daisies tolerate traditional garden soil. Zones 4–10.

Growing
Daisies grow 9 inches to 4 feet tall (36 inches or more in bloom) and 24 inches wide. Stake tall varieties with grow-through supports. Some varieties rebloom after deadheading.

Cut back plants in fall after the foliage dies. Divide every three years in spring or fall to renew the clump and maintain strong blooming. When dividing, discard the central portion of the clump, which often harbors pests.

Design ideas
Shasta daisies pair well with spiky-flowered perennials, such as mullein and speedwell.

varieties:

❶ 'ALASKA' 3-inch-wide, single daisies on long stems. Good for cutting.

'CRAZY DAISY' Semidouble to double white daisies with small, butter yellow centers.

Showy Sedum
(*Sedum spectabile*)

Showy sedum offers four-season interest: fresh foliage in spring, chartreuse flower buds in summer, blooms in late summer to fall, and faded flowers in winter. The blooms attract butterflies and bees. The thick, succulent foliage is often tinted various shades of blue, purple, red, or gray.

Best site
Plant showy sedum in full sun to part sun in well-drained soil. Sedum tolerates heat, high humidity, and wind, making it a good choice for Southern gardens. Plants don't withstand wet soil or poor drainage. Zones 3–10.

Growing
Showy sedum grows 12 to 18 inches tall (24 inches in bloom) and 24 inches wide. Typically, plants rarely need division, but flop-prone plants often benefit from division every five years or so in early spring. In this case, you're using division as a way to maintain the plant's health, shape, and overall vigor. Lift the plant, discarding central portions of the clump that may show little growth. Also break off any woody roots. Refresh the soil in the planting hole. If your planting bed has a rich, fertile base, add a little sharp sand to enhance drainage and reduce fertility, which contributes to stem flop.

Allow plants to remain through winter to add interest. Trim flowers and stems in spring. Aphids occasionally attack plants in spring.

Design ideas
Showy sedum holds its own in a border planting, forming a sturdy clump. Its four seasons of interest and tough-as-nails constitution make it a great choice for low-maintenance plantings. Sedum grows fast; add it to new planting beds as a smaller plant and you'll have full-size beauty the next growing season.

In narrow spaces, plant showy sedum in a row to form a no-fuss, hedge-style planting. In perennial borders, combine it with late-flowering perennials, such as joe-pye weed, goldenrod, ornamental grasses, or asters.

Names to watch for

SHOWY SEDUM (*S. spectabile*)
'Autumn Fire' Improved 'Autumn Joy' with bigger flowers and stronger stems.

'Neon' Rosy magenta flowers top foliage that is neon yellow green in late summer. Leaves take on a golden hue in fall.
'Purple Emperor' Deep pink flowers top foliage which turns burgundy-purple by late summer.

GOLDMOSS STONECROP (*S. acre*)
Groundcover to 3 inches tall with tiny round leaves. Flowers open bright yellow in spring. Avoid planting fast-growing groundcover sedums in alpine gardens; plants will crowd out slow-growing alpines. Zones 3–10.
'Iceberg' White blooms.

KAMCHATKA STONECROP

(*S. kamtschaticum*) Toothed leaves on stems growing 4 to 9 inches tall; flat-head yellow flowers in summer. Zones 3–9.
'Variegatum' Scalloped green leaves edged in pink and yellow.
'Tricolor' Variegated deep green, white, and pink foliage with pink flowers.

TWO-ROW STONECROP (*S. spurium*)
Groundcover 2 to 6 inches tall. White or rose flowers in midsummer. Same care as showy sedum. Zones 3–10.

'Dragon's Blood' Deep pink flowers on bronze-tinged foliage that turns dark burgundy in fall. Low-growing groundcover. Zones 3–10.
'Red Carpet' Red-tint leaves turn burgundy in fall; sparse red blooms.

BLUE SPRUCE SEDUM (*S. pruniatum* 'Blue

Spruce') Groundcover with smooth, blue-green leaves on stems less than 6 inches tall. Bright yellow blossoms in midsummer. Zones 4–9.

ANGELINA SEDUM (*S. reflexum* 'Angelina')

Tidy groundcover with stems 6 to 12 inches tall. Bright chartreuse foliage fades to lighter green in summer. Zones 6–9.

species and varieties:

❶ 'AUTUMN JOY' (*S. spectabile*) Denser blooms with richer color, starting rose, aging to bronze, and turning chocolate brown in winter.

❷ 'BLACK JACK' (*S. spectabile*) Deep purple, almost black leaves; 8-inch-wide, pink flower clusters.

❸ 'BRILLIANT' (*S. spectabile*) Large clusters of bright rose pink flowers.

❹ 'FROSTY MORN' (*S. telephium*) White flower clusters, gray-green foliage edged in white.

❺ GOLDMOSS STONECROP (*S. acre*) Ground-hugging succulent is rabbit and deer resistant. Plants tolerate salt spray and road salt.

❻ KAMCHATKA STONECROP (*S. kamtschaticum*) Gold starlike flowers blanket this groundcover in early summer. Foliage is whorled and toothed on the edges, very attractive when not in bloom.

❼ 'MATRONA' (*S. telephium*) Large pink blooms on reddish purple stems; gray-green leaves with rosy margins.

Spiderwort
(*Tradescantia*)

With a foolproof, easy-growing nature, spiderwort opens three-petaled flowers in purple, pink, or white from spring to fall. The blossoms close daily at dusk. Whenever the foliage looks less than ideal, cut the plant to the ground to stimulate new flowers.

Best site
Plant in part shade in moist, well drained soil. Zones 3–11.

Growing
Spiderwort grows 12 to 24 inches tall and wide. Cut the foliage to the ground after spring bloom to prevent self-sowing and renew the clump. New shoots and leaves emerge, followed by fresh flowers. Keep plants watered. Spider mites attack when heat arrives; cut plants to the ground and water them. Spiderwort can be invasive by self-sowing and sprouting from pieces of root left in the ground when moving plants.

Design ideas
Use spiderwort as an edging along paths or a groundcover in shady spots. Plants blend well with centranthus and columbine.

varieties:

❶ 'SWEET KATE' (also sold as 'Blue and Gold') Chartreuse foliage and deep violet-blue blooms.

Spike Speedwell
(*Veronica*)

For long-season color, it's tough to beat spike speedwell. Spikes in white, blue, pink, or violet open in summer and continue until frost. Spike speedwell provides some of the truest and richest blues in the garden. The plants are easy-to-grow and undemanding.

Best site
Plant in full sun to part shade in moist, well drained, fertile soil. Poor winter drainage will kill plants. Zones 4–10.

Growing
Spike speedwell grows 8 to 18 inches tall (12 to 24 inches in bloom) and 18 inches wide. Plants prefer some fertility; mix compost into holes at planting time. Water regularly the first year after planting. Speedwell is drought tolerant once established.

In spring, fertilize plants with a complete organic fertilizer, and continue to build soil fertility by adding a layer of compost around plants. Deadhead after flowering to keep blooms coming all season long. If plants become floppy, prune stems hard, removing all leggy growth.

Divide speedwell in fall or early spring. Poor winter drainage can kill plants. In some regions, powdery mildew may attack foliage. Give plants a slightly moister site to prevent the disease. Afternoon shade helps diminish leaf browning.

Design ideas
Spike speedwell makes a charming addition to cottage gardens. Planted with lady's mantle, clematis, centranthus, and coreopsis, it orchestrates a blooming combination that plays a flowery tune all summer long.

Speedwell is a natural choice for wildlife gardens, where the flower spikes beckon butterflies and bees. In a cutting garden, combine it with peony, bearded iris, black-eyed susan, balloon flower, and aster for beautiful bouquets. Select small, mat-forming species for rock gardens. In general garden settings, good planting companions include daylily, coneflower, hollyhock, and Siberian iris.

Names to watch for

CREEPING VERONICA (*V. umbrosa*)
'Georgia Blue' Low, mat-forming veronica that grows 4 to 6 inches tall and 12 inches wide. Round, saucer-shape, clear blue flowers with white eyes appear in late winter or early spring. Leaves turn bronze-purple in winter. Plant in full sun to part shade. Good choice for rock gardens or rocky edgings of planting beds. Zones 3–8.

LONG-LEAF VERONICA (*V. longifolia*) A larger version of spike speedwell, growing 24 to 36 inches tall and 18 inches wide with tall violet, pink, or fuchsia spikes. Plants don't tolerate drought, wet soil, or high humidity, but do withstand wind. Staking is sometimes necessary; use grow-through supports. Zones 4–10.

SPIKE SPEEDWELL (*V. spicata*) Forms low-growing mat and tall-flowering clump. Flowers open from the bottom of the spike up. Spikes appear from summer through fall in shades of blue, white, pink, and purple. Deer resistant. Zones 3–8.
'Alba' White flowers on 15-inch-tall spikes in midsummer.
'Blue Carpet' Groundcover, creeping form with stems 6 inches tall and spreads to 15 inches wide.
'Red Fox' Deep rose-red flowers on plant 12 to 18 inches tall and wide.

TURKISH SPEEDWELL (*V. liwanensis*)
Vigorous groundcover veronica covered with blue flowers in spring. Forms a thick green carpet 3 inches tall and 12 to 18 inches wide. Reblooms lightly in summer if given water. Needs afternoon shade in hot climes. Great choice for western regions; forms fast-growing groundcover. Zones 4–10.

YOU SHOULD KNOW

Spike speedwell makes an excellent cut flower. For longest vase life, snip stems when blooms at the bottom of the spike are beginning to open and tiny flower buds show color nearly to the tip of the spire.

species and varieties:

1 **'GEORGIA BLUE'** (*V. spicata* hybrid)
2 **'GOODNESS GROWS'** (*V. spicata* hybrid) Dark violet-blue spikes on 12-inch-tall and -wide plant.
3 **LONG-LEAF VERONICA** (*V. longifolia*)
4 **'PURPLELICIOUS'** (*V. spicata* hybrid) Dark purple blooms on 10-inch-long spikes. Zones 3–8.
5 **SPIKE SPEEDWELL** (*V. spicata*) 'Red Fox' is pictured here.
6 **'SUNNY BORDER BLUE'** (*V. spicata* hybrid) Deep violet-blue flowers above crinkled leaves. 18 to 24 inches tall, 12 to 18 inches wide. Zones 4–9.
7 **'WATERPERRY BLUE'** (*V.* hybrid) Pale blue blooms in early summer on 4- to 6-inch-tall plants. Good in rock gardens. Zones 4–8.

Spurge *(Euphorbia)*

There's a spurge that will flourish in every garden setting—from dry shade to moist soil or a sunny rock garden. The foliage is showy, and the flowers feature colorful, eyecatching bracts in bright shades. (Poinsettia is a member of this genus.) Use deer- and rabbit-resistant spurge as a filler or focal point in the garden.

Best site

Plant in full sun to full shade, well-drained to moist soil, depending on species. Zones 3–11.

Growing

Spurge can grow from 4 inches to 5 feet tall and 3 to 8 feet wide, depending on species. Deadhead after flowering to prevent self-sowing. Many species fall open after flowering; cut back by at least half to rejuvenate the plant. Divide plants every three to five years to reduce crowding and renew clumps. Spurges are pest free.

The stems leak a milky sap that causes an allergic reaction in some individuals. Wear gloves when working with spurge. If these plants are staples in your garden, consider using a separate pair of gloves for working with them. Spurge blooms make good cut flowers; seal the stem bases in boiling water to stop sap leakage.

Names to watch for

CUSHION SPURGE (*E. polychroma*) Chartreuse flower bracts open atop 12- to 20-inch stems in early to midspring (pictured top right). Grows 24 inches wide. Plant in full to part sun in well drained soil. Combine with midseason tulips, creeping phlox, dwarf bearded iris, and peonies. Zones 3–10.

CYPRESS SPURGE (*E. cyparissias*) Lime yellow flower bracts appear in spring; they fade to red. Site in full sun in dry soil . Tolerates sandy soil. Grows 9 to 12 inches tall and 12 to 18 inches wide. Forms a dense groundcover; use 8 plants per square yard. Spreads by underground stems and self-sowing. In rich soils, plant is invasive. Zones 4–10.

MEDITERRANEAN SPURGE (*E. characias*) Chartreuse bloom bracts persist from spring to early summer. Purple stems and blue-green leaves on plant 3 to 5 feet tall and 24 to 36 inches wide. Grow in full sun in dry, rocky soil. Zones 7–10.

E. c. wulfenii Chartreuse flower bracts from late spring to midsummer on plant 2 to 4 feet tall and 24 to 36 inches wide. Pair with iris, centranthus, or artemisia.

MYRTLE SPURGE (*E. myrsinites*) Bright yellow bracts on trailing stems with geometrically arranged blue-green leaves. Grows 6 inches tall and 12 inches wide. Site in full sun in well-drained soil. Commonly used in rock gardens and trailing over stone walls. A noxious weed in some western regions, such as Colorado. Zones 5–10.

'PURPUREA' PURPLE WOOD SPURGE (*E. amygdaloides*) Burgundy-purple leaves make chartreuse flower bracts pop in mid- to late spring. 12 to 18 inches tall and wide. Site in part to full shade in moist to dry soil. Grows in dry shade. Prune right after flowering. Short lived in Zones 5–6, but self-sowing ensures a presence in the garden. Use as groundcover. Zones 5–10.

Stokes' Aster
(Stokesia laevis)

Long-blooming stokes' aster decorates the garden with shaggy pink, blue, white, or yellow flowers from summer to fall. The 3- to 5-inch-wide daisies with fringed petals and fluffy centers last for weeks. This Southern native opens nectar-rich blooms that lure bees and butterflies.

Best site
Plant in full sun to light shade in moist, well drained, acid soil. Zones 5–10.

Growing
Stokes' aster grows 12 to 18 inches tall and 18 inches wide (up to 24 inches in flower). Give it full sun in the North and afternoon shade in the South. Deadhead to extend bloom, cutting flower stems to foliage. Use grow-through supports to keep plants upright. Mulch in Zone 5 winters. Remove dead or damaged leaves in spring. Divide clumps every three to five years.

Design ideas
Use stokes' aster in container, cottage, or wildlife gardens. Blossoms make long-lasting cut flowers. Good planting companions include aster, 'Happy Returns' daylily, and blanket flower.

varieties:

❶ **'BLUE DANUBE'** Lavender-blue blooms.
'COLORWHEEL' Flowers open white, change to lavender, mature to purple.

Sweet Woodruff
(Galium odoratum)

In shady settings, sweet woodruff creates a dense groundcover with bright green, fine-textured leaves. White blooms open in spring, dotting the green mat with sparkling stars. Dried leaves smell like sweet, freshly mown hay and are often added to potpourri.

Best site
Plant in part to full shade in moist, well-drained soil. This groundcover also tolerates average, thin soils of various pH. Zones 4–9.

Growing
Sweet woodruff grows 4 inches tall (up to 12 inches tall in flower) and 8 inches wide. It requires frequent irrigation in areas with hot, dry summers. Sweet woodruff spreads by creeping roots, filling in around other plants. It tends to die back during summer heat and drought, and especially in dry, sunny settings. Divide in spring or fall; propagate by digging up edges of clumps.

Design ideas
Use this spring bloomer in woodland settings or shady borders or rock gardens. Plants work well on shady slopes where grass won't grow.

species:

❶ **SWEET WOODRUFF** (*G. odoratum*) White flowers decorate plants in spring.

Thyme *(Thymus praecox)*

Also called creeping thyme or mother-of-thyme, this ground-hugging herb forms a dense mat of scented, edible foliage that sparkles with brightly tinted blooms from late spring to early summer. The flowers attract bees, and the plants offer good drought tolerance and rabbit resistance. Look for cultivars with variegated gold and silver leaves.

YOU SHOULD KNOW
Harvesting thyme for the kitchen is easy: Just snip a few stems from the plant and peel off the leaves. Don't eat the woody stems. With new plantings, avoid harvesting more than one-third of stems. It's nearly impossible to overharvest established thyme plants.

Best site
Plant in full or part sun in well-drained soil with low fertility. Thyme tolerates wind, heat, light foot traffic, and organic or clay soil if it's well drained. Plants will grow beneath the high shade of deciduous trees. Zones 4–10.

Growing
Thyme grows 1 to 8 inches tall and 12 to 24 inches wide. Plants spread by layering, with stems rooting wherever they touch the ground. Thyme grows at a medium to fast pace. Too much fertilizer causes vigorous growth with lanky stems and diminished leaf flavor. Shear or mow plants after flowering to promote branching and dense growth. Cutting plants back in fall or early spring isn't necessary.

Divide plantings every three to four years to renew the clump. Thyme transplants easily. Cut a portion of the plant, and lift stems and roots from the soil. When planting divisions, amend soil in planting holes with equal parts compost and sand. Plants in full sun in desert areas can be hard to establish. Water well until plants are actively producing new growth. Providing a little shade during the afternoon is helpful in southern regions.

Design ideas
Thyme is versatile in the perennial garden. Use it to camouflage bare lower stems of plants like butterfly weed or spike speedwell. It forms an eye-pleasing balance when planted with tall vase-shape perennials such as fountain grass, white gaura, yarrow, and caryopteris.

Thyme does an excellent job covering spots of bare soil along edges of planting beds. Alternate it with creeping phlox for a textural tapestry. Use thyme between stepping-stones or to add a green carpet to a rock garden.

With silver-tone perennials, such as artemisia and lamb's-ears, thyme makes a lovely partner. It also pairs well with coarse-textured plants such as upright-growing showy sedum or globe thistle. Golden cultivars shine when planted with purple-leaf plants such as coral bells or 'Matrona' or 'Purple Emperor' sedum.

Names to watch for
DOONE VALLEY THYME (*T.* 'Doone Valley') Green leaves variegated gold in spring; mature leaves fade to green. Stems sprawl to 18 inches; pink flowers on 3- to 4-inch stems in late spring or early summer. Trim flower stems after bloom, otherwise stems will creep over faded blooms, forming gentle mounds. Leaves have lemon flavor, which doesn't hold up in cooking. Use as a garnish.

ELFIN THYME (*T. serpyllum* 'Elfin') Lilac blooms blanket stems in early summer. Plant grows 1 to 2 inches tall. One of the smallest-leaved thymes and slowest growing. Excellent choice for filling in around tightly spaced stepping-stones. Zones 5–10.

ENGLISH THYME (*T. vulgaris*) This is the common culinary thyme. Plants grow 12 inches tall and flower in spring, luring honeybees and beneficial wasps. Best flavor develops when plants are in full sun in fertile, well-drained soil. Trim stems after flowering, cutting back to just past blooms. Best flavored leaves for drying occur on new growth that emerges after flowering.

LEMON THYME (*T.* ×*citriodorus*) Plant grows 12 inches tall and wide. Leaves smell like lemons when crushed. Blossoms open pale lilac to pink. **'Aureus'** Dark green leaves edged in gold. **'Archer's Gold'** Dark golden-yellow foliage.

thyme varieties:

1 **'COCCINEUS'** (*T. praecox*) Magenta blooms from early to midsummer. Dark green leaves turn bronze in fall.

2 **LEMON THYME** Use as a substitute in recipes for lemon juice, zest, or flavoring.

3 **'RUBY GLOW'** (*T. praecox*) Ruby-purple flower clusters to 6 inches long. Crushed blooms smell like lemons.

4 **WOOLLY THYME** (*T. pseudolanuginosus*) Tiny leaves with furry hairs. Needs good drainage.

5 **'SILVER QUEEN'** (*T. citriodorus,* also sold as 'Argenteus') Green leaves edged in white on plants 6 to 12 inches tall and wide. Upright, twiggy stems bear pink blooms in midsummer.

Torch Lily (*Kniphofia*)

Set off floral fireworks with torch lily's towering spikes. From summer to fall the blossoms open in sizzling hues that lure hummingbirds. Red buds open to orange flowers, which fade to yellow, giving the elongated flower stems a two-tone appearance. This deer-resistant plant unfurls sword-shape, blue-green leaves.

Best site
Plant in full sun in moist, well-drained soil. Avoid windy spots. Zones 6–10.

Growing
Torch lily grows 18 to 24 inches tall (to twice that height in bloom) and 3 to 4 feet wide. Drainage is key; too much moisture leads to crown rot. Deadhead individual flowers after bloom. Cut stalks to ground level when flowering is finished. Divide plants if clumps become crowded, though rarely needed.

Design ideas
Plant torch lily in the back of the border or give it center stage in a container. Blooms make excellent cut flowers, and the plant's showy nature makes it a natural choice for a focal point plant.

varieties:

1 **'BRESSINGHAM COMET'** Scarlet to yellow flowers on 24-inch plants from late summer to fall. **'CANDLELIGHT'** Creamy yellow flower buds open to white.

Tree Mallow
(*Lavatera thuringiaca*)

Tree mallow opens pink or white trumpet-shape blooms along stems all summer long. The 3-inch-wide flowers resemble hollyhock blossoms and attract butterflies and bees. Group several tree mallows to create a shrubby planting.

Best site
Plant in full sun in continuously moist, fertile, well-drained soil. Site in afternoon shade in the South or other hot climes. Tree mallow tolerates heat and humidity. Zones 6–10.

Growing
Tree mallow grows 5 to 7 feet tall and 4 feet wide. Cut flowering stems back after blossoms fade. In spring, cut the entire plant back to 24 inches. Water during dry spells. Clean up fallen leaves from around plants in late fall. Japanese beetles can attack plants; hand pick them.

Design ideas
Tree mallow creates a striking specimen in a container. In the border, it adds season-long color and stature. Good companion plants include Shasta daisy, goldenrod, joe-pye weed, and bee balm.

Variegated Solomon's Seal
(*Polygonatum odoratum*)

Tiny, fragrant, bell-shape blooms dangle beneath the leaves, luring bumblebees to weave among plants. The foliage fades to gold in fall. Plants decay in place over winter with no need for fall cutback.

Best site
Plant in part shade in moist soil with abundant organic matter. Variegated solomon's seal will adapt to dry shade conditions. Zones 4–9.

Growing
Plants grow 36 inches tall and 12 inches wide. They often go dormant during hot summers. Small plants are slow to grow in the garden; start with the largest plants you can find. Space them 12 inches apart. There's no need to deadhead or cut plants down in fall. They spread by rhizomes to form large colonies. Divide every five years or so in early spring or fall.

Design ideas
Use variegated solomon's seal to brighten a moist, shady border. Companion plantings include Japanese painted fern, 'Jack Frost' heart-leaf brunnera, hosta, and barrenwort.

species:

❶ PINK TREE MALLOW (*L. thuringiaca*). Blooms add a delicate sparkle to summer perennial gardens.

varieties:

❶ 'VARIEGATUM' FRAGRANT SOLOMON'S SEAL Leaf margins edged in white provide season-long interest. Foliage fades to buff-gold in autumn.

Wall Germander
(*Teucrium chamaedrys*)

Wall germander is ideal for creating knot gardens or formal hedges. In early summer, pinkish purple flowers unfurl against lustrous, deep green foliage. The blooms attract bees and butterflies. Plants are drought tolerant once established, needing only occasional water during dry spells.

Best site
Plant in full sun in well-drained soil. Wall germander also flourishes in heat and rocky soil. Zones 5–9.

Growing
The plant grows 10 to 12 inches tall (up to 20 inches in bloom) and 12 to 18 inches wide. Space 6 inches apart for hedges. Add slow-release fertilizer in spring. Prune in early spring, cutting stems to 2 to 6 inches. Deadhead by removing the top third of plants. Shear hedges regularly. Divide plants in spring or fall.

Design ideas
Use this plant to outline a knot garden or add order to a cottage garden. It thrives in rock gardens, in containers, or as edging. Plant with geraniums, lavender, or perennial salvia.

White Gaura
(*Gaura lindheimeri*)

Star-shape pink or white flowers open on airy stems from midsummer to early fall. The blossoms, which attract butterflies, fall from stems when faded. Gaura can be short-lived but may self-sow. Use plants as a gauzy screen around other perennials.

Best site
Plant in full sun in moderately fertile, well drained soil. Gaura tolerates part shade, heat, drought, and high humidity. Wet soil kills plants. Zones 5–10.

Growing
White gaura grows 12 to 36 inches tall (up to 5 feet in bloom) and 36 inches wide. Fertile soil causes stems to flop; insert supports. In early summer, prune plants to reduce height and increase blooms. Shear stems occasionally after flowering to promote more blossoms. In late fall or early spring, cut plants to the ground. Divide every two to three years.

Design ideas
Good companions include false indigo, blue oat grass, and moss phlox.

varieties:

❶ **'SUMMER SUNSHINE'** Short pink flowers in late summer on plant 6 to 8 inches tall and 15 inches wide with chartreuse leaves.

varieties:

❶ **'WHIRLING BUTTERFLIES'** White blossoms fade to pink on 24-inch-tall, red stems. Sterile plant that doesn't reseed. Zones 5–10.

Yarrow (*Achillea*)

For season-long color, plant yarrow. This hardy North American native has ferny foliage that deer and rabbits find distasteful. Sturdy, flat-top flowers in red, white, pink, salmon, or yellow open from late spring to fall. Butterflies and bees flock to the blooms. The drought tolerant leaves form tufted mounds or creeping mats that can be used in many ways in the garden. Yarrow grows fast, creating full clumps in one growing season.

Best site

Plant in full sun in well-drained, average soil. Yarrow tends to suffer winter kill in poorly drained soils. Zones 2–10.

Growing

Plants grow 4 inches to 5 feet tall and 12 to 36 inches wide, depending on species. The first round of flowers in early summer features tall, floppy stems. Cut these stems back after bloom, even if a few buds along flowerhead edges remain unopened. Subsequent flower stems will rise in a few weeks; these stems will be shorter and sturdier. Continue to deadhead through summer to extend flowering until frost.

Fertile soil or light shade can cause plants to flop. In these growing conditions, insert grow-through supports in early spring. Established plants are drought tolerant but perform best when they receive water during dry spells.

Some yarrow species (especially common yarrow) self-sow to the point of invasiveness. To prevent self-sowing, deadhead faithfully. You can clean up plants before winter, or if you want to savor flowerheads through winter, cut plants back in early spring.

To gather flowers for drying, cut flowerheads in full bloom but with a firm feel. Blossoms harvested too early tend to wilt; picked too late, the flowers turn brown.

Design ideas

Yarrow offers versatility for the perennial garden. Use this undemanding bloomer en masse in planting beds for a drift of color all season long. Yarrow is a natural choice for planting in wildlife or butterfly gardens. Low-growing species are good choices for rock gardens. Yarrow forms a dense, eye-catching groundcover in sunny settings where grass doesn't thrive, such as strips along driveways, sidewalks, or streets.

Use yarrow with its low mound of foliage to edge planting beds. Add this tough-as-nails perennial to cutting gardens, and harvest the blooms for fresh or dried bouquets. Good planting partners include gayfeather, spike speedwell, daylily, penstemon, and perennial salvia.

Names to watch for

COMMON YARROW (*A. millefolium*) This low-growing, fast-spreading species has white flowers and fine-textured green leaves on plant 18 to 24 inches tall and 24 to 36 inches wide. Spreads by self-sowing and rhizomes. Zones 3–10.
'Red Velvet' Red blossoms are fade resistant.

FERN-LEAF YARROW (*A. filipendulina*) Not aggressive like its cousins. Flat, yellow flower clusters from mid- to late summer. Plants reach 3 to 5 feet tall in bloom and 24 to 36 inches wide. Zones 3–10.
'Gold Coin Dwarf' Mustard yellow flowers on 36-inch stems in early to midsummer.
'Gold Plate' Deep mustard yellow blooms on 4- to 5-foot stems.

SERBIAN YARROW (*A. serbica*) Evergreen with gray leaves. Plant grows 4 inches tall and 15 inches wide and is topped with yellow-centered white daisies in early summer. Zones 4–10.

WESTERN YARROW (*A. lanulosa*) Small white flowers open atop 12- to 18-inch stems in summer. Plant grows 6 to 12 inches tall and wide. Adapted to cold, high desert regions in the West, and elevations to 11,000 feet. Zones 2–10.

WOOLLY YARROW (*A. tomentosa*) Ferny leaves

look white thanks to a coating of fine hairs. Plant grows 6 to 12 inches tall and 18 inches wide. Clear yellow, flat-top flower clusters in early summer. Performs poorly in hot, humid, or wet climates. Zones 3–10.

YOU SHOULD KNOW
Sometimes yarrow foliage can become tattered and tired looking during the growing season. Renew the plant's appearance by cutting foliage to the ground. New, fresh leaves will emerge.

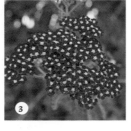

common yarrow varieties:

① **'APPLEBLOSSOM'** Pale lilac blossoms.
② **'CHRISTEL'** Magenta-pink blooms.
③ **'PAPRIKA'** Brilliant scarlet flowers.

yarrow hybrid varieties:

④ **'CORONATION GOLD'** Fern-leaf yarrow with flat, yellow blossoms on 36-inch stems; good for drying. Plants spread 18 inches. Zones 3–10.
⑤ **'MOONSHINE'** Woolly yarrow with lemon yellow flowers on plant 24 inches tall and 18 to 24 inches wide. Zones 3–10.
⑥ **'TERRACOTTA'** Common yarrow type with burnt yellow blooms. Zones 3–10.
⑦ **'POMEGRANATE'** Common yarrow type with deep reddish pink blooms. Zones 3–10.
⑧ **'PINK GRAPEFRUIT'** Common yarrow type with clear pink blooms. Zones 3–10.

Yellow Corydalis
(*Corydalis lutea*)

Shade gardens shine when you plant yellow corydalis. The yellow blooms, appearing on plants from midspring through fall, cluster together to create a showy effect. The fine-textured leaves resemble bleeding heart foliage. Plants self-sow readily.

Best site
Plant in moist, well-drained, neutral to slightly alkaline soil. Heat, humidity, and poorly draining soil can kill corydalis. Zones 5–10.

Growing
Corydalis grows 8 to 12 inches tall and 12 inches wide. To give roots slightly alkaline soil, insert a piece of blackboard chalk near roots in spring. Deadheading isn't necessary. Corydalis rarely needs division; divisions are slow to re-establish. Dig seedlings to propagate the plant.

Design ideas
Tuck yellow corydalis at the front of a shady border as edging or use it as a groundcover in a woodland setting where it can self-sow. Plants thrive in shady rock crevices in walls or along pathways. Good companions include heart-leaf brunnera, hosta, or heart-leaf bergenia.

Yellow Foxglove
(*Digitalis grandiflora*)

Dress woodland or shady settings with the buttery blooms of yellow foxglove. In June and July, flowers appear on tall spikes, forming a strong vertical accent in the garden. The blossoms are packed with sweet nectar that hummingbirds find irresistible.

Best site
Plant in part shade and moist, well-drained soil high in organic matter. Provide afternoon shade in hot regions. Zones 3–10.

Growing
Yellow foxglove grows 12 inches tall (2 to 4 feet in bloom) and 18 to 24 inches wide. Remove flower spikes before seeds set and you might be rewarded with a second bloom. Foxglove self-sows in good growing conditions. Cut off all flower spikes unless you want plants to spread. Divide clumps any time plants aren't flowering.

Design ideas
Use yellow foxglove in woodland areas or shady planting beds. Its flowers' allure for hummingbirds makes it an excellent choice for a wildlife garden. Pair it with lady's mantle, ferns, pulmonaria, hosta, or heart-leaf brunnera.

species:

1 **YELLOW CORYDALIS** Cheery yellow flowers contrast with blue-tone, fern-like foliage. In the right conditions, plants self-sow freely to form a carpet of color.

species and varieties:

1 **'CARILLON'** Dwarf (to 10 inches tall) with yellow blooms all summer. Cream-edged green leaves.

2 **COMMON FOXGLOVE** (*D. purpurea*) Biennial or short-lived perennial. Zones 4–8.

Yucca (*Yucca*)

Clusters of white flowers open in early to midsummer, towering 5 feet above leaves. Individual blooms are 2-inch-wide bells that exude a sweet perfume. Some blooms are blushed with purple. Sword-shape, stiff leaves form an evergreen tuft that's deer resistant and adds a touch of green to snowy landscapes in winter.

Best site

Plant yucca in full sun in light, sandy, well-drained soil for best results. However, yucca tolerates many kinds of soil, including heavy clay. Site plants away from pedestrian traffic to avoid injury from the sharp, spiny leaves. Zones 4–11.

Growing

Yucca grows 2 to 10 feet tall and 5 or more feet wide, depending on the species. Space plants at least 36 inches apart. Keep plants clean by trimming damaged leaves, removing faded flowers, and cutting down spent blossom stalks. With pointed leaf tips that penetrate skin, yucca can be dangerous to work around. Wear long-cuffed gauntlet gloves and eye protection. Use a leaf blower to remove debris from around plants.

Design ideas

Yucca adds architectural interest to any setting. It tolerates neglect, drought, and heat, making it a great choice for planting spaces alongside parking areas or driveways. Yucca gives a tropical appearance to poolside plantings—just keep it well beyond the reach of bathers or inflatable pool toys.

Use this sturdy perennial as a specimen plant; a clump of several creates a striking focal point. For a combination with vertical interest, plant yucca with coneflowers or tall ornamental grasses such as 'Silver Feather' miscanthus grass or 'Cloud Nine' switch grass. Yucca's straight leaves partner nicely with plants that have fine-textured foliage, such as Russian sage, globe thistle, or artemisia.

YOU SHOULD KNOW

Established yucca plants can be difficult to remove. Large roots require a chainsaw to cut. Plants regrow from the smallest piece of root. When digging yucca for removal, sift through soil to remove every bit of the tuberous root system.

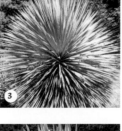

species and varieties:

1 'COLOR GUARD' Green leaves with yellow centers flush coral in winter; flowers on 5-foot stems; plants 20 inches tall and 36 inches wide.

2 ADAM'S NEEDLE (*Y. filamentosa*) White flowers rise 5 feet above foliage; leaves have curly hairs along edges. Plant grows 36 inches tall and wide. Tolerates light shade. Zones 5–10.

3 BLUE-BEAKED YUCCA (*Y. rostrata*) White flowers in 24-inch clusters that barely rise above leaves. Powder blue, sharp-tip leaves remain on trunks when they die. Slow growing, reaching 4 feet tall in 10 years. New Mexico native. Zones 5–10. 'Sapphire Skies' (bluer foliage).

4 SPANISH DAGGER (*Y. gloriosa*) White flowers 4 inches wide in late summer above 18-inch-long, stiff leaves with soft points. 'Variegata' (blue-green leaves edged with yellow, and white blooms with purple blush on 6- to 8-foot spikes. Grows 4 to 5 feet tall and wide). Zones 6–11.

USDA Plant Hardiness Zone Map

Perennials, such as these fall bloomers, have Hardiness Zone ratings. Select plants that are hardy in your area and they will likely overwinter well.

Each plant has an ability to withstand cold temperatures.

The temperature range is expressed as a zone—and a hardiness zone map shows where you can grow each plant.

Planting for your zone

There are 11 zones from Canada to Mexico, and each zone represents the lowest expected winter temperature in that area. Each zone is based on a 10-degree difference in minimum temperatures. Once you know your hardiness zone, you can choose plants for your garden that will flourish. Look for the hardiness zone on the plant tags of the perennials, trees, and shrubs you buy.

Microclimates in your yard

Not all areas in your yard are the same. Depending on your geography, trees, and structures, some spots may receive differing sunlight and wind and, consequently, experience temperature variations. Take a look around your yard and you may notice that the same plant comes up sooner in one place than another. This is the microclimate concept in action. A microclimate is an area in your yard that is slightly cooler or hotter (or wetter or drier) than other areas of your yard.

Create a microclimate

Once you're aware of your yard's microclimates, you can use them to your advantage. For example, you may be able to grow plants in a sheltered south-facing garden bed that you can't grow elsewhere in your yard. You can create a microclimate by planting evergreens on the north side of a property to block prevailing winds. Or plant deciduous trees on the south side to provide shade in summer.

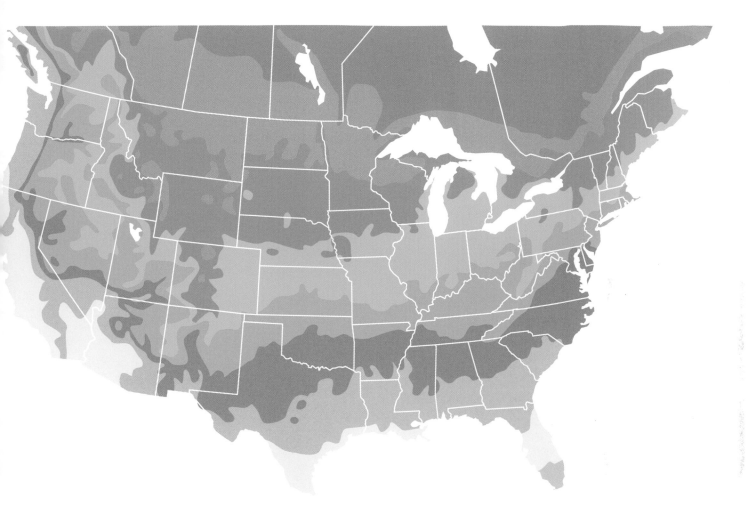

Range of Average Annual Minimum Temperatures for Each Zone

- Zone 2: -50 to -40° F (-45 to -40°C)
- Zone 3: -40 to -30° F (-40 to -35°C)
- Zone 4: -30 to -20° F (-34 to -29°C)
- Zone 5: -20 to -10° F (-29 to -23°C)
- Zone 6: -10 to 0° F (-23 to -18°C)

- Zone 7: 0 to 10° F (-18 to -12°C)
- Zone 8: 10 to 20° F (-12 to -7°C)
- Zone 9: 20 to 30° F (-7 to -1°C)
- Zone 10: 30 to 40° F (-1 to 4°C)

Resources

Mail-Order Perennials

Look for perennials in local garden centers and retail outlets, but when you can't find a particular plant, turn to perennial specialists—nurseries that grow perennials for shipping. Search online for specialists, or use one of these reputable perennial retailers. Some sell nationally; some do not. Visit websites or call for more information.

BLUEBIRD NURSERY, INC.
519 Bryan Street
Clarkson, NE 68629
(402) 892-3457
www.bluebirdnursery.com

BLUESTONE PERENNIALS
7211 Middle Ridge Rd.
Madison, OH 44057
(800) 852-5243
www.bluestoneperennials.com

BRENT AND BECKY'S BULBS
7900 Daffodil Lane
Gloucester, VA 23061
(877) 661-2852
www.brentandbeckysbulbs.com

DIGGING DOG NURSERY
P.O. Box 471
Albion, CA 95410
(707) 937-1130
www.diggingdog.com

GILBERT H. WILD & SON
2944 State Hwy 37
Reeds, MO 64859
(888) 449-4537
www.gilberthwild.com
Specialize in daylilies, peonies, iris, and perennials

GREEN HILL HOSTAS
P.O. Box 16306
Chapel Hill, NC 27516
(919) 309-0649
www.hostahosta.com

HERONSWOOD NURSERY
Attn: Customer Service
300 Park Avenue
Warminster, PA 18974-4818
(877) 674-4714
www.heronswood.com
Specialize in lenten roses, perennials

HIGH COUNTRY GARDENS
2902 Rufina Street
Santa Fe, NM 87507
(800) 925-9387
www.highcountrygardens.com

KLEHM'S SONG SPARROW NURSERY
13101 E. Rye Road
Avalon, WI 53505
(800) 553-3715
www.songsparrow.com

KURT BLUEMEL INC.
2740 Greene Lane
Baldwin, MD 21013
(800)498-1560
www.kurtbluemel.com
Specialize in ornamental grasses

LANDSCAPE ALTERNATIVES, INC.
25316 St. Croix Trail
Shafer, MN 55074
(651) 257-4460
www.landscapealternatives.com
Specialize in prairie plants

MCCLURE & ZIMMERMAN
P.O. Box 368
Friesland, WI 53935
(800) 546.4053
www.mzbulbspring.com
Specialize in bulbs

MOUNTAIN VALLEY GROWERS
38325 Pepperweed Road
Squaw Valley, CA 93675
www.mountainvalleygrowers.com
Specialize in herbs and perennials

NAYLOR CREEK NURSERY
P.O. Box 309
Chimacum, WA 98325
(360) 732-4983
Specialize in shade plants

NICHE GARDENS
1111 Dawson Road
Chapel Hill, NC 27516
(919) 967-0078
www.nichegardens.com
Specialize in native perennials

NICHOLLS GARDENS
4724 Angus Drive
Gainesville, VA 20155-1217
(703) 754-9623
www.nichollsgardens.com
Specialize in iris (bearded, Japanese, Louisiana, Siberian), hosta, daylilies, and perennials

OLD HOUSE GARDENS
536 Third St.
Ann Arbor, MI 48103
(734) 995-1486
www.oldhousegardens.com

PLANT DELIGHTS NURSERY, INC.
9241 Sauls Road
Raleigh, NC 27603
(919) 772-4794
www.plantdelights.com

PLANTER'S PALETTE
28W571 Roosevelt Rd.
Winfield, IL 60190-1530
(630) 293-1040
www.planterspalette.com

PRAIRIE RESTORATION
P.O. Box 327
Princeton, MN 55371
(763) 389-4342
www.prairieresto.com

PRAIRIE NURSERY
P.O. Box 306
Westfield, WI 53964
(800) 476-9453
www.prairienursery.com

RARE FIND NURSERY
957 Patterson Road
Jackson, NJ 08527
(732) 833-0613
www.rarefindnursery.com
Specialize in coral bells, foam flower, foamy bells, and perennials, including deer-resistant and shade perennials

ROOTS & RHIZOMES
PO Box 9
Randolph, WI 53956
(800) 374-5035
www.rootsrhizomes.com
Specialize in daylilies, Siberian iris, hostas, and perennials

SCHREINER'S IRIS GARDENS
3625 Quinaby Road NE
Keizer, OR 97303
(800) 525-2367
www.schreinersgardens.com
Specialize in iris: bearded, dwarf, Louisiana, Siberian

SISKIYOU RARE PLANT NURSERY
2115 Talent Avenue
Talent, OR 97540
(541)535-7103
www.siskiyourareplantnursery.com

SUNLIGHT GARDENS
174 Golden Lane
Andersonville, TN 37705
(800) 272-7396
www.sunlightgardens.com
Specialize in wildflowers and perennials

VIETTE NURSERIES
994 Long Meadow Road
Fishersville, VA 22939
(800) 575-5538
www.viette.com

WAYSIDE GARDENS
1 Garden Lane
Hodges, SC 29695
(800) 213-0379
www.waysidegardens.com

WHITE FLOWER FARM
P.O. Box 50, Route 63
Litchfield, CT 06759
(800) 503-9624
www.whiteflowerfarm.com

YUCCA DO
P.O. Box 1039
Giddings, TX 7894
(979) 542-8811
www.yuccado.com

Tools and supplies

Look for tools and supplies at local nurseries and garden centers. The following mail-order suppliers also carry a range of perennial garden specialty supplies.

A.M. LEONARD
241 Fox Drive/ P.O. Box 816
Piqua, OH 45356-0816
(800) 543-8955
www.amleo.com

GARDENERS SUPPLY
128 Intervale Rd.
Burlington, VT 05401
(888) 833-1412
www.gardeners.com

GARDENS ALIVE!
5100 Schenley Place
Lawrenceburg, IN 47025
(513) 354-1482
www.gardensalive.com

LEE VALLEY TOOLS LTD.
P.O. Box 1780
Ogdensburg, NY 13669-6780
(800) 267-8735
www.leevalley.com

SPRAY-N-GROW
P.O. Box 2137
Rockport, TX 78382
(800) 323-2363
www.spray-n-grow.com

index

index

index

Looking for more
gardening inspiration?

See what the experts at
Better Homes & Gardens have to offer.

WILEY